MASTER VISUALLY®

Windows Mobile™ 2003

Visual™

by Bill Landon and Matthew Miller

From

maranGraphics®

&

Wiley Publishing, Inc.

G000020265

Master VISUALLY® Windows Mobile™ 2003

Published by
Wiley Publishing, Inc.
111 River Street
Hoboken, NJ 07030-5774

Published simultaneously in Canada

Library of Congress Control Number: 2004103154

ISBN: 0-7645-5889-7

Manufactured in the United States of America

10 9 8 7 6 5 4 3 2 1

1V/RX/QY/QU/IN

Trademark Acknowledgments

Important Numbers

For U.S. corporate orders, please call maranGraphics at 800-469-6616 or fax
905-890-9434.

For general information on our other products and services or to obtain technical
support please contact our Customer Care Department within the U.S. at
800-762-2974, outside the U.S. at 317-572-3993 or fax 317-572-4002.

Permissions

WILEY

U.S. Corporate Sales	U.S. Trade Sales
Contact maranGraphics at (800) 469-6616 or fax (905) 890-9434.	Contact Wiley at (800) 762-2974 or fax (317) 572-4002.

Praise for Visual books...

"If you have to see it to believe it, this is the book for you!"
   –*PC World*

"A master tutorial/reference – from the leaders in visual learning!"
   –*Infoworld*

"A publishing concept whose time has come!"
   –*The Globe and Mail*

"Just wanted to say THANK YOU to your company for providing books which make learning fast, easy, and exciting! I learn visually so your books have helped me greatly – from Windows instruction to Web page development. I'm looking forward to using more of your Master VISUALLY series in the future, as I am now a computer support specialist. Best wishes for continued success."
   –*Angela J. Barker (Springfield, MO)*

"I have over the last 10-15 years purchased thousands of dollars worth of computer books but find your books the most easily read, best set out, and most helpful and easily understood books on software and computers I have ever read. Please keep up the good work."
   –*John Gatt (Adamstown Heights, Australia)*

"I am an avid fan of your Visual books. If I need to learn anything, I just buy one of your books and learn the topic in no time. Wonders! I have even trained my friends to give me Visual books as gifts."
   –*Illona Bergstrom (Aventura, FL)*

"The Greatest. This whole series is the best computer-learning tool of any kind I've ever seen."
   –*Joe Orr (Brooklyn, NY)*

"What fantastic teaching books you have produced! Congratulations to you and your staff."
   –*Bruno Tonon (Melbourne, Australia)*

"I have quite a few of your Visual books and have been very pleased with all of them. I love the way the lessons are presented!"
   –*Mary Jane Newman (Yorba Linda, CA)*

"Like a lot of other people, I understand things best when I see them visually. Your books really make learning easy and life more fun."
   –*John T. Frey (Cadillac, MI)*

"Your Visual books have been a great help to me. I now have a number of your books and they are all great. My friends always ask to borrow my Visual books - trouble is, I always have to ask for them back!"
   –*John Robson (Brampton, Ontario, Canada)*

"I would like to take this time to compliment maranGraphics on creating such great books. I work for a leading manufacturer of office products, and sometimes they tend to NOT give you the meat and potatoes of certain subjects, which causes great confusion. Thank you for making it clear. Keep up the good work."
   –*Kirk Santoro (Burbank, CA)*

"I write to extend my thanks and appreciation for your books. They are clear, easy to follow, and straight to the point. Keep up the good work! I bought several of your books and they are just right! No regrets! I will always buy your books because they are the best."
   –*Seward Kollie (Dakar, Senegal)*

"You're marvelous! I am greatly in your debt."
   –*Patrick Baird (Lacey, WA)*

maranGraphics is a family-run business
located near Toronto, Canada.

At maranGraphics, we believe in producing great computer books — one book at a time.

maranGraphics has been producing high-technology products for over 25 years, which enables us to offer the computer book community a unique communication process.

Our computer books use an integrated communication process, which is very different from the approach used in other computer books. Each spread is, in essence, a flow chart — the text and screen shots are totally incorporated into the layout of the spread. Introductory text

and helpful tips complete the learning experience.

maranGraphics' approach encourages the left and right sides of the brain to work together — resulting in faster orientation and greater memory retention.

Above all, we are very proud of the handcrafted nature of our books. Our carefully chosen writers are experts in their fields and spend countless hours researching and organizing the content for each topic. Our artists rebuild every screen shot to provide the best clarity possible, making our screen

shots the most precise and easiest to read in the industry. We strive for perfection and believe that the time spent handcrafting each element results in the best computer books money can buy.

Thank you for purchasing this book. We hope you enjoy it!

Sincerely,

Robert Maran
President
maranGraphics
Rob@maran.com
www.maran.com

CREDITS

Project Editor
Dana Rhodes Lesh

Acquisitions Editor
Jody Lefevere

Product Development Manager
Lindsay Sandman

Copy Editor
Dana Rhodes Lesh

Technical Editor
Chris De Herrera

Editorial Manager
Robyn Siesky

Manufacturing
Allan Conley
Linda Cook
Paul Gilchrist
Jennifer Guynn

Vice President and Executive Group Publisher
Richard Swadley

Vice President and Publisher
Barry Pruett

Book Design
maranGraphics®

Project Coordinator
Maridee Ennis

Layout
Beth Brooks
Carrie Foster
Jennifer Heleine
Heather Pope

Screen Artist
Jill A. Proll

Illustrator
Ronda David-Burroughs

Proofreaders
Vickie Broyles
Susan Sims

Quality Control
John Greenough
Susan Moritz

Indexer
Johnna VanHoose

Composition Director
Debbie Stailey

ABOUT THE AUTHORS

Bill Landon is a mobile technology professional with 17 years combined experience in the computer and mobile technology field. Bill started his computer technology interests in the mid 1980s, programming software and modifying system hardware. He is the founder and senior editor of MaximumPDA.com and the recently developed PDAToday.com, both of which offer news and reviews of personal data assistant and mobile technology. In addition, through Bill's Web site, PDAToday.com, Bill helps in sponsoring and organizing the Puget Sound Handheld Users Group. PSHUG.org is the largest handheld/Pocket PC club in North America.

Bill lives in the Pacific Northwest and enjoys snowboarding during the winter and taking weekend trips hiking and camping with his family during the summer.

Matthew (palmsolo) Miller has been using PDAs since 1997 and is an avid PDA enthusiast when not working his day job as a professional engineer and naval architect at a firm in Seattle, WA. He served 12 years in the U.S. Coast Guard before joining his current marine consulting employer in 2001.

Matthew began writing daily news blurbs and conducting reviews for Geek.com in August 2001. He also wrote reviews for PocketPCLife.co.uk for a couple years. Matthew has owned over 25 models of mobile devices and currently uses an HP iPAQ 4350 for his Windows Mobile 2003 device. You can find him as palmsolo in online discussion forums, at local user group meetings, at national conferences, at his blog (www.palmsolo.com), and at Geek.com.

Matthew is also a husband to his wife of 11 years, Dayna, and a father to his three daughters, Danika, Maloree, and Kari. Matthew enjoys participating in his local church, camping with the family, and watching his girls play sports.

AUTHORS' ACKNOWLEDGMENTS

From Bill: Special thanks to my wife, Erin, for her patience and immense help during the author review process. Thanks to my son, Ethan, and my daughter, Ashley, for allowing me to miss many family nights during the writing of this book. I would like thank Matt Miller for taking on the additional role as coauthor of this book. Without Matt's help, this book would not have been completed.

I would also like take a moment to thank the additional following people who helped make this book possible: the Puget Sound Handheld Users Group (PSHUG.org), the PDAToday.com editorial staff (Robert Hartley, Tucker Hatfield, and Harvey Lee), Jeff McKean, the very dedicated staff of editors at Wiley Publishing (Dana Lesh and Jody Lefevere), Pavel Koza of PDAGold.com, all my readers at PDAToday.com and MaximumPDA.com, and finally to the many people I forgot to list here.

From Matthew: I would like to thank my best friend and lovely wife, Dayna, for her patience and understanding with my late nights and deadlines and for helping keep me motivated. I thank my three wonderful daughters, Danika, Maloree, and Kari, for letting Daddy have his quiet time and for their love. Joel Evans deserves my gratitude for allowing me to write for Geek.com for the last three years. I have been able to gain an incredible amount of experience and knowledge working with Joel and consider him a good friend and mentor. Finally, I thank Bill Landon for increasing my role from a single chapter to coauthor and for giving me the opportunity to assist in writing this book.

In memory of Grace Ann Fordyce: Blessed Be

— Bill Landon

My Saviour, Jesus Christ, has blessed me with the technical and writing abilities necessary to contribute to this book and the PDA community, and I owe all I have to Him.

— Matthew (palmsolo) Miller

I
GETTING STARTED

II
PERSONAL AND SYSTEM SETTINGS

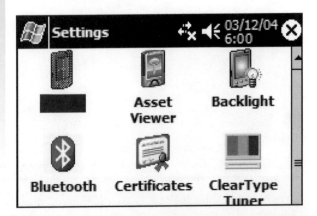

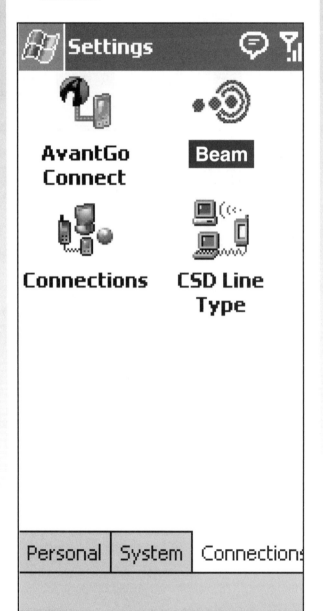

1

1) USING WINDOWS MOBILE 2003

2) USING THE TODAY SCREEN

3) USING THE START MENU

TABLE OF CONTENTS

2
PERSONAL AND SYSTEM SETTINGS

4) CUSTOMIZING PERSONAL SETTINGS

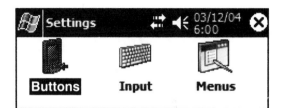

5) CUSTOMIZING GENERAL SYSTEM SETTINGS

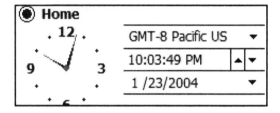

6) MODIFYING POWER USAGE AND BACKLIGHT SETTINGS

7) MODIFYING MEMORY USAGE

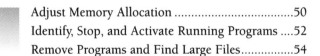

8) MANAGING BLUETOOTH COMMUNICATIONS

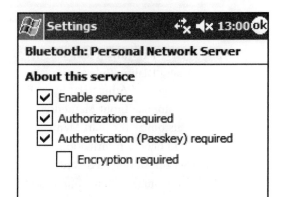

3

CONNECTION SETTINGS

9) PREPARING YOUR DEVICE TO RECEIVE INFRARED BEAMS

Receive an infrared beam from a Pocket PC
2000 or H/PC device

10) SETTING UP NETWORK CONNECTIONS

TABLE OF CONTENTS

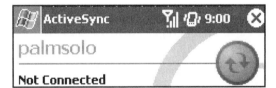

4 *APPLICATIONS*

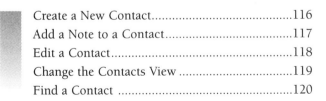

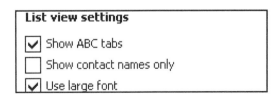

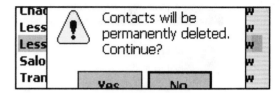

15) E-MAILING WITH THE INBOX

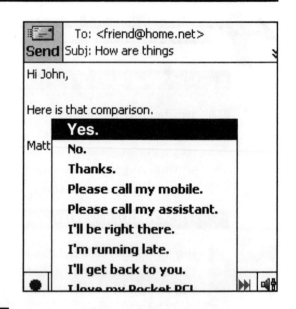

16) BROWSING WITH INTERNET EXPLORER

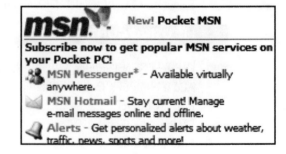

TABLE OF CONTENTS

17) USING NOTES

18) PLAYING MULTIMEDIA WITH WINDOWS MEDIA PLAYER

19) PLAYING GAMES AND USING THE CALCULATOR

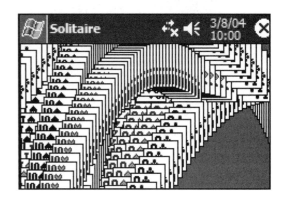

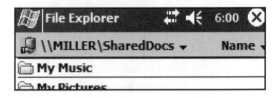

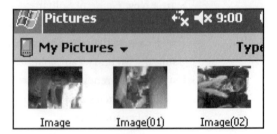

TABLE OF CONTENTS

24) USING SPREADSHEETS WITH POCKET EXCEL

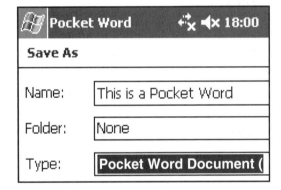

25) WORKING WITH DOCUMENTS IN POCKET WORD

26) WORKING WITH TASKS

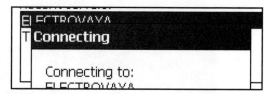

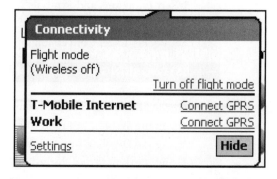

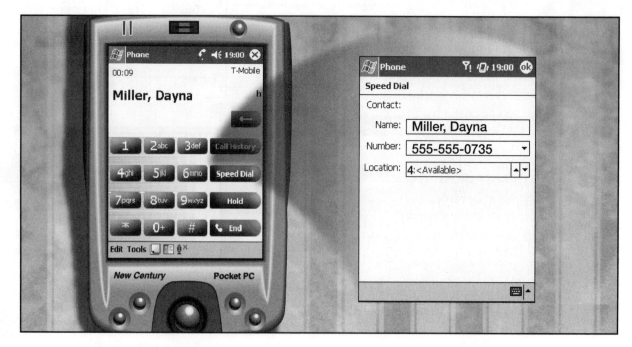

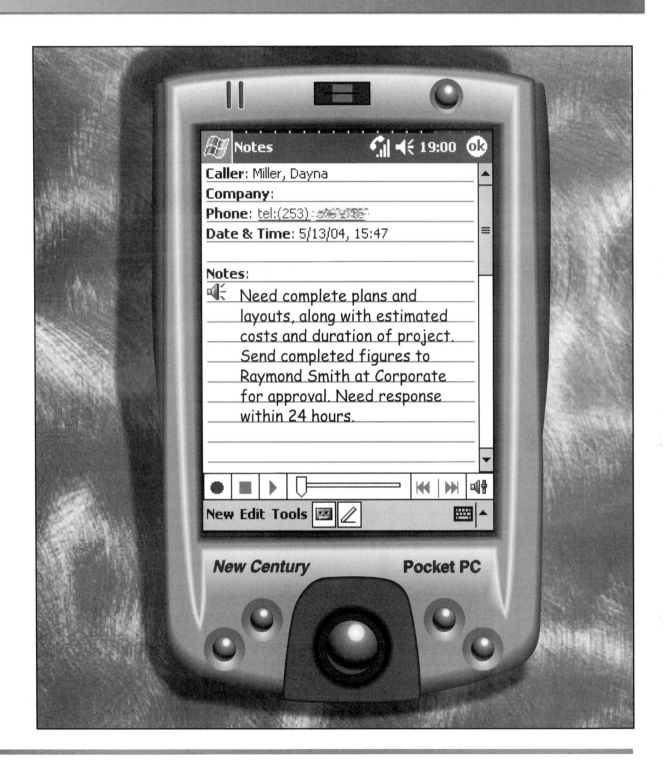

Master VISUALLY Windows Mobile 2003 contains straightforward examples to teach you how to use Windows Mobile 2003 on the Pocket PC.

This book is designed to help readers receive quick access to any area of question. You can simply look up a subject within the table of contents or index and go immediately to the task of concern. A *section* is a self-contained unit that walks you through a computer operation step-by-step. That is, with rare exception, all the information that you need regarding an area of interest is contained within one section.

The Organization of Each Chapter

Each chapter is organized into a collection of related sections. Each section contains an introduction, a set of screen shots with steps, and, if the steps goes beyond one page, a set of tips. The introduction tells why you want to perform the steps, the advantages and disadvantages of performing the steps, a general explanation of any procedures, and references to other related tasks in the book. The screens, located on the bottom half of each page, show a series of steps that you must complete to perform a given task. The tip area gives you an opportunity to further understand the task at hand, to learn about other related tasks in other areas of the book, or to apply more complicated or alternative methods.

A chapter may also contain an illustrated group of pages that gives you background information that you need to understand the tasks in the chapter.

The Organization of This Book

Master VISUALLY Windows Mobile 2003 has 28 chapters and is divided into four parts. Part I, "Getting Started," shows you how to get up and running with your new device and become familiar with its operation. Part II, "Personal and System Settings," covers how to customize the Personal and System settings to match your needs. Part III, "Connection Settings," discusses how to set up and modify the Connection settings. Part IV, "Applications," offers information about the various applications that are included with most Windows Mobile 2003 devices.

Who This Book is For

This book is for the beginner, who is unfamiliar with Windows Mobile 2003 and the various Pocket PC programs. It is also for more computer-literate individuals who want to expand their knowledge of the different features that Windows Mobile 2003 and the Pocket PC has to offer.

What You Need to Use This Book

To perform the tasks in this book, you must use some type of Pocket PC device that is running Windows Mobile 2003.

Conventions When Using the Stylus

This book uses the following conventions to describe the actions you perform when using the stylus:

- **Tap:** Press with the stylus and release. You use a tap to select an item on the screen.
- **Tap and hold:** You tap and hold the stylus down on the item to display a shortcut menu, which is a list of commands specially related to the selected program.

The Conventions in This Book

A number of typographic and layout styles have been used throughout *Master VISUALLY Windows Mobile 2003* to distinguish different types of information:

- **Bold** indicates information that must be typed.

- *Italics* indicates a new term being introduced.

- Numbered steps indicate that you must perform these steps in order to successfully perform the task.

- Bulleted steps offer you alternative methods, explain various options, or present what a program will do in response to the numbered steps.

- Notes give you additional information to help you complete a task. The purpose of a note is three-fold: It can explain special conditions that may occur during the course of the task, warn you of potentially dangerous situations, or refer you to tasks in the same or a different chapter. References to tasks within the chapter are indicated by the phrase "See the section . . .," followed by the name of the task. References to sections in other chapters are indicated by "See Chapter . . .," followed by the chapter number.

- Icons in the steps indicate a button that you must press.

- areas are included in most of the sections in this book. The Master It area supplements a section with tips, hints, and tricks that extend your use of the task at hand beyond what you learned by performing the steps in the section.

SECTION I

1) USING WINDOWS MOBILE 2003

2) USING THE TODAY SCREEN

3) USING THE START MENU

AN INTRODUCTION TO WINDOWS MOBILE 2003

Windows Mobile 2003 is the latest version of the software (built upon Microsoft Windows CE 4.2) that is included on Windows Mobile–based Pocket PCs.

Many vendors make PDAs based on Windows Mobile 2003. Some vendors design their devices with different consumer needs in mind. They may add additional memory, biometric security, extra expansion slots, GPS, high-resolution screens, and other value-added features.

There are a few basic hardware features that all Windows Mobile

2003 devices have in common, such as an ARM-based processor (Intel StrongARM, XScale, or Texas Instruments OMAP processor). These processors are interoperable for application compatibility with Windows Mobile 2003. They have at least 32MB of RAM for internal storage and application use. These devices contain at least one storage card slot for use with storage media such as Compact Flash or Secure Digital cards. They also have a transflective display, providing superior image clarity, indoors and outdoors, over previous generation devices.

The focus of this book is to provide you with an intimate knowledge of all aspects of Windows Mobile 2003–based devices. Each chapter contains tasks that walk you through the functions of your device in easy-to-follow steps.

Windows Mobile 2003 comes with certain built-in applications. Some vendors include additional applications and omit others. You will learn how to use the most commonly included applications found in Windows Mobile 2003.

Customize Personal and System Settings

Most aspects of Windows Mobile 2003 can be customized or modified to fit your specific needs. You will learn how to change the personal settings of your device such as how you enter data. You will also learn to add security features to your device. Screen settings can be changed, and you can alter the appearance of your device's display. Regional settings can be localized to your area of the world. Memory and power usage can be optimized.

Create a Mobile Office

You will learn how to synchronize your device data with your home or office PC. You can schedule meetings and appointments with the built-in calendar. You can collect all of your contacts in one easy-to-use location and access them anytime. You will learn how to send and receive e-mail, take notes, and schedule tasks.

You will also learn how to take Word and Excel documents with you and edit them on-the-go with Pocket Word and Pocket Excel.

Entertain On-the-Go

You can take movies and music with you with Windows Media Player 9 and entertain yourself and others for hours. You can show your favorite pictures with the Pictures program and create a slideshow of your next family or office outing.

You can also take books with you in electronic format with Microsoft Reader and spend hours reading the classics or latest novel.

Stay Connected

You will learn how to connect your device to another device via infrared, Bluetooth, and wireless networks.

You will learn how to set your device to use network cards, modems, virtual private networks, and more.

With Internet connectivity, you can browse the Internet for the latest news, weather, and sports scores. You can communicate with friends, colleagues, and family with MSN Messenger. You can also connect to Terminal Services with the Terminal Services Client.

EXPLORE WHAT'S NEW IN WINDOWS MOBILE 2003

Microsoft has spent the last couple of years fine-tuning the Windows CE .NET OS to enhance your daily mobile computing experience, and Windows Mobile 2003 is the result.

Zero Configuration WiFi

Windows Mobile 2003 has greatly simplified connecting to 802.11 wireless local area networks, also called WiFi or WLAN networks. When your WiFi–enabled device comes within range of a WiFi network, your wireless-enabled device asks you if you want to connect to the hotspot that it just found. If you accept the connection, you may be prompted for additional information such as a WEP key. Your device will remember your connections, simplifying the next time that you connect to that hotspot.

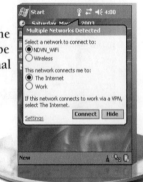

Integrated Bluetooth Support

Windows Mobile 2003 has added support for Bluetooth-enabled devices and accessories, simplifying connections between Bluetooth-equipped devices, such as mobile phones, printers, GPS units, and more.

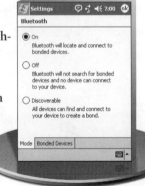

A Simplified Connections Manager

The Connections Manager has been completely redesigned with a simplified wizard, enabling a quick and easy setup of connections for VPN, proxy servers, 802.1x, secure VPN, and encrypted connections.

Enhanced Messaging and Keyboard Support

Communicating on-the-go just got easier with enhanced e-mail capabilities such as signatures and auto-suggest, which suggests the e-mail address that you are entering from your list of contacts. The Inbox also auto-corrects commonly misspelled words as you type your e-mail text. Common tasks in the Inbox can now be accomplished with new keyboard shortcuts.

Improved Contacts and Calendar

Improved search functions in Contacts enable you to find a contact in a matter of seconds by entering only part of the contact's name. The improved search feature filters out all other names but the one you are typing, and with improved keyboard integration, you can do this without the use of the stylus. The Calendar application has been redesigned to show weekends in different colors, offering a clear representation of your weekly schedule. Saturdays are presented in blue, contrasting with Sunday and holidays, which now appear in red.

Additionally, vCards and vCals support has been added for the Inbox and Calendar to provide better integration with your desktop's Outlook application.

Advanced Imaging and Entertainment

Moving a compatible storage card from your digital camera to your Pocket PC just got easier. With new support for photos in the program Pictures, you can take your favorite pictures with you and show them as a slideshow to friends, family, and colleagues. You can edit your photos with basic features such as cropping, image rotation, and brightness and contrast modifications.

Windows Media Player 9 for Pocket PC has been added for improved performance and compatibility with today's music and video entertainment. Streaming audio and video content up to 300KB from your storage card or the Internet makes streaming media delivery the perfect companion to Media Player 9 for the PC.

A new game called Jawbreaker has been added to the game lineup as a welcome alternative to Solitaire.

Improved Pocket Internet Explorer Features

Pocket Internet Explorer has been improved with new features and a faster speed. Improved style sheet support, added SSL compatibility, and improved Web site rendering provide a rich Web browsing experience.

EXPLORE WHAT'S NEW IN WINDOWS MOBILE 2003 SECOND EDITION

Microsoft announced Windows Mobile 2003 Second Edition on March 24, 2004, and Dell, Motorola, HP, and Toshiba announced that new devices with this updated operating system will be released in the summer and fall of 2004.

The major updates in the operating system include the ability to use

Landscape, Portrait, or Square mode while allowing for dynamic switching between modes and support for high-resolution VGA displays up to 480 x 640 pixels. Windows Mobile 2003 is limited to a 240 x 320 display resolution in portrait-only mode.

Other new features in Windows Mobile 2003 Second Edition include

customizing the Start menu and OK buttons, a font size slider for smaller or larger systemwide fonts, the improvement of page formatting in Internet Explorer, the ability to use shortcuts with Transcriber, a most frequently used applications area of the Start menu, and support for WiFi Protected Access (WPA).

Portrait and Landscape Orientation

The ability to dynamically switch between Portrait and Landscape modes without using a third-party solution or soft resetting your device is the most noticeable change in Second Edition. Many current Windows Mobile 2003 devices have the option to upgrade to Second Edition, and switching between modes will work on the current devices, which have 240 x 320 pixel displays. Both right-handed and left-handed Landscape modes are supported, and hardware buttons can be assigned to switch between the modes.

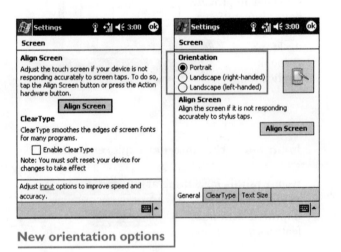

New orientation options

New Font Settings

The Screen settings have been changed from one entry screen to three. Screen orientation and alignment is on the first tab, General, enabling systemwide ClearType is on the ClearType tab, and the font size adjustment slider is on the Text Size tab.

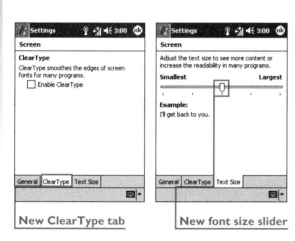

New ClearType tab   New font size slider

Using Landscape Mode

Landscape mode has been a feature requested by users and will be especially beneficial for using Internet Explorer and Pocket Excel. Spreadsheets are commonly used in Landscape mode on desktop computers, and now you will be able to experience the same layout on your mobile device.

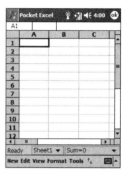

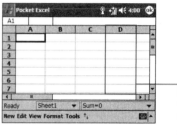

More columns are visible in Landscape mode

Internet Explorer Updates

Many Web sites still do not have mobile format options, so Internet Explorer attempts to reformat them to mobile format. The new version of Internet Explorer improves this formatting ability and offers you some more options. You can choose One Column, Default, or Desktop formats for Web sites.

New layout options

CONTINUED

EXPLORE WHAT'S NEW IN WINDOWS MOBILE 2003 SECOND EDITION (CONTINUED)

New Buttons Settings

You have been able to customize what actions will occur when pressing the hardware buttons on your mobile device, and the Second Edition update now enables you to customize the Start menu and OK/X button as well.

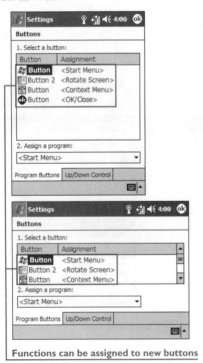

Functions can be assigned to new buttons

The Square Display Option

The majority of Windows Mobile 2003 devices used a 240 x 320 pixel display due to requirements of the operating system. Microsoft now allows manufacturers to use square 240 x 240 and 480 x 480 pixel resolutions. This will allow Pocket PC Phone Edition devices or devices with integrated keyboards to be smaller and easier to carry in your pocket.

Windows Media Player on a square display

GET ACQUAINTED WITH YOUR WINDOWS MOBILE 2003 DEVICE

Windows Mobile devices vary in features from manufacturer to manufacturer. Some companies include a built-in camera, extra card slots, wireless capability, and such. However, the basic layout of a Windows Mobile device remains fairly similar from brand to brand.

Power button

Indicator lights

Screen

Directional pad

Action buttons

Chassis

Head phone jack

Stylus

Card slot

Sync and docking port

Battery compartment

Speaker

UNDERSTANDING THE TODAY SCREEN

The Today screen is the first display that you see after going through the initial device configuration; it serves as the desktop for your mobile device. Like the main desktop display on your home or work computer, the Today screen can be customized to your personal preferences.

There are five items included on Windows Mobile 2003 devices that you can choose to have shown on the Today screen. You can select to view the date, owner information, Calendar, Tasks, and Inbox items. You can further specify display options for the Calendar and Tasks.

There are also several third-party applications that you can use to customize your Today screen so that you can view news briefs, movie updates, weather forecasts, Real Simple Syndication (RSS) news feeds, and more.

You can use pictures on your device or storage card for backgrounds on your Today screen. A free download is also available from Microsoft to create custom Today screen backgrounds and themes.

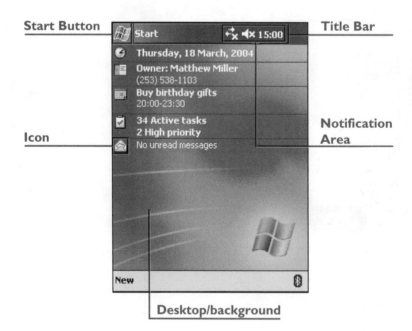

Start Button · Title Bar · Icon · Notification Area · Desktop/background

IDENTIFY TODAY SCREEN INDICATOR ICONS

Time and Next Appointment Notification

Tapping the time in the top title bar launches a notification that presents the date, time, battery status, and next appointment in your Calendar.

Connectivity Notification

Tapping the icon to the left of the speaker in the top title bar launches a notification that shows the current status of connectivity enabled on your particular piece of hardware. All devices show sync status, whether you sync via USB, IR, or serial. These notifications vary depending on the wireless capabilities of your device. If you have a WiFi (802.11b) enabled device, a list of available hotspots appears when they are in range of your device. If you connect via a Bluetooth phone or via GPRS or 1xRTT, the notification allows you to tap to connect to your service. You can also turn off the integrated wireless capabilities of your device and put it into "flight mode."

Volume Notification

Tapping the speaker icon in the top title bar launches a notification that shows a slider control for the volume. You can move the slider up or down to increase or decrease, respectively, the system volume. On Phone Edition devices, a second slider adjusts the ringer volume, and an option to have the ringer or notification vibrate is available.

E-mail Notification

If you are using an application other than the Inbox and e-mail is received on your device, an e-mail notification appears automatically. The notification informs you how many new e-mails have arrived and enables you to view them in the Inbox or close the notification.

Bluetooth Manager

Tapping the bottom-right icon on the Today screen of a Bluetooth-enabled device presents three options for managing Bluetooth communications — On, Off, or Discoverable. The HP manager shown here offers you more Bluetooth options.

CUSTOMIZE THE TODAY SCREEN APPEARANCE

Y ou can customize the Today screen on your device with different theme files, which you can create yourself or find online for free or for a small fee. Thousands of theme files are available online for different movies, nature scenes, cartoons, and many more. You can also use .gif or .jpg images stored on

your device, found in internal or external memory, for background images.

Microsoft has a free Theme Generator that you can use on your desktop computer. Themes enable you to change the background image and colors of the text, menus, navigation bars, and

notification bubbles. There is also a third-party application, Animated Today, that enables you to create animated Today themes.

Theme files have a .tsk extension. When you place them in the My Documents or Windows folders of your device, they appear in the Today settings preferences screen.

CUSTOMIZE THE TODAY SCREEN APPEARANCE

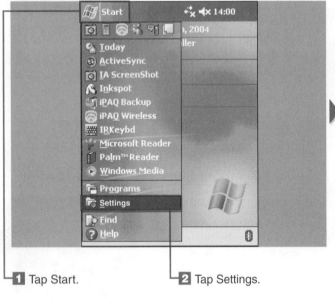

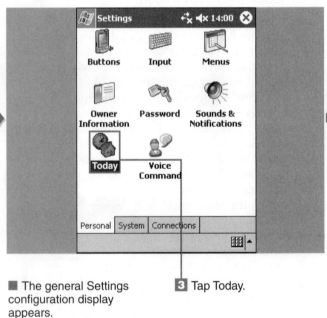

1 Tap Start.

2 Tap Settings.

■ The general Settings configuration display appears.

3 Tap Today.

Do I have to resize images to fit on my device?

✔ No, the images do not have to be resized to work on your device, but only a portion of images greater than 240 x 320 pixels will show.

Can I create Today themes on my device instead of having to use a desktop computer?

✔ No, .tsk theme files can be created only on a Windows desktop computer.

What are the general file sizes of Today themes?

✔ Theme files usually range from 15KB to 45KB in size.

Can I rotate themes automatically?

✔ This functionality is not built into Windows Mobile 2003, but a plug-in is available for free with the Microsoft Theme Generator. The plug-in enables you to set the interval at which Today themes switch.

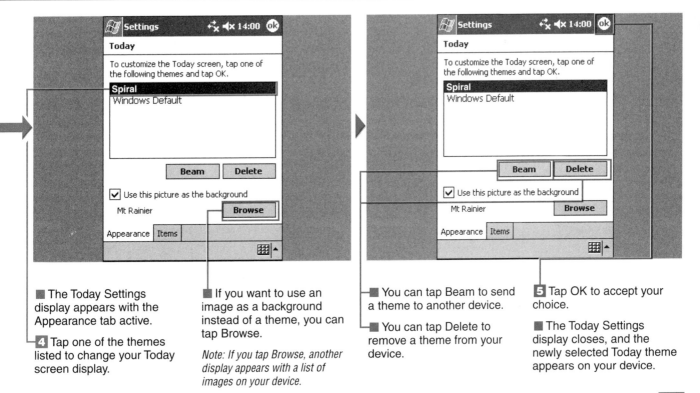

■ The Today Settings display appears with the Appearance tab active.

4 Tap one of the themes listed to change your Today screen display.

■ If you want to use an image as a background instead of a theme, you can tap Browse.

Note: If you tap Browse, another display appears with a list of images on your device.

■ You can tap Beam to send a theme to another device.

■ You can tap Delete to remove a theme from your device.

5 Tap OK to accept your choice.

■ The Today Settings display closes, and the newly selected Today theme appears on your device.

SELECT THE ITEMS APPEARING ON THE TODAY SCREEN

In addition to a background image or theme, you can select from five items to appear on the Today screen: You can have the date, owner information, Calendar, Tasks, and Inbox information shown.

The date always appears at the top, but the other four items can be arranged in any order that you want by using the Move Up or Move Down functions.

The date, owner information, and Inbox items cannot be further customized, so you will see the date as you have selected in the Date settings (which are discussed in Chapter 5), your name and phone number for owner information, and a note listing how many messages you have in your Inbox.

You can specify what appointments are shown on the Today screen and

if all-day events will be displayed. You can also select the type and category of tasks that you want to appear.

There are also several third-party applications that enable you to use the Today screen to launch applications and show news updates, weather forecasts, movie times, and other handy information.

SELECT THE ITEMS APPEARING ON THE TODAY SCREEN

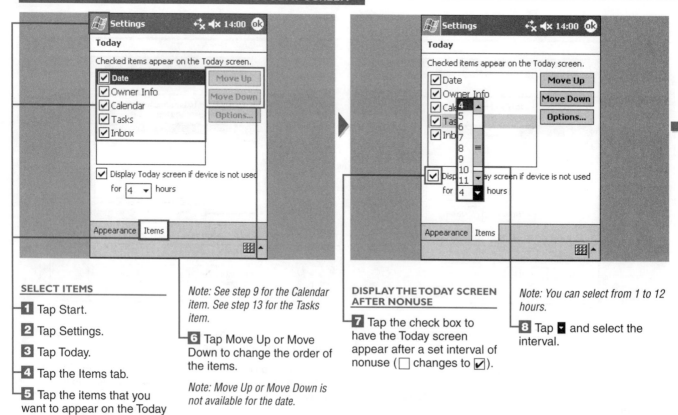

SELECT ITEMS

1 Tap Start.

2 Tap Settings.

3 Tap Today.

4 Tap the Items tab.

5 Tap the items that you want to appear on the Today screen (☐ changes to ☑).

Note: See step 9 for the Calendar item. See step 13 for the Tasks item.

6 Tap Move Up or Move Down to change the order of the items.

Note: Move Up or Move Down is not available for the date.

DISPLAY THE TODAY SCREEN AFTER NONUSE

7 Tap the check box to have the Today screen appear after a set interval of nonuse (☐ changes to ☑).

Note: You can select from 1 to 12 hours.

8 Tap ▾ and select the interval.

Can I hide all the items in the Today settings from the Today screen?

✔ Yes, any item can be unchecked and will not appear on the Today screen. However, you cannot delete the Today screen itself.

What is the maximum number of appointments that I can view on my Today screen?

✔ The next three appointments and the scheduled time can appear on the Today screen. After the time for one appointment has passed, the next one in line is automatically shown, if you have the Calendar settings established.

What happens if I tap in the block or on the icon of any item on the Today screen?

✔ The application is launched, so you can enter appointments, modify tasks, or read e-mails. If you tap the owner information, its display appears in case you want to make changes. If you tap the date, the Alarms Settings utility is launched so that you can set up an alarm.

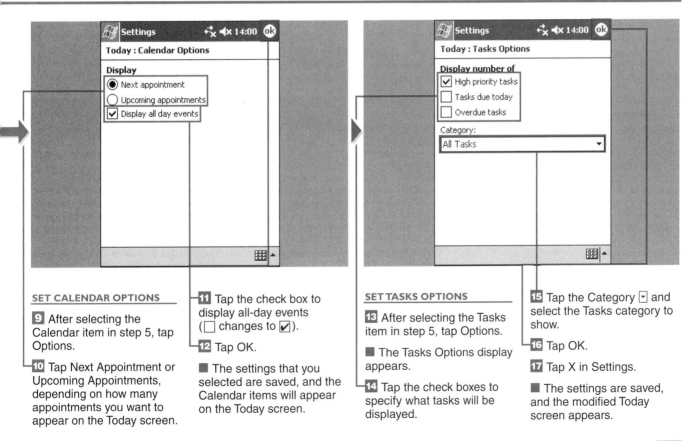

SET CALENDAR OPTIONS

■9 After selecting the Calendar item in step 5, tap Options.

■10 Tap Next Appointment or Upcoming Appointments, depending on how many appointments you want to appear on the Today screen.

■11 Tap the check box to display all-day events (☐ changes to ☑).

■12 Tap OK.

■ The settings that you selected are saved, and the Calendar items will appear on the Today screen.

SET TASKS OPTIONS

■13 After selecting the Tasks item in step 5, tap Options.

■ The Tasks Options display appears.

■14 Tap the check boxes to specify what tasks will be displayed.

■15 Tap the Category ⊡ and select the Tasks category to show.

■16 Tap OK.

■17 Tap X in Settings.

■ The settings are saved, and the modified Today screen appears.

USING NEW TO LAUNCH A PROGRAM

You can activate a setting that enables you to start creating a new document right from your Today screen by using the New command.

Windows Mobile 2003 includes the options to create a new appointment, contact, message, task, note, Excel spreadsheet, and

Word document. In addition, when an application is installed on your device, it may install a plug-in that allows a new document of its type to be created from the New menu.

The Menus settings enable you to activate the New menu and select the specific documents that you can create.

In addition to having the New menu appear on the Today screen, you can have the New menu appear in other applications such as Pocket Word or Pocket Excel. Tapping the arrow to the right of New brings up a list of items that you can create.

USING NEW TO LAUNCH A PROGRAM

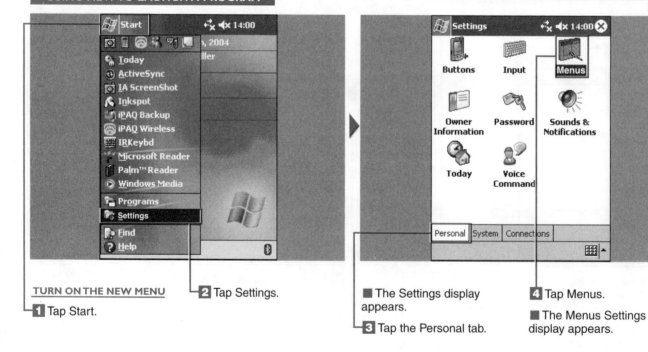

TURN ON THE NEW MENU

■1 Tap Start.

■2 Tap Settings.

■ The Settings display appears.

■3 Tap the Personal tab.

■4 Tap Menus.

■ The Menus Settings display appears.

Can I use the New menu to launch any application?

✔ No, the New menu launches only those applications that have a plug-in to the New menu settings. These applications generally enable you to create new documents, so games, Web browsers, and other applications without much text entry will not be able to be launched.

Why does the New menu not appear in some applications?

✔ Generally, the New menu appears in applications that allow text entry, such as the Calendar, Notes, Pocket Word, and Pocket Excel.

Is there a limit to the number of items that I can have in the New menu?

✔ No, you can check as many items as you want in the Menus settings.

Can I reorganize the order of items in the New menu?

✔ No, the items appear in alphabetical order. Some applications use techniques in the plug-ins to rearrange their shortcuts. For example, Pocket Informant adds a dot to the beginning of its shortcuts so that its items appear at the top of the menu.

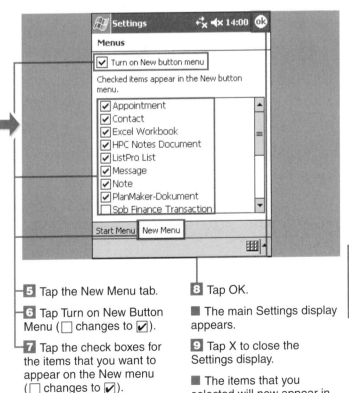

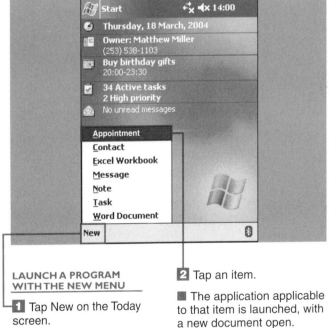

5 Tap the New Menu tab.

6 Tap Turn on New Button Menu (☐ changes to ☑).

7 Tap the check boxes for the items that you want to appear on the New menu (☐ changes to ☑).

8 Tap OK.

■ The main Settings display appears.

9 Tap X to close the Settings display.

■ The items that you selected will now appear in the New menu.

LAUNCH A PROGRAM WITH THE NEW MENU

1 Tap New on the Today screen.

■ The menu of items that you selected appears.

2 Tap an item.

■ The application applicable to that item is launched, with a new document open.

CUSTOMIZE THE START MENU

Windows Mobile 2003 includes a Start menu similar to the one on a Windows desktop computer. With the Start menu, you can launch any application stored on your device, launch a recently used application, access your Programs or Settings folder, launch the Find utility, and view the Help files.

You can customize the Start menu by adding shortcuts to it. The default menu settings allow only nine application shortcuts to be placed on the Start menu, but you can copy and paste more by using File Explorer. The Today shortcut cannot be removed from the device and will always appear at the top of the Start menu. The other items on the menu are listed in alphabetical order.

You can access the Start menu directly from almost any application, except games. This enables you to move quickly between applications.

The Start menu is more limited than what you may be familiar with on a Windows desktop, but it is intended just for quick access to your most common applications.

CUSTOMIZE THE START MENU

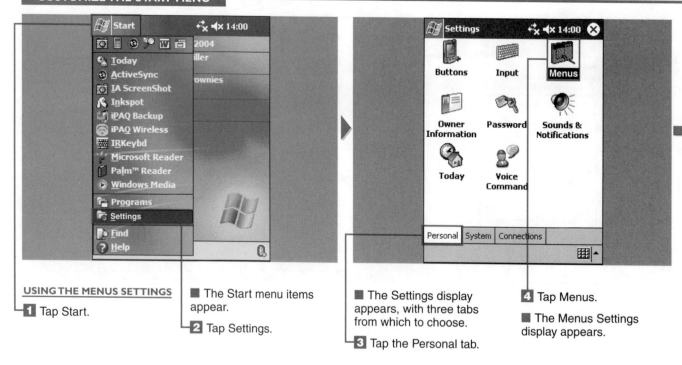

USING THE MENUS SETTINGS

1 Tap Start.

■ The Start menu items appear.

2 Tap Settings.

■ The Settings display appears, with three tabs from which to choose.

3 Tap the Personal tab.

4 Tap Menus.

■ The Menus Settings display appears.

Can I move the Start menu elsewhere on my display as in Windows?

✔ No, the Start menu cannot be moved in Windows Mobile 2003; it always remains in the upper-left corner.

Can I use folders to add more shortcuts to the Start menu so that I do not have to scroll down the menu?

✔ You cannot add folders as you can in Windows for your desktop. However, there are third-party applications that enable you to add more customization and organization to your Start menu.

Can I paste shortcuts to documents or Web site links in the Start menu?

✔ Yes, but a Web site link first needs to be saved in Internet Explorer as a favorite. You can then go to your Favorites folder in File Explorer and copy and paste the shortcut into the Windows\Start Menu folder. You can paste shortcuts only to documents that are supported by the applications in the Windows Mobile 2003 operating system. For example, you can paste shortcuts to Notes, Word documents, and Excel spreadsheets but not to documents run with third-party applications.

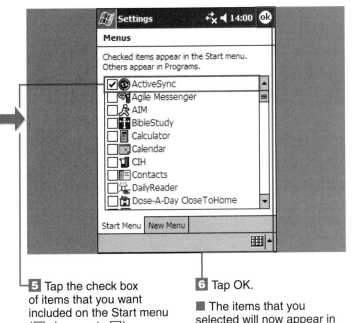

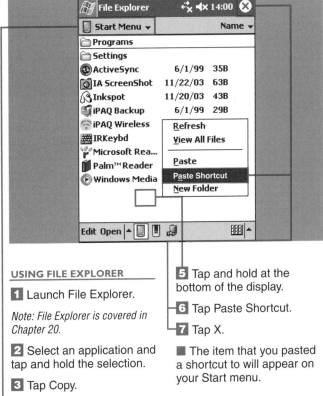

5 Tap the check box of items that you want included on the Start menu (☐ changes to ☑).

Note: If you tap more than nine items, a warning pop-up box will appear.

6 Tap OK.

■ The items that you selected will now appear in the Start menu.

USING FILE EXPLORER

1 Launch File Explorer.

Note: File Explorer is covered in Chapter 20.

2 Select an application and tap and hold the selection.

3 Tap Copy.

4 Open the Start menu in File Explorer.

5 Tap and hold at the bottom of the display.

6 Tap Paste Shortcut.

7 Tap X.

■ The item that you pasted a shortcut to will appear on your Start menu.

START AN APPLICATION

You can start an application from the Start menu with a single tap on the application shortcut — even when you are running another application. Windows Mobile 2003 manages the open applications in the background, so you do not have to close one to start another.

If you do not have an application shortcut shown on your Start menu, you can still launch the application by using Start to go to the Programs folder. The Programs folder lists all the applications that you have installed on your device.

How many applications can I start by using the Start menu?
✔ You can use the Start menu to launch any application.

Can I start multiple copies of a single application by using the Start menu?
✔ No, Windows Mobile 2003 does not allow multiple copies of an application to be launched.

START AN APPLICATION

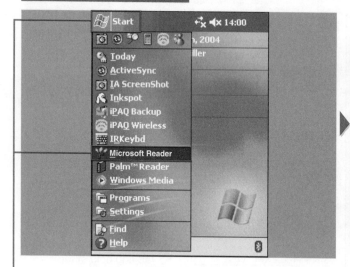

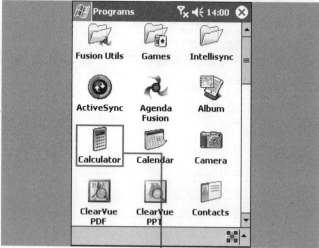

START AN APPLICATION

1 Tap Start.

■ The Start menu appears.

2 Tap an application shortcut.

■ If another application is already running, it is minimized.

■ The selected application starts.

USE PROGRAMS

3 If an application is not on your Start menu, tap Start ➪ Programs.

■ The Programs folder opens, listing all the installed applications.

4 Tap the application.

■ The application starts.

SWITCH TO A RECENT APPLICATION

You may want to use a few applications repeatedly, so with the Recent Applications bar of the Start menu, you can launch your most recently used applications. The Recent Applications bar contains up to eight applications.

Because the Windows Mobile 2003 operating system enables users to

run multiple applications at once, it is handy to be able to start one application and initiate an action, such as starting to download e-mail with the Inbox, and then switch to another application to work, such as creating a Word document.

Will only applications that I have listed in my main Start menu appear in the Recent Applictions bar?

✔ No, application shortcuts that are not shown on your Start menu also appear in the Recent Applications bar.

SWITCH TO A RECENT APPLICATION

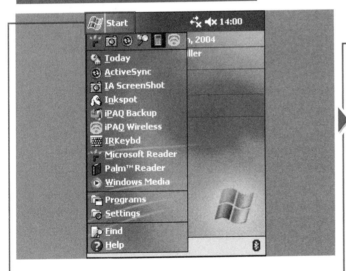

1 Tap Start.

■ The Start menu appears.

2 Tap the shortcut in the Recent Applications bar to the application that you want to open.

■ The selected application is launched.

FIND A DOCUMENT

One of the most powerful features of the Windows Mobile 2003 platform compared to using a paper organizer or planner is the capability to quickly find a word, document, task, appointment, and so on by using a search engine. You can find what you are looking for on your device by using the Start menu and Find utility.

Find is easy to use because you simply enter the term that you are searching for.

What is the small memory card icon next to the item returned by my search?

✔ This icon indicates that the item is saved on an external storage card.

How else can I use the Find function, aside from searching for a specific item?

✔ You can leave the Find line blank and select Larger Than 64KB from the Type drop-down list to quickly find large files that are stored on your device.

FIND A DOCUMENT

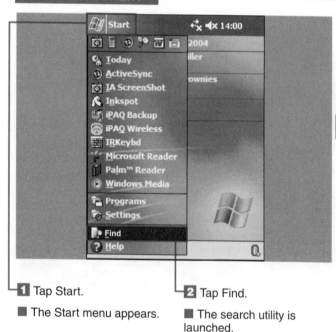

1 Tap Start.

■ The Start menu appears.

2 Tap Find.

■ The search utility is launched.

3 Enter the search term.

Note: You can also use the Find ⊡ to access recent search terms.

4 Tap the Type ⊡ and select the type of data that you are looking for.

5 Tap Go.

■ Go changes to Stop so that you can tap it again to stop your search.

6 Tap a selected item.

■ The item's application starts, and the document with your found item appears.

GET HELP

Microsoft has included quick access to the Help files on the Start menu. You can view Help files for most applications and utilities that are part of the Windows Mobile 2003 operating system.

In addition to the Help files installed in the operating system, when you install an application on your device, you may find that the application's developer installed a useful Help file in HTML format. Some applications enable you to access this file from within the application, but others do not include this capability. You can use your Start menu to access all the Help files stored on your device.

The Help files are written in HTML code so that you can use the Help interface like a Web browser — in which you can tap a link to go to the next page, tap Back or Forward to go back or forward a page, and go back to the contents file for all Help files.

GET HELP

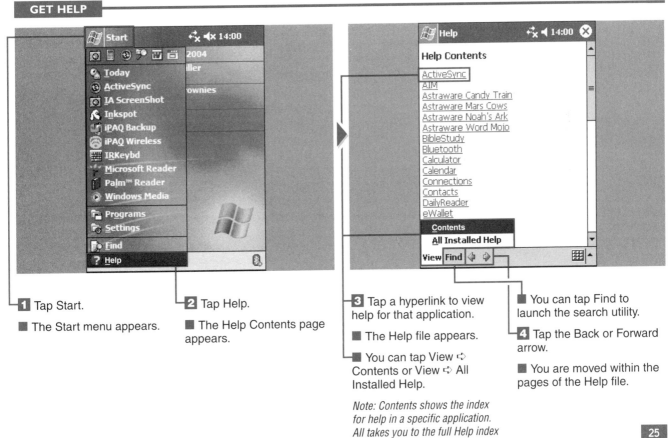

1 Tap Start.

■ The Start menu appears.

2 Tap Help.

■ The Help Contents page appears.

3 Tap a hyperlink to view help for that application.

■ The Help file appears.

■ You can tap View ➪ Contents or View ➪ All Installed Help.

■ You can tap Find to launch the search utility.

4 Tap the Back or Forward arrow.

■ You are moved within the pages of the Help file.

Note: Contents shows the index for help in a specific application. All takes you to the full Help index display.

4) CUSTOMIZING PERSONAL SETTINGS

5) CUSTOMIZING GENERAL SYSTEM SETTINGS

6) MODIFYING POWER USAGE AND BACKLIGHT SETTINGS

PERSONAL AND SYSTEM SETTINGS

7) MODIFYING MEMORY USAGE

8) MANAGING BLUETOOTH COMMUNICATIONS

ASSIGN AND ADJUST HARDWARE BUTTONS

Your device is equipped with four assignable hardware buttons. Your device manufacturer sets a default action for each button. Assigning Calendar to button one is typical, so when button one is pressed, the calendar launches.

You can assign a program or function to any of these four programmable buttons; doing so

can give you easy access to a frequently used program or function. For example, if you frequently use GPS software, you can assign the GPS software to a hardware button so that when the button is pressed, it launches your GPS software.

The directional pad on your device is used for scrolling through items on a list. If scrolling is too fast or

slow, you can adjust the delay before the first repeat and the repeat rate of the directional pad. The Delay Before First Repeat option adjusts the length of the delay before scrolling begins, and the Repeat Rate option adjusts how long it takes to scroll from item to item.

ASSIGN AND ADJUST HARDWARE BUTTONS

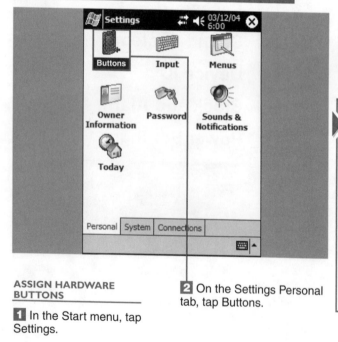

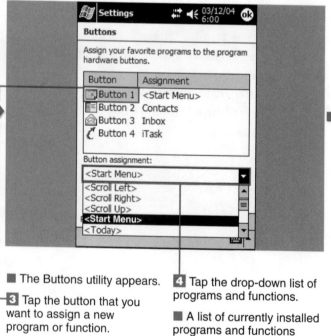

ASSIGN HARDWARE BUTTONS

1 In the Start menu, tap Settings.

2 On the Settings Personal tab, tap Buttons.

■ The Buttons utility appears.

3 Tap the button that you want to assign a new program or function.

4 Tap the drop-down list of programs and functions.

■ A list of currently installed programs and functions appears.

Can I reset my device's hardware buttons back to the default settings?

✔ Yes. In the bottom-right corner of the Program Buttons tab, you can tap Restore Defaults to return the hardware buttons to their original assignments.

What can I do on the Lock tab?

✔ Some device manufacturers add in additional functions. Lock enables you to disable the hardware buttons when your device is in standby. Check with your device vendor for additional information about the Lock feature. If you are using a Phone Edition of Windows Mobile 2003, this feature is located under the Phone options.

Why is the Restore Defaults button grayed out?

✔ You have to change one of the existing default button assignments before the Restore Defaults button becomes available. Until then, the button is disabled, or grayed out. When you select Restore Defaults, all the buttons return to their defualt settings.

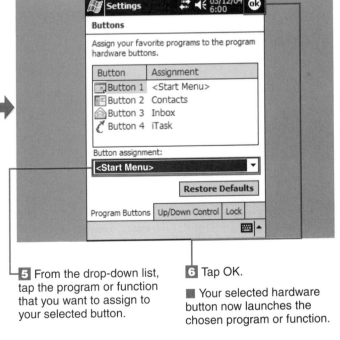

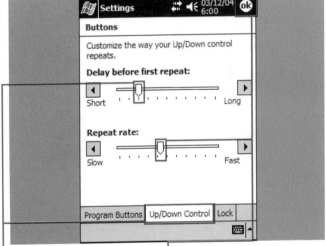

■5 From the drop-down list, tap the program or function that you want to assign to your selected button.

■6 Tap OK.

■ Your selected hardware button now launches the chosen program or function.

ADJUST HARDWARE SCROLL AND REPEAT RATE

■1 Tap the Up/Down Control tab.

■2 Tap and drag the Delay Before First Repeat slider control to the delay that you want.

■3 Tap and drag the Repeat Rate slider control to the rate that you want.

■4 Tap OK.

■ Your directional control pad now scrolls through items on a list according to your settings.

CUSTOMIZE INPUT METHODS

Y ou can customize many aspects of your device's input methods.

The most common text input method for your device is the on-screen keyboard. You can change the way the on-screen keyboard is displayed and used. Other input methods include the block recognizer, letter recognizer, and transcriber. The block recognizer supports the Graffiti writing strokes that existed on the Palm.

Many third-party input methods are available as well.

When you enter text into programs such as Pocket Word, Notes, or Messenger, Windows Mobile 2003 suggests the word you are trying to type and offers to complete the word for you. You can customize how suggested words are displayed and offered.

Additionally, you can customize various other input options for

entering text input or audio input. You can change the default voice recording format for audio input, the default zoom level for writing and typing, whether to capitalize the first letter of a sentence, or whether to have the screen scroll when it reaches its last visible line.

Windows Mobile 2003 makes entering data into your device simple and natural, providing you with a robust set of tools.

CUSTOMIZE INPUT METHODS

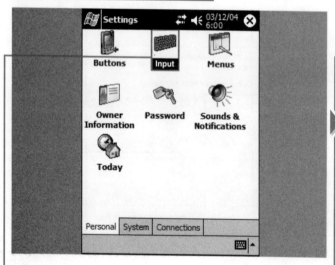

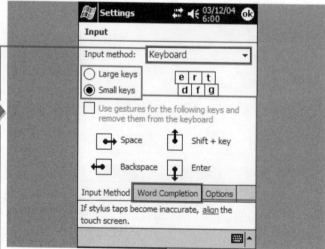

1 On the Settings Personal tab, tap Input.

■ The Input utility is displayed.

2 Tap the drop-down list and select the input method that you want to customize.

Note: Different methods have different options that you can choose.

■ For the keyboard options, you can select to use the large key or small key on-screen keyboard (○ changes to ●).

3 Tap the Word Completion tab.

■ The Word Completion tab is displayed.

Why is the Use Gestures option on the Keyboard page grayed out?

✔ If you choose to use large keys for your on-screen keyboard, the Use Gestures check box becomes enabled, or no longer grayed out. Using large keys for your on-screen keyboard can make entering text easier to tap but gives up easy access to some characters such as numbers and certain symbols that are displayed on the small key on-screen keyboard. When using the large keys, you have to access those characters from the number and symbols on-screen keyboard, but there is an extra step to using them. Using gestures brings many of those numbers and symbols back to the main large key on-screen keyboard by sacrificing the Space, Shift, Backspace, and Enter keys. When the Use Gestures box is checked, you tap and move your stylus as shown for each of the sacrificed keys.

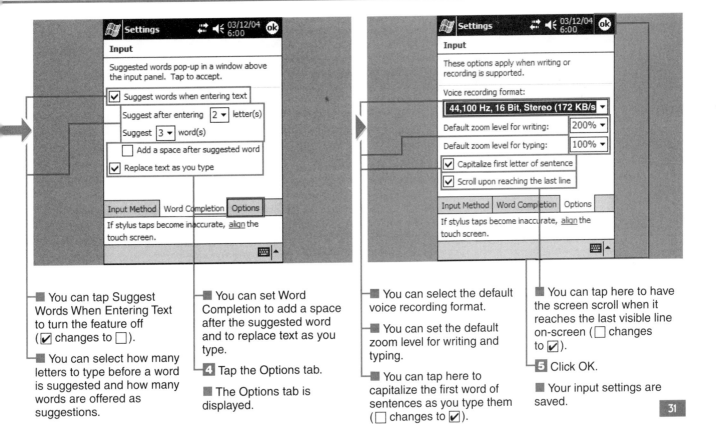

■ You can tap Suggest Words When Entering Text to turn the feature off (☑ changes to ☐).

■ You can select how many letters to type before a word is suggested and how many words are offered as suggestions.

■ You can set Word Completion to add a space after the suggested word and to replace text as you type.

4 Tap the Options tab.

■ The Options tab is displayed.

■ You can select the default voice recording format.

■ You can set the default zoom level for writing and typing.

■ You can tap here to capitalize the first word of sentences as you type them (☐ changes to ☑).

■ You can tap here to have the screen scroll when it reaches the last visible line on-screen (☐ changes to ☑).

5 Click OK.

■ Your input settings are saved.

CUSTOMIZE THE START MENU

You can customize the appearance of your Start menu by selecting what programs appear on it. Any installed program can be added to or removed from the Start menu. Removing a program from the Start menu does not uninstall the program; it only removes it from being displayed on the Start menu. To remove a program, you can refer to Chapter 7.

Adding programs that you use frequently to the Start menu makes them more convenient to locate when you need to run them.

How do I add subfolders or shortcuts to the Start menu?

✔ In ActiveSync on your PC, click Explore and open up My PocketPC; click Windows, click Start Menu, and then add or create folders and shortcuts that you want to appear on the Start menu. You can find more information about ActiveSync in Chapter 12.

CUSTOMIZE THE START MENU

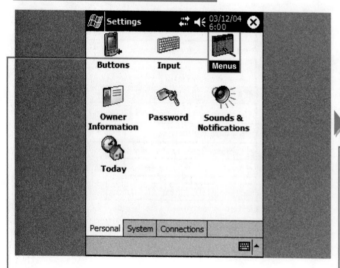

1 On the Settings Personal tab, tap Menus.

■ The Menus utility appears.

2 Tap the application that you want to appear on the Start menu (☐ changes to ☑).

Note: You are limited to only nine items in the Start menu.

■ You can uncheck a box next to an application that you do not want to appear on the Start menu (☑ changes to ☐).

3 Tap OK.

■ Your Start menu has been updated.

ADD OWNER INFORMATION

You can set your personal information, such as your name, address, and phone number, for your device. Additionally, you can include your company name and e-mail address.

You can choose to have your owner information displayed when the device is turned on. When this

featured is enabled, the information you added will be displayed every time that you turn on your device until you tap the screen.

Adding your identification to the device can be helpful in the return of a lost or recovered PDA.

Can I add additional owner information, such as offering a reward if the device is found?

✔ Yes. Simply tap the Notes tab and add your personal message. You can select to have your personal message displayed when the device is turned on just like your standard owner information.

ADD OWNER INFORMATION

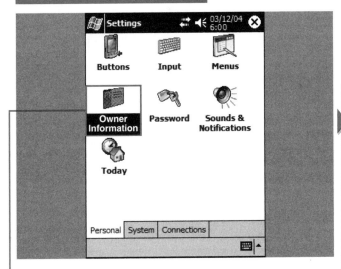

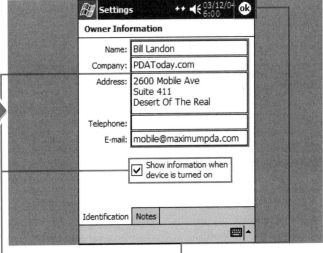

1 On the Settings Personal tab, tap Owner Information.

■ The Owner Information utility appears.

2 Enter your owner information.

3 Tap Show Information When Device Is Turned On (☐ changes to ☑).

4 Tap OK.

■ The next time that you turn on your device, the owner information will be displayed until you tap the screen.

SET THE DEVICE PASSWORD

You can set your device to require a password to be entered before it can be accessed or used.

You can set a simple four-digit password to access your device. A four-digit password provides a minimum amount of security for your device's data but should not be used for more sensitive data or if your device connects to a network.

For added security, you can use a strong password. A strong password needs to include at least seven characters and combine upper- and lowercase letters, numerals, and punctuation. You should use a strong password if your device contains sensitive data or connects to a network.

You can set how long your device must be turned off before the password is needed to access the device.

Additionally, you can add a password hint in case you forget your password. The hint is shown after four unsuccessful password attempts.

SET THE DEVICE PASSWORD

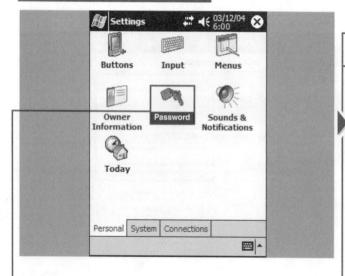

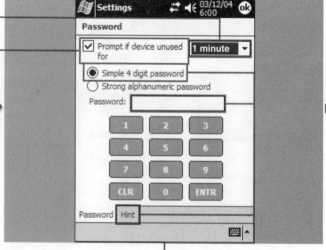

SET A SIMPLE PASSWORD

1 On the Settings Personal tab, tap Password.

■ The Password utility appears.

2 Tap Prompt If Device Unused For (□ changes to ☑).

3 From the drop-down list, select how long your device must be unused before the password is needed to access your device.

4 Tap Simple 4 Digit Password (○ changes to ◉).

5 Enter your four-digit password using the keypad provided.

6 Tap the Hint tab.

MASTER IT

I forgot my password, and I didn't have a password hint; what can I do now?

✔ If you forget your password, you need to refer to your owner's manual and follow the directions on how to perform a hard reset. Performing a hard reset results in the loss of any data on the device and the removal of any programs that you have installed. If you have created a backup file, you will still be able to restore data from the date of your last backup.

Can a hacker use my device to gain access to my company's network?

✔ Yes. If your device has been configured to connect to your company's network and the network password is stored on the device, an unauthorized person may be able to gain access. Also, any other confidential information such as credit card numbers, birthdays, or contact information is available to the user. You should always use a strong password to help protect networked devices.

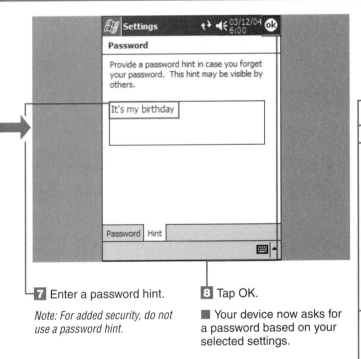

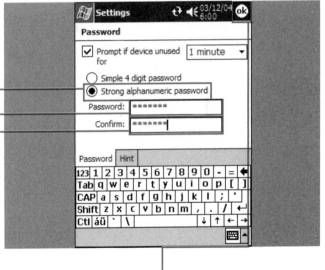

7 Enter a password hint.

Note: For added security, do not use a password hint.

8 Tap OK.

■ Your device now asks for a password based on your selected settings.

SET A STRONG PASSWORD

1 On the Password tab, tap Strong Alphanumeric Password (○ changes to ⦿).

2 Enter your strong password.

3 Confirm your strong password by reentering it.

Note: You need to use at least seven characters, including a combination of upper- and lowercase letters, numbers, and symbols.

4 Tap OK.

■ Your device now asks for a password based on your selected settings.

35

CUSTOMIZE SYSTEM SOUNDS AND NOTIFICATIONS

Y ou can customize many aspects of your device's system sounds and notifications. The most basic change that you can make is adjusting the volume. You can easily adjust the device volume with varying levels from silent to loud.

You can enable sounds for features such as warnings and system

events. You can enable sounds for programs and set those programs that have notifications such as alarms or reminders to become active.

You can set the device to provide you with an auditory tap sound when the screen is tapped or a hardware button is used.

You can customize the sound that is played when a program event occurs, such as when you receive an infrared beam from another device. Along with playing a sound with an event, you can have your device display a message on-screen. Additionally, you can set your device to flash its indicator light for a specific amount of time.

CUSTOMIZE SYSTEM SOUNDS AND NOTIFICATIONS

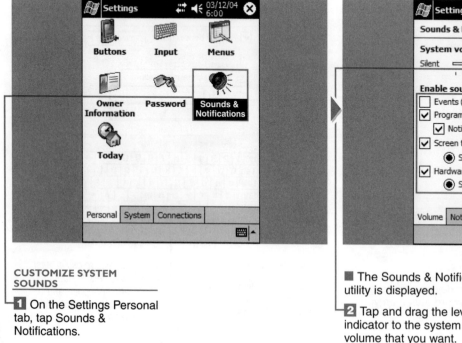

CUSTOMIZE SYSTEM SOUNDS

1 On the Settings Personal tab, tap Sounds & Notifications.

■ The Sounds & Notifications utility is displayed.

2 Tap and drag the level indicator to the system volume that you want.

3 Tap the features for which you want to enable sound (□ changes to ☑).

4 Tap OK.

■ Your system sounds have been set.

Is the system volume setting the same as the volume setting found in Chapter 2?

✔ Yes. This is another way to adjust the system volume that enables greater control over other system sound aspects such event and notification sounds.

Does using system sounds and the notification light use additional battery power?

✔ Yes. Turning off system sounds and the notification light increases your device's battery life between charges.

Is there a way to add my own system sounds?

✔ Yes. There are many third-party tools for customizing the system sounds. A search in Google for "Pocket PC system sounds" is a good place to start. Additionally, you may want to look at several Pocket PC software vendors for more custom sound solutions.

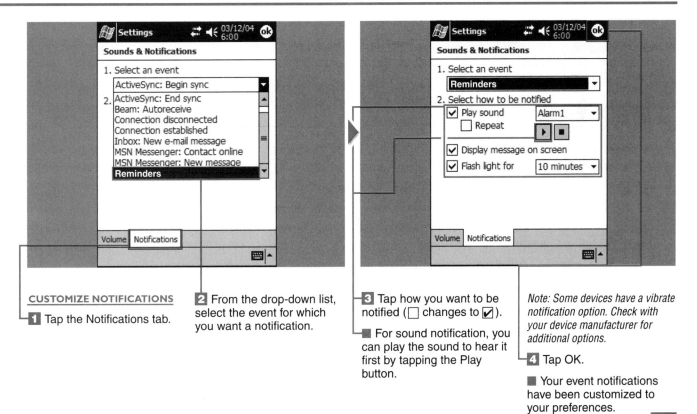

CUSTOMIZE NOTIFICATIONS

1 Tap the Notifications tab.

2 From the drop-down list, select the event for which you want a notification.

3 Tap how you want to be notified (☐ changes to ☑).

■ For sound notification, you can play the sound to hear it first by tapping the Play button.

Note: Some devices have a vibrate notification option. Check with your device manufacturer for additional options.

4 Tap OK.

■ Your event notifications have been customized to your preferences.

IDENTIFY THE SYSTEM VERSION AND SET THE DEVICE ID

Many Windows Mobile devices vary in specifications depending on the device manufacturer and model within a particular manufacture's product line. The key differences to be aware of are the device's processor and amount of installed memory, along with what version of Windows Mobile is installed on the device. You can view this kind of valuable

information about your device in the About settings.

You can replace your device's default device ID with a custom device ID to help distinguish your device from other devices. You can add an additional description to your device to help further identify it.

Changing your PDA's device ID and adding a description to your device

is a recommended task that helps avoid confusion when working with multiple Windows Mobile devices on the same desktop. *Note:* The device ID is used for synchronization, so changing it may require that you reestablish your device partnership with your PC.

IDENTIFY THE SYSTEM VERSION AND SET THE DEVICE ID

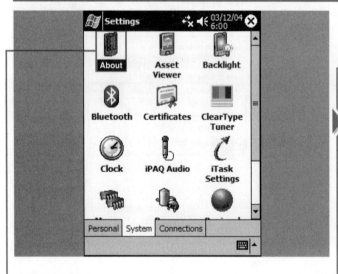

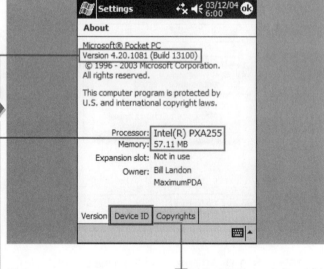

1 In System Settings, tap About.

■ The About utility appears.

■ You can view various device statistics, such as the processor, installed memory, and Windows Mobile version.

2 Tap the Device ID tab.

If I change my device name, will I have to reestablish my device partnership?

✔ No. Your device has a unique key that your PC uses to distinguish your Windows Mobile device from other Windows Mobile devices. ActiveSync will display your new device name. You can find more information about ActiveSync in Chapter 12. *Note:* In some cases, you may have to reestablish the partnership.

Can I use two Windows Mobile device with the same name?

✔ No. ActiveSync will prompt you to change the name of your device if you set up a partnership with a name that already exists.

Can someone with the same device name use ActiveSync on my PC and access my personal information?

✔ No, your device has a unique key with your PC. You would have to delete the partnership with your current device to synchronize the new device. You can have another device attach to your PC as a guest. Again, you can find more information about ActiveSync in Chapter 12.

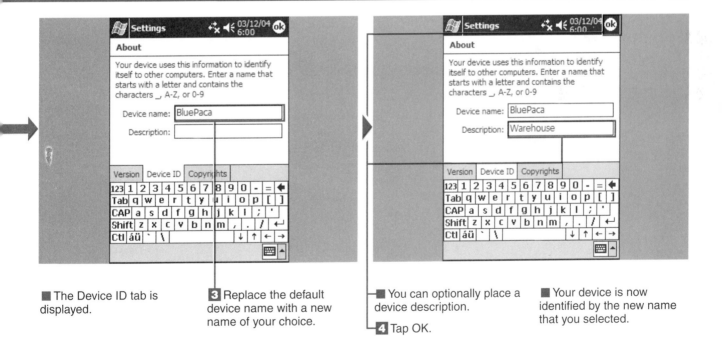

■ The Device ID tab is displayed.

3 Replace the default device name with a new name of your choice.

━ You can optionally place a device description.

4 Tap OK.

■ Your device is now identified by the new name that you selected.

ADJUST THE CLOCK AND ALARM SETTINGS

Keeping the date and time and setting the alarm are integral parts of Windows Mobile 2003. These features are a basic part of the underpinnings of a Personal Information Manager (PIM) for your Calendar, Tasks, e-mail, and file date stamps.

You can adjust the date and time for your local time zone on your device. This also automatically sets the daylight saving time adjustment for your time zone based on what city you choose. You can additionally set a separate time zone if you travel, which you manually select when in the other time zone.

You can set up to four daily alarms with your device, similar to a travel alarm. Setting an alarm can be useful for reminding you about an important reoccurring event such as taking medication at a required daily interval.

ADJUST THE CLOCK AND ALARM SETTINGS

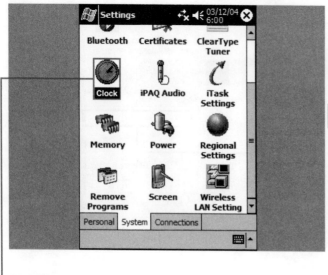

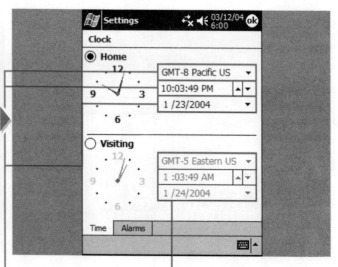

ADJUST THE CLOCK

■ In System Settings, tap Clock.

■ The Clock utility appears.

2 Tap the time zone ⊡ and select your local time zone.

3 Tap ⊡ and ⊡ to adjust the time.

4 Tap the date ⊡ and select your current date.

■ Your time and date are updated.

■ You can repeat steps 2 to 4 in the Visiting section to set a traveling time zone, date, and time.

How do I change the format for how the time and date are displayed?

✔ You can change your time and date format using the Regional Settings utility. You can find more information about the Regional Settings utility in the section "Change Regional Number Formatting."

Can I change the way the clock is displayed on the navigation bar?

✔ Yes. You can tap and hold the clock display and select an analog or digital display.

What is GMT?

✔ GMT is short for *Greenwich Mean Time,* which is measured at the Royal Observatory in Greenwich, England. GMT is the universal time zone (UTC) for the world; all other time zones are measured plus or minus GMT.

Can I set an alarm to "snooze," as I do with my regular alarm clock?

✔ Yes. You can snooze the alarm, similar to the reminders for your tasks and schedules.

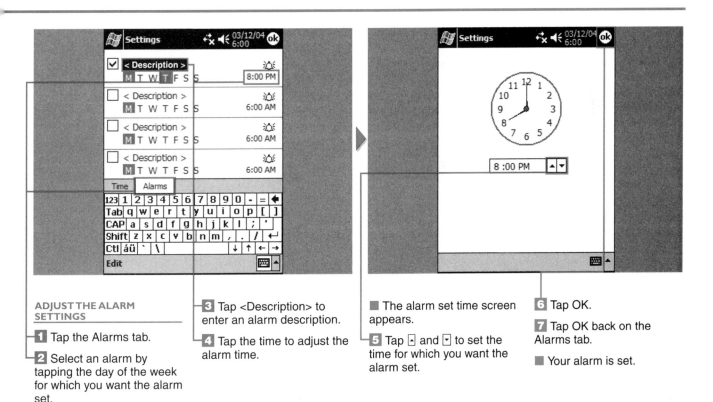

ADJUST THE ALARM SETTINGS

1 Tap the Alarms tab.

2 Select an alarm by tapping the day of the week for which you want the alarm set.

3 Tap <Description> to enter an alarm description.

4 Tap the time to adjust the alarm time.

■ The alarm set time screen appears.

5 Tap ▲ and ▼ to set the time for which you want the alarm set.

6 Tap OK.

7 Tap OK back on the Alarms tab.

■ Your alarm is set.

CHANGE REGIONAL NUMBER FORMATTING

Using the Regional Settings utility, you can change how the numbers, currency, times, and dates are displayed on your device. This enables you to use the settings common to your language and region of the world.

You can select a new regional setting for your device. On the Appearance Samples screen, your device displays a preview of how the new settings will affect numbers, currency, times, and dates. The new settings will also affect how these items are sorted in some programs.

You can customize every aspect of how numbers are displayed and treated on your device. For example, in North America, the period (.) is used to indicate a decimal point, and a comma (,) is used to separate large numbers. In many regions around the world, these settings are reversed.

You can customize how currency is displayed and treated on your device. Additionally, you can change how time, dates, and calendar information are shown.

CHANGE REGIONAL NUMBER FORMATTING

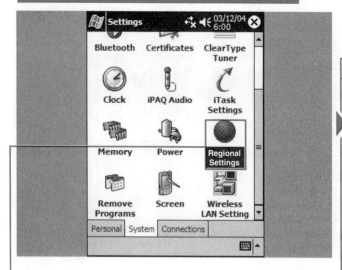

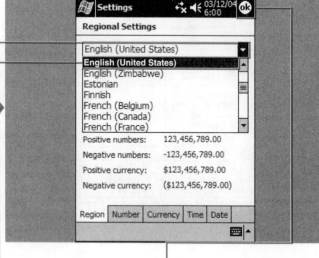

SET THE REGION

1 In System Settings, tap Regional Settings.

■ The Appearance Samples screen is displayed.

2 Tap ▼.

3 Select the language and region in which you are located.

■ The Appearance Samples screen shows how time, date, numbers, and currency will be displayed.

4 Tap OK.

■ Your language and region are saved.

How do I customize the Time settings?

✔ On the Time tab, use the ▼s to select the format that you want. You are able to change the time style, time separator, and A.M. and P.M. symbols. There is a time sample at the top of the screen that displays the time in the format that you have chosen. When you have made all of your changes, tap OK to save them.

How do I customize the Date settings?

✔ On the Date tab, use the ▼s to select the date format that you want. You can change both the long date format and the short date format. Sample formats are displayed at the top of the screen. When your changes are complete, tap OK to save them.

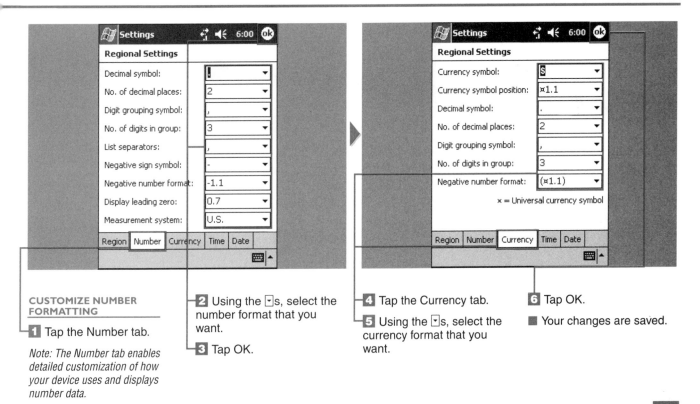

CUSTOMIZE NUMBER FORMATTING

1 Tap the Number tab.

Note: The Number tab enables detailed customization of how your device uses and displays number data.

2 Using the ⊡s, select the number format that you want.

3 Tap OK.

4 Tap the Currency tab.

5 Using the ⊡s, select the currency format that you want.

6 Tap OK.

■ Your changes are saved.

MANAGE PERSONAL AND ROOT CERTIFICATES

You can add and use personal certificates as well as designated root certificates in Windows Mobile 2003. You can use personal certificates to control what devices have access to the Web sites that you manage. Several common root certificates are included that enable you to visit banks, credit card companies, or other selected secure sites.

Third-party applications, such as Crtimprt, enable you to import personal and root certificates that may not be included in Windows Mobile 2003.

Can I add personal certificates from the Settings display?

✔ No, personal certificates are added through the use of a desktop utility.

Why would I want to add a personal certificate to my device?

✔ You may need authentication for a VPN, Internet Explorer, or your WiFi network.

MANAGE PERSONAL AND ROOT CERTIFICATES

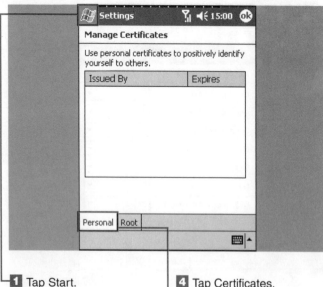

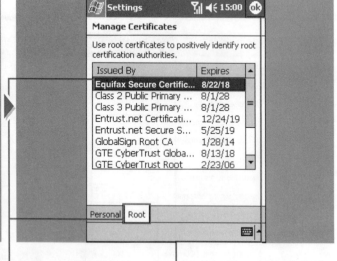

1 Tap Start.

2 Tap Settings.

3 Tap the System tab.

4 Tap Certificates.

5 Tap the Personal tab.

Note: Here you can view any certificates that you loaded onto your device.

6 Tap the Root tab.

7 Tap the name of a certificate to view its details.

■ A detail page listing who the certificate was issued to and by, along with the valid dates, appears.

Note: On the detail page, you also have the option to delete the certificate.

8 Tap OK to close the details.

9 Tap OK to close the certificate management settings.

■ The main System Settings display appears.

ALIGN THE DISPLAY AND ENABLE CLEARTYPE

I f you test or evaluate a lot of software or use your device to play games regularly, you may find that the touch panel loses a bit of accuracy. Windows Mobile 2003 includes a utility that enables you to recalibrate and align your display so that accurate screen taps can be made.

Also, Windows Mobile 2003 devices can use ClearType fonts on a global scale; they are no longer limited to just eBook applications. A ClearType Tuner utility is included on some models of Windows Mobile 2003 devices that enables you to use a slider to further refine ClearType settings.

What is the difference between ClearType fonts and standard fonts?

✔ ClearType technology allows the device to display pieces of text on fractions of pixels rather than on a single pixel, which enables text to be almost as clear and sharp as text found on paper.

ALIGN THE DISPLAY AND ENABLE CLEARTYPE

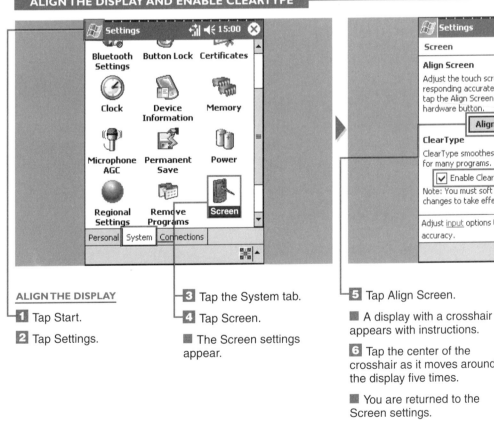

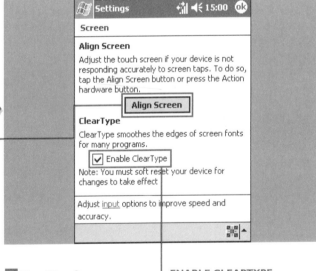

ALIGN THE DISPLAY

1 Tap Start.

2 Tap Settings.

3 Tap the System tab.

4 Tap Screen.

■ The Screen settings appear.

5 Tap Align Screen.

■ A display with a crosshair appears with instructions.

6 Tap the center of the crosshair as it moves around the display five times.

■ You are returned to the Screen settings.

ENABLE CLEARTYPE

7 Tap Enable ClearType (☐ changes to ☑).

8 Soft reset your device so that the ClearType setting takes effect.

■ You will notice that the readability of text throughout your device is improved.

ADJUST THE BACKLIGHT AND BRIGHTNESS SETTINGS

With the Backlight settings, you can control how your mobile device uses backlighting and power consumption, ensuring that you get the most time between charges out of your device's battery while still getting ample screen brightness.

You can further define these settings by telling your device to turn off the backlight after a predetermined amount of time or to turn on the backlight when a button is pressed or the screen is tapped. These settings are divided into two distinct tabs — Battery Power and External Power. This gives you more flexibility on the device's power consumption, enabling you to maximize battery life between charges.

In addition to defining when and how the device's backlight is activated, you can control the amount of brightness the screen has. You can control the level of brightness independently when the device is on battery power and when the device is on external power.

Note: The backlight and brightness settings are OEM specific, so the features and functions may vary on your device.

ADJUST THE BACKLIGHT AND BRIGHTNESS SETTINGS

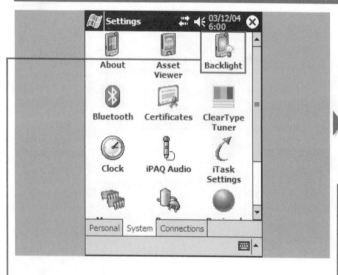

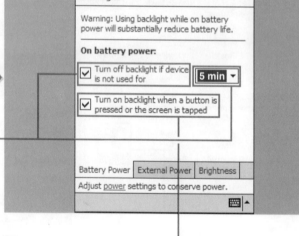

ADJUST THE BACKLIGHT ON BATTERY POWER

1 On the Settings System tab, tap Backlight.

■ The Backlight utility appears.

2 Tap the first check box to set the elapsed time to turn off the backlight when the device is not in use (□ changes to ☑).

■ You can select the amount of time to elapse until your backlight turns off.

3 Tap the second check box to set the device to turn on its backlight when a button is pressed or the screen is tapped.

■ Your device is now set to use its backlight while on battery power as you have specified.

Do I need to use the backlight when outside?

✔ It depends on your mobile device. Mobile devices have optimized screens that enable easy visibility when used outside or in bright light; check with your device manufacturer for more information regarding this type of use.

Is there a shortcut to adjust my power settings?

✔ Yes. In the Backlight utility at the bottom of the screen, there is a shortcut labeled Adjust Power Settings to Conserver Power that takes you to the power settings.

How do I force my device to always have the backlight on when it is on battery power?

✔ On the Battery Power tab, uncheck the Turn Off Backlight If Device Is Not Used For box. The elapsed time drop-down box will become grayed out. Note, however, that using the backlight while on battery power will substantially reduce your device's battery life.

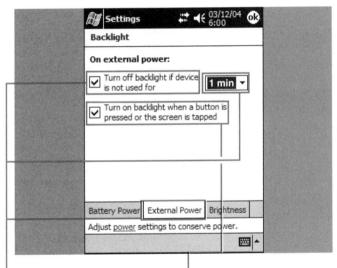

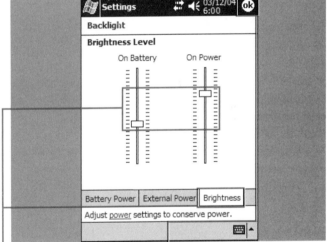

ADJUST THE BACKLIGHT ON EXTERNAL POWER

1 Tap the External Power tab.

2 Tap the first check box to set the elapsed time to turn off the backlight when the device is not used.

■ You can select the amount of time to elapse until your backlight turns off.

3 Tap the second check box to set the device to turn on its backlight when a button is pressed or the screen is tapped.

■ Your device is now set to use its backlight while on external power as you have specified.

ADJUST BACKLIGHT BRIGHTNESS

1 Tap the Brightness tab.

2 Tap and drag the level indicator buttons to the brightness level that you want for the On Battery and On Power settings.

Note: If your device is on battery power, you will see the backlight change as you move the On Battery slider button. This is also the case if you are on external power and you move the On Power slider button.

3 Tap OK to finish.

MODIFY POWER SETTINGS

With the Power utility, you can modify how your device consumes power, thus maximizing your device's battery life between charges. You can also view how much power is left on your main battery and your backup battery.

Depending on the manufacturer of your device, you may be able to adjust a power-conservation mode called *standby*. The Standby utility reserves a portion of battery life, and you can modify the Standby settings to meet your needs. When the unit goes into standby, it cannot be used until it is recharged. This prevents program and data loss.

You can adjust when the unit powers itself off when it is not being used while it is on battery power as well as on external power. Allowing the device to turn itself off after a period of inactivity greatly increases the battery life between charges.

MODIFY POWER SETTINGS

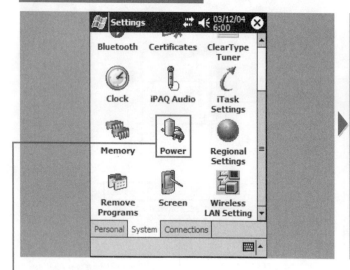

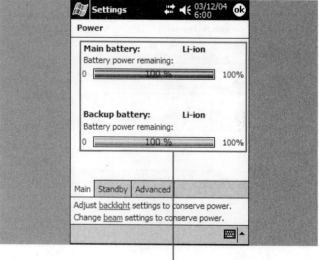

VIEW REMAINING POWER

1 From the System Settings, tap Power.

■ The Power utility appears.

■ You can check the remaining battery life for your device's main battery. Some devices also show the strength of the backup battery.

How do I force my device to always stay powered on?

✔ On the Advanced tab, you can uncheck the box under On Battery Power to force the device to always stay on while using battery power. You can additionally uncheck the box under On External Power to force the device to stay on while on external power.

Why do I not have a Standby tab on my device?

✔ Not all devices offer the standby power-saving feature. It is found on HP iPAQ devices; other device manufacturers may implement similar features.

How come my battery power does not last very long when I use a Compact Flash card or other peripheral?

✔ Many of these devices draw power from your PDA's main battery. I recommend that you use the AC adapter or another form of external power when using Compact Flash or other peripheral devices for extended periods of time.

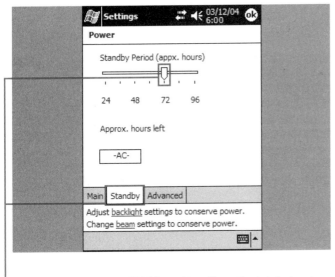

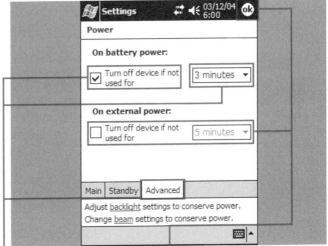

ADJUST STANDBY SETTINGS

■1 Tap the Standby tab.

■2 Tap and drag the indicator button to the standby time that you want.

Note: The estimated displayed hours of time remaining may vary, depending on other system settings.

Note: This feature is specific to the HP iPAQ devices only.

ADJUST POWER SETTINGS

■1 Tap the Advanced tab.

■2 Tap the first check box to adjust when your device will power off while on battery power.

■ You can select how many minutes until your device will power off.

■3 Tap the second check box and adjust when your device will power off while on external power.

■4 Tap OK.

■ Your device is now set to conserve and use power based on your custom settings.

ADJUST MEMORY ALLOCATION

With the Memory utility, you can view and modify a variety of memory-related tasks on your mobile device.

The Main tab of the Memory utility displays how much memory is currently allocated for storage memory and program memory. The Windows Mobile 2003 operating system automatically manages your device's memory usage; however,

you can temporarily change those allocations to increase or decrease your program memory or storage memory.

On the Storage Card tab, you can view the size of inserted storage devices. Some examples of attached storage devices are Secure Digital (SD) memory cards, Compact Flash (CF) memory cards, and similar types of storage peripherals.

Additionally, you can view how much storage is being used and how much storage is available for use.

Some devices include built-in nonvolatile memory storage for placing valuable data. This type of storage is sometimes called a *file store*, and you can view this information on the Storage Card tab as well.

ADJUST MEMORY ALLOCATION

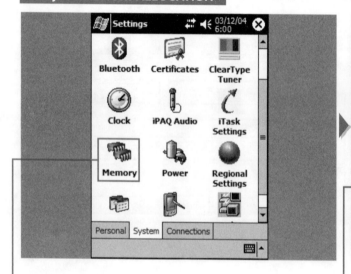

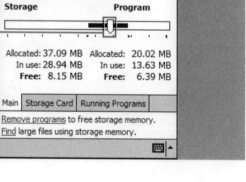

ADJUST MEMORY ALLOCATION

1 In System Settings, tap Memory.

■ The Memory utility appears.

2 Tap and drag the level indicator button to the memory setting that you want.

Note: Drag the button toward Storage to increase the amount of available program memory. Drag the button toward Program to increase the amount of available storage memory.

Note: Some programs require you to allocate more memory for them to run efficiently.

■ Windows Mobile 2003 will continue to manage memory usage.

When I place files in storage, they appear to take up less space than they do on my PC. Is there something wrong with my internal storage?

✔ No. Windows Mobile 2003 manages your memory usage and compresses RAM that is used for storage at a rate of 2:1.

How come files in the file store do not disappear after a hard reset?

✔ Files located in the file store are stored in what is called *nonvolatile memory.* Nonvolatile memory retains its memory after power is removed, similar to an SD card or a CF card.

How do I add additional internal storage memory and not use my SD or CF slots?

✔ Most Windows Mobile devices are not designed with user-replaceble parts in mind. However, there are third-party companies who specialize in adding additional internal storage to mobile devices.

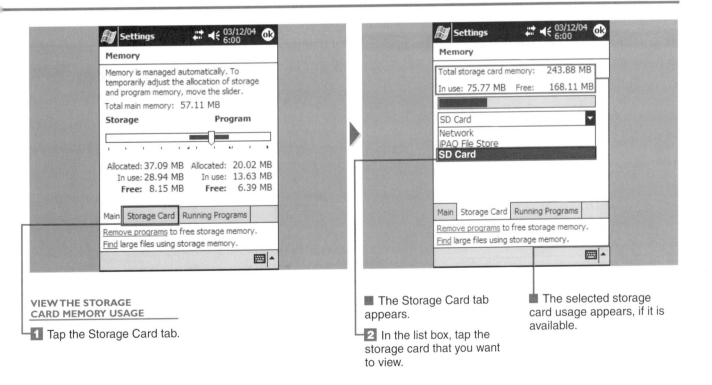

VIEW THE STORAGE CARD MEMORY USAGE

1 Tap the Storage Card tab.

■ The Storage Card tab appears.

2 In the list box, tap the storage card that you want to view.

■ The selected storage card usage appears, if it is available.

IDENTIFY, STOP, AND ACTIVATE RUNNING PROGRAMS

On the Running Programs tab of the Memory utility, you can view all the currently running programs.

After a program is started, it remains running in the background — *smart minimized* — until it is manually stopped, even if you are not using it. However, the OS does stop programs as needed to keep the system running smoothly.

On the Running Programs tab, you can manually stop a smart-minimized program or activate a program. You can also stop all running programs, freeing up system and program memory.

Stopping running programs that you are not using helps free up memory for the operating system and other programs and, potentially, can increase system performance. Additionally, you may need to stop

a program if it becomes unstable and program or system memory becomes low.

Performing a soft or hard reset can also free up memory and stop running programs; however, these procedures can result in lost data. Before performing a soft reset, be sure to save any data in running programs. Performing a hard reset will erase all your data.

IDENTIFY, STOP, AND ACTIVATE RUNNING PROGRAMS

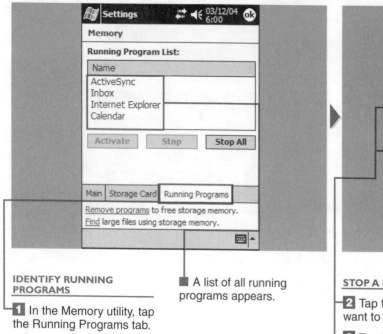

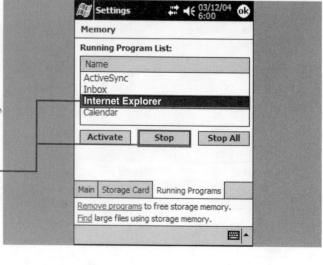

IDENTIFY RUNNING PROGRAMS

1 In the Memory utility, tap the Running Programs tab.

■ A list of all running programs appears.

STOP A RUNNING PROGRAM

2 Tap the program that you want to stop.

3 Tap Stop.

■ The selected program is stopped, and the memory that the program was using is returned to the system.

Will performing a soft reset stop all running programs?

✔ Yes and no. Most currently running programs will stop until you open them again. However, some programs may be activated from the startup folder and launch when your device resets.

Do I have to stop each program individually?

✔ No, on the Running Programs tab, you can tap Stop All to stop all the running programs.

Is the Running Programs tab the only place that I can stop or close a program?

✔ Not necessarily. Some device vendors include a program that brings up a list of running programs that can be accessed by pressing a button on the device, enabling you to easily stop running programs. There are a number of third-party applications for stopping or closing applications as well.

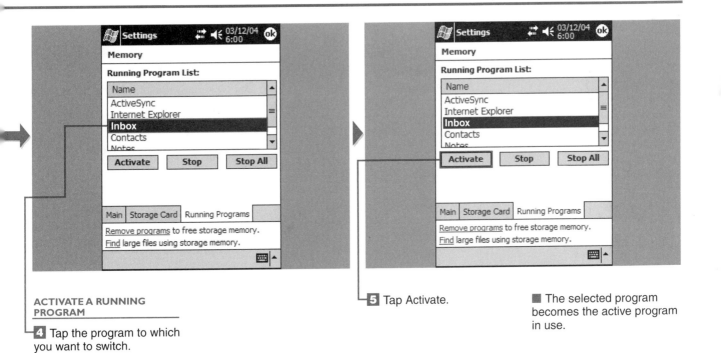

ACTIVATE A RUNNING PROGRAM

4 Tap the program to which you want to switch.

5 Tap Activate.

■ The selected program becomes the active program in use.

REMOVE PROGRAMS AND FIND LARGE FILES

You can choose to remove any or all of the programs that you have installed in storage memory. Removing unused installed programs can free up valuable memory space. The total storage available on your device is displayed and updated when you remove programs.

Unused large files can also take up valuable storage space that could otherwise be used for more storage memory or program memory. You can find such large files by using the Find tool. If the files are no longer used or needed, you can make note of them and delete them

later in File Explorer. You can find additional information about File Explorer in Chapter 20.

The Remove Programs utility includes an Adjust Memory Allocation hyperlink that enables you to quickly switch between utilities while fine-tuning your memory and storage space.

REMOVE PROGRAMS

1 On the Running Programs tab of the Memory utility, tap the Remove Programs link.

■ The Remove Programs utility appears.

2 Tap the program that you want to remove.

3 Tap Remove.

■ A dialog box appears, verifying that you want to remove the selected program.

4 Tap Yes.

5 Tap OK to return to the Memory utility.

■ The selected program is removed.

There still seems to be missing storage space, and I have deleted all my installed programs. What am I missing?

✔ Some programs leave data and temporary files on your device. Additionally, remnants of programs can be left from an unsuccessful or corrupted install or uninstall. In these cases, you may want to perform a complete hard reset of your device. Note that *all data* on your device will be erased.

Also, you can delete temporary Internet files from Pocket Internet Explorer.

Can I remove applications like Word or Excel?

✔ You can remove only programs installed in storage memory. Programs that come on the device or do not appear in the Remove Programs list cannot be removed. Note that these programs reside in ROM rather than storage memory, so there is no advantage to removing them.

Can I delete files that are in the Find Large Files list?

✔ No. You can delete files only from File Explorer.

FIND LARGE FILES

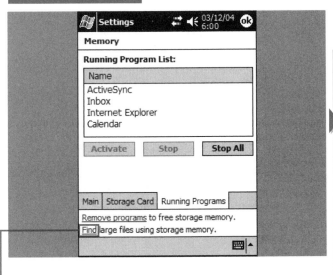

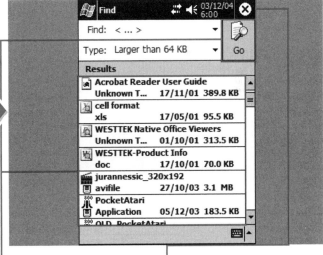

1 On the Running Programs tab of the Memory utility, tap the Find Large Files link.

■ The Find utility appears, ready to find files larger than 64KB.

2 Tap Go.

■ A list of all files larger than 64KB appears.

3 Make a note of which files you want to delete.

Note: You will need to delete the files from File Explorer. You can find information on how to use File Explorer in Chapter 20.

4 Tap X to return to the Memory utility.

CREATE AND CHANGE A PROFILE

With your Windows Mobile 2003 device and either integrated Bluetooth or a Bluetooth expansion card, you can connect to your desktop, laptop, cell phone, headset (select models only), or other Bluetooth-enabled Palm or Pocket PC device.

Using a Bluetooth connection, you can transfer files, exchange business cards, connect to the Internet, or ActiveSync with your computer.

Bluetooth is a wireless radio frequency-based standard that is designed to replace cables. It is a short range wireless technology with a maximum range of approximately 300 feet (100m) with a dedicated Bluetooth access point. A range of about 30 feet (10m) is standard with a Bluetooth USB dongle connected to your desktop.

To be more specific, there are three classes: Class 1 — 100mw, 7dbm or higher — about 100 meters;

Class 2 — 2.5mw, 4dbm — about 30 meters; and Class 3 — 1mw, 0dbm — about 10 meters. Each device has a different class, and any class can talk to another if the two are in range.

Windows Mobile 2003 devices use the default profile unless you create other profiles or modify existing profiles specifically for your personal Bluetooth settings. You can create, edit, or delete Bluetooth profiles.

CREATE AND CHANGE A PROFILE

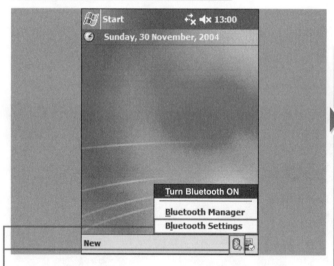

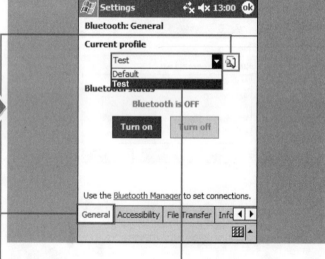

1 Tap the Bluetooth icon on the Today screen.

■ A small pop-up list appears with three options for you to select.

2 Tap Bluetooth Settings.

■ The Bluetooth settings appear.

Note: You can also tap Start ⇨ Settings ⇨ Connections ⇨ Bluetooth to get here.

Note: These steps show the most common implementation using the Widcomm configuration found on the HP iPAQ devices.

3 Tap the General tab.

4 Tap the Add/Delete Profiles button to add or delete a profile.

■ Alternatively, you can tap the ▼ to select an existing account.

Do I have to create a new profile to use Bluetooth?

✔ No, the default profile is adequate for many users and enables you to connect to most Bluetooth devices.

Why would I want or need to create a new profile or change the default profile?

✔ The default profile is set up for standard connection settings but will not save any changes that you make. Your device will always be seen as a Pocket PC by other Bluetooth devices if you do not create and select a new profile. Multiple profiles are commonly established for home, office, and travel settings. Multiple profiles are also convenient for designating different shared folders and setting different security restrictions.

Can I get more help on profiles on my Pocket PC?

✔ Yes, tap Start ➪ Help while on the main General display, and an HTML help file will be launched.

Do I have to go to the General display to switch from the default profile every time that I use Bluetooth?

✔ No, Windows Mobile 2003 saves and reloads your last used profile when the device is turned off and then on again.

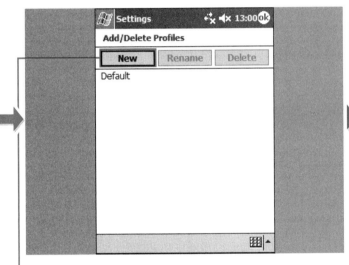

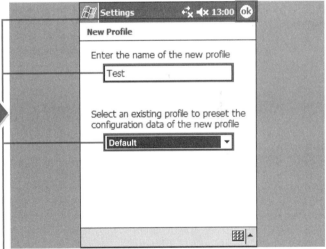

■ The Add/Delete Profiles settings appear.

5 Tap New to create a new profile.

Note: You can tap Rename to change the name or Delete to delete the selected profile.

Note: You cannot delete the default profile or the active profile.

■ The New Profile entry screen appears.

6 Type in a name for the new profile.

7 Tap the drop-down list to select a profile to copy existing configuration data.

8 Tap OK to return to the profile list.

9 Tap OK to return to the General tab.

10 Tap OK once more to save the settings and exit the Bluetooth Settings area.

■ The Today screen reappears, and your new Bluetooth profile is saved.

57

ACTIVATE BLUETOOTH

The Bluetooth radio sends out signals to maintain the connection between devices and requires constant power. You can choose to turn your Bluetooth radio on and off to conserve power when you are not using Bluetooth communications.

The integrated Bluetooth radio or radio contained on an external card must be turned on before communications can be initiated.

Can I set my Bluetooth radio to turn on automatically?

✔ No, you must manually turn on the radio to start communications.

Why would I want to turn off the Bluetooth radio?

✔ The radio consumes power, and eventually the Windows Mobile 2003 device battery will die. Microsoft and device manufacturers have made it a quick two-tap process to turn on the Bluetooth radio.

ACTIVATE BLUETOOTH

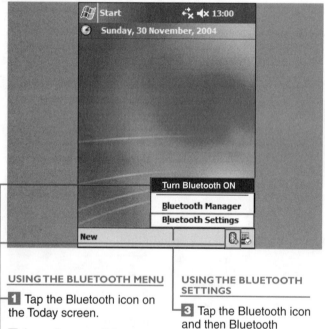

USING THE BLUETOOTH MENU

1 Tap the Bluetooth icon on the Today screen.

■ A small pop-up list appears.

2 Tap Turn Bluetooth On to activate the radio.

■ The blue indicator light on your Pocket PC or Bluetooth card starts flashing.

USING THE BLUETOOTH SETTINGS

3 Tap the Bluetooth icon and then Bluetooth Settings.

4 Tap Turn On on the General tab.

■ The Bluetooth settings appear.

■ The blue indicator light on the device or Bluetooth card starts flashing when the radio is turned on, and the Turn Off button turns red.

VIEW BLUETOOTH AND MODULE VERSIONS

The Bluetooth radio — integrated into Windows Mobile 2003 devices or on external cards — is controlled by drivers. You can view the driver developer's information and version of the modules that are loaded onto your device or external card.

New versions of the Bluetooth radio drivers are generally released with newer devices and through updates to existing Windows Mobile 2003 devices or external Bluetooth cards.

Can I change the version of my modules?

✔ The Bluetooth drivers may be updated by the device or Bluetooth card manufacturer with RAM or ROM updates. Check your device or Bluetooth card manufacturer's Web site for information.

VIEW BLUETOOTH AND MODULE VERSIONS

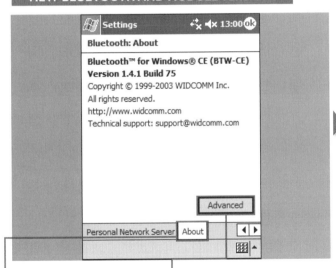

■1 In the Bluetooth settings, tap the About tab.

Note: See the section "Create and Change a Profile" to access the Bluetooth settings.

■ The current version of the Bluetooth drivers and the developer of the drivers are shown.

■2 Tap Advanced.

■ Each Bluetooth module loaded on your device is shown.

Note: Modules include the Bluetooth Wizard, File Explorer, and business card.

■3 Tap OK to close the module viewing area.

■4 Tap OK again to close the About screen.

■ The Bluetooth settings close, and the Today screen appears.

LAUNCH THE BLUETOOTH MANAGER

You can easily manage Bluetooth communications between your Windows Mobile 2003 device and other Bluetooth-enabled devices with the Bluetooth Manager.

Hewlett-Packard (HP) includes its own Bluetooth Manager to help make the Bluetooth experience easier for owners and facilitate communications between devices.

Do other manufacturers have the Bluetooth Manager?

✔ No, only HP Windows Mobile 2003 devices use the Bluetooth Manager.

What can I do with the Bluetooth Manager?

✔ The Bluetooth Manager enables you to follow step-by-step Connection Wizards

to set up communciations between Bluetooth devices. You can manage the following communications: exploring a Bluetooth device, connecting to the Internet via a phone, ActiveSyncing via Bluetooth, browsing files on a remote device, connecting to a network, joining a personal network, or exchanging business cards.

LAUNCH THE BLUETOOTH MANAGER

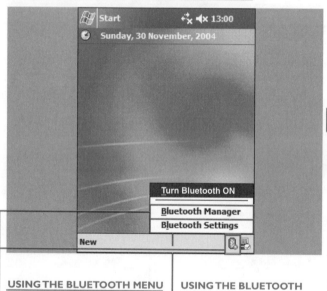

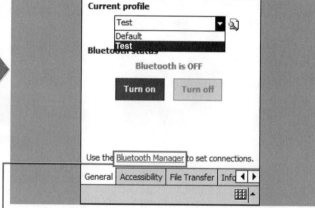

USING THE BLUETOOTH MENU

1 Tap the Bluetooth icon on the Today screen.

■ A small pop-up list appears.

2 Tap Bluetooth Manager.

■ The blue indicator light on your Pocket PC or Bluetooth card starts flashing, and the Bluetooth Manager screen opens.

USING THE BLUETOOTH SETTINGS

3 Tap the Bluetooth icon and then Bluetooth Settings.

■ The Bluetooth settings appear with the General tab selected.

4 Tap the Bluetooth Manager hyperlink.

■ The blue indicator light on your Pocket PC or Bluetooth card starts flashing, and the Bluetooth Manager screen opens.

SET THE DEVICE IDENTIFICATION

Every Bluetooth device has a unique name to identify it when Bluetooth communications are established. Each Windows Mobile 2003 device uses "PocketPC" as the default device name. After creating a new profile as detailed in the section

"Create and Change a Profile," you can create a unique identity for your device.

You should change the name to something other than "PocketPC" so that you can communicate with other Windows Mobile 2003 devices without all having the same name.

Can I change the name of my device in the default profile?

✔ No, you must create a new profile to make changes to the Bluetooth settings. This procedure is described in the section "Create and Change a Profile."

SET THE DEVICE IDENTIFICATION

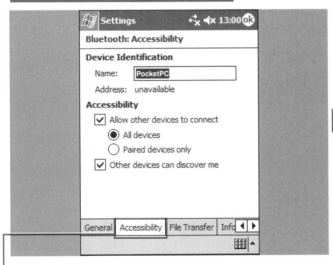

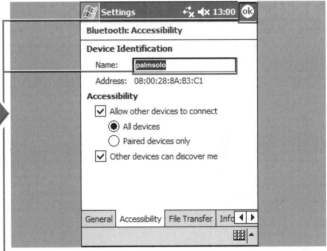

1 In the Bluetooth settings, tap the Accessibility tab.

Note: See the section "Create and Change a Profile" to access the Bluetooth settings.

■ The default name of "PocketPC" appears in the Name box.

2 Type in a unique name for your device.

3 Tap OK to save the name and exit the Bluetooth settings.

■ Your Windows Mobile 2003 device identification is now saved, and other devices will see your device with this unique name.

MODIFY DEVICE ACCESSIBILITIES

When you turn on your Bluetooth radio, your device begins sending out a signal that other Bluetooth devices can discover and identify.

So that you can maintain security of the information on your device, you have options for controlling who may connect to or discover your Windows Mobile 2003 device. Unless you give specific permission and a PIN code to other people, your device cannot be connected to other devices.

What does paired devices mean?

✔ When a connection is made between two devices, the option to pair them up and recognize each other for future connections is presented. This pairing process includes entering a PIN number on both devices that must match for a successful pairing. After devices are paired, they can be connected more quickly during subsequent connections.

MODIFY DEVICE ACCESSIBILITIES

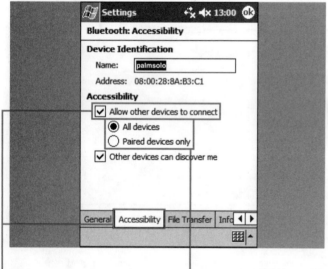

1 In the Bluetooth settings, tap the Accessibility tab.

■ The Accessibility settings appear.

2 Tap the first check box to allow other devices to connect to your device (☐ changes to ☑).

3 Tap the top radio button to allow all devices to connect or tap the bottom button to allow only paired devices to connect (○ changes to ◉).

4 Tap the bottom check box to allow other devices to discover your device (☐ changes to ☑).

5 Tap OK.

■ The Bluetooth settings close, and your Accessibility settings are saved for your custom profile.

DEFINE FILE TRANSFER SETTINGS

B ecause Bluetooth is a short range wireless technology designed to replace cables, one of the main functions of the technology is to transfer files wirelessly. You can transfer files to other Windows Mobile 2003 devices, Pocket PCs, Palm-powered devices, desktop/laptop computers, and cell phones. File transfer speeds can reach up to 768K compared to the 11Mbps rating of 802.11b WiFi connections.

How does the passkey work?

✔ When someone attempts to send you a file via Bluetooth, a dialog box appears on your device in which you enter a passkey (PIN code) that you define. The other person must then enter the same passkey on his or her device in order to transfer the file.

DEFINE FILE TRANSFER SETTINGS

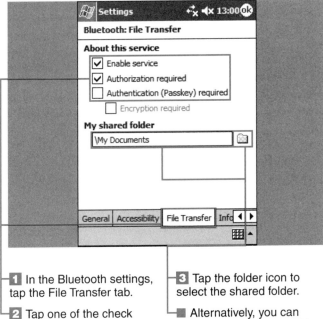

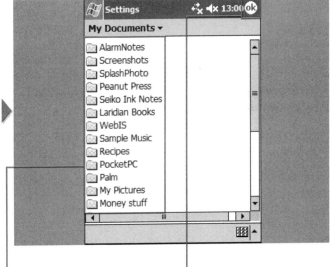

1 In the Bluetooth settings, tap the File Transfer tab.

2 Tap one of the check boxes.

Note: The first box enables the file transfer service; the second requires you to authorize file transfers. The third box requires a passkey.

3 Tap the folder icon to select the shared folder.

■ Alternatively, you can enter the name of the folder that you want to use for sharing files.

■ All the existing folders on your device are shown.

4 Tap one of the folders to designate it as the shared folder.

5 Tap OK.

6 Tap OK again.

■ The Bluetooth settings close, and the file transfer settings are saved.

CUSTOMIZE INFORMATION EXCHANGE SETTINGS

With the Information Exchange settings, you can quickly send your business card, also known as a *vCard,* to other Windows Mobile 2003, Pocket PC, or Palm devices via Bluetooth. You specify a Pocket

Outlook contact that is designated as your business card. You can send your business card to others, or they can request your business card — with different permissions set on incoming communications.

Can I designate more than one business card?

✔ No, the Information Exchange settings are designed to allow you to designate only one business card and have it readily available for other Bluetooth users.

CUSTOMIZE INFORMATION EXCHANGE SETTINGS

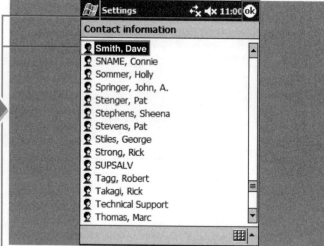

1 In the Bluetooth settings, tap the Information Exchange tab.

2 Tap one of the check boxes.

Note: The first box enables the information exchange service; the second requires you to authorize exchanges. The third box requires a passkey.

3 Tap the vCard icon to select an existing contact for your business card.

■ A list of all contacts in your Pocket Outlook database appears.

4 Tap your contact information.

5 Tap OK.

■ The Information Exchange screen appears with your contact information in blue text.

Note: You can tap the contact icon to enter new contact information. To do so, follow the steps in Chapter 14.

6 Tap OK.

■ The Bluetooth settings close, and the information exchange settings are saved.

CUSTOMIZE SERIAL PORT SETTINGS

You can connect to Global Positioning System (GPS) devices and print from your Pocket PC using the serial port profile. Bluetooth is primarily intended as a cable replacement wireless technology, and the serial port profile included in Windows Mobile 2003 provides serial port emulation.

The serial port profile is based on radio frequency communications

(RFCOMM). This profile provides virtual COM ports that applications can use to connect to various devices. The inbound and outbound COM ports in Windows Mobile 2003 are nonconfigurable. Both ports are bidirectional and support sending and receiving data.

The most common use for the serial port profile is connecting to a Bluetooth GPS. With a Bluetooth GPS and Bluetooth-enabled

Windows Mobile 2003 device, you can place your GPS anywhere in your vehicle, within Bluetooth range, and navigate on your Pocket PC.

Most Windows Mobile 2003 devices do not include a headset profile. The Pocket PC Phone Edition devices include this profile, which enables users to listen to their phone calls, music, and so on on a Bluetooth headset instead of using the internal speaker on the device.

CUSTOMIZE SERIAL PORT SETTINGS

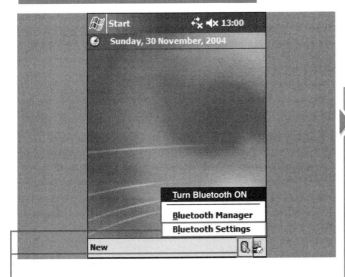

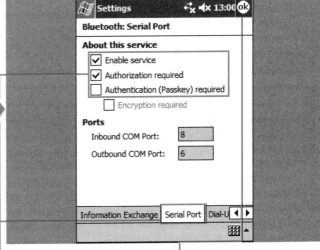

1 Tap the Bluetooth icon on the Today screen.

■ A pop-up menu appears with three options.

2 Tap Bluetooth Settings.

■ The Bluetooth settings appear.

Note: You can also tap Start ⇨ Settings ⇨ Connections ⇨ Bluetooth to get to this same settings area.

3 Tap the Serial Port tab.

4 Tap one of the check boxes.

Note: The first box enables the serial port service; the second requires you to authorize connections. The third box requires a passkey.

5 Tap OK.

■ The Bluetooth settings close, and the serial port settings are saved.

CUSTOMIZE DIAL-UP NETWORKING SETTINGS

With your Bluetooth-enabled Windows Mobile 2003 device and a Bluetooth cell phone, you can connect to the Internet anywhere that you have a satisfactory wireless signal.

Your Bluetooth cell phone serves as a dial-up modem and enables you to connect directly to your wireless

provider's data network or to dial in to your ISP with your cell phone. Wireless data connection speeds vary by provider, but generally range between 40Kbps to 56Kbps on current networks. Many wireless data providers will be offering higher speeds as the technology evolves.

You can use your Inbox to check e-mail or Internet Explorer to surf the Internet virtually anywhere you travel with a successful dial-up connection. Most wireless carriers charge a nominal data fee based on how many kilobytes of data are used; check with your wireless carrier for additional fees and services.

CUSTOMIZE DIAL-UP NETWORKING SETTINGS

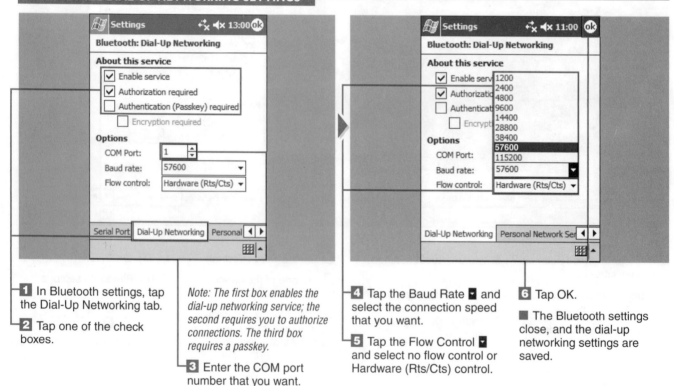

■1 In Bluetooth settings, tap the Dial-Up Networking tab.

■2 Tap one of the check boxes.

Note: The first box enables the dial-up networking service; the second requires you to authorize connections. The third box requires a passkey.

■3 Enter the COM port number that you want.

■4 Tap the Baud Rate ■ and select the connection speed that you want.

■5 Tap the Flow Control ■ and select no flow control or Hardware (Rts/Cts) control.

■6 Tap OK.

■ The Bluetooth settings close, and the dial-up networking settings are saved.

CUSTOMIZE PERSONAL NETWORK SERVER SETTINGS

Instead of connecting to external devices to transfer files or establish communications, you can use your Windows Mobile 2003 device as a server for other Bluetooth-enabled devices. The local network that you create with your Bluetooth device is usually called a personal area network (PAN).

With other devices connected to your PAN server, you can chat, transfer files, or exchange other data.

Can I have more than one device connected to my personal network?

✔ Yes, multiple devices can join or leave the network as long as they satisfy your connection security settings.

CUSTOMIZE PERSONAL NETWORK SERVER SETTINGS

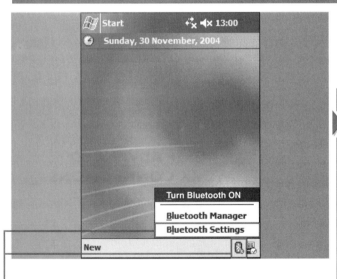

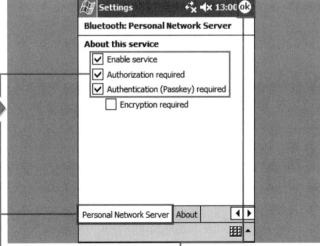

1 Tap the Bluetooth icon on the Today screen.

■ A pop-up menu appears with three options.

2 Tap Bluetooth Settings.

■ The Bluetooth settings appear.

Note: You can also tap Start ➪ Settings ➪ Connections ➪ Bluetooth to get to this same settings area.

3 Tap the Personal Network Server tab.

4 Tap one of the check boxes.

Note: The first box enables the personal network server; the second requires you to authorize connections. The third box requires a passkey.

5 Tap OK.

■ The Bluetooth settings close, and the personal network server settings are saved.

SECTION III

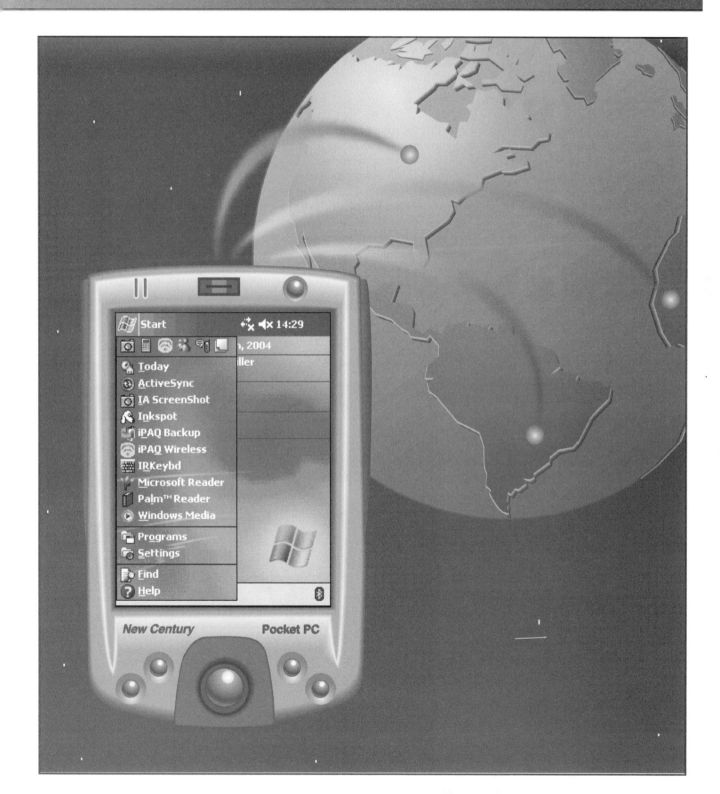

RECEIVE ALL INCOMING INFRARED BEAMS

Transferring files and personal data from one device to another is probably one of the most commonly used features of mobile devices. All Windows Mobile devices currently available include an infrared (IR) port for device-to device communication.

You can transfer files, contacts, appointments, and other files. You can set your device to automatically receive data files from other devices that are in range. When a file is sent to your device, you will receive a prompt asking if you want to accept the file.

Where are files stored after I receive them via IR?

✔ They are stored in the My Documents folder.

Can I send and receive files from a Palm device?

✔ Many other OS-based devices include an IR port as well, so you will usually be able to transfer files between your devices. However, files that are designed to run on another device plaform such as Palm may not open or run on your Windows Mobile device.

RECEIVE ALL INCOMING INFRARED BEAMS

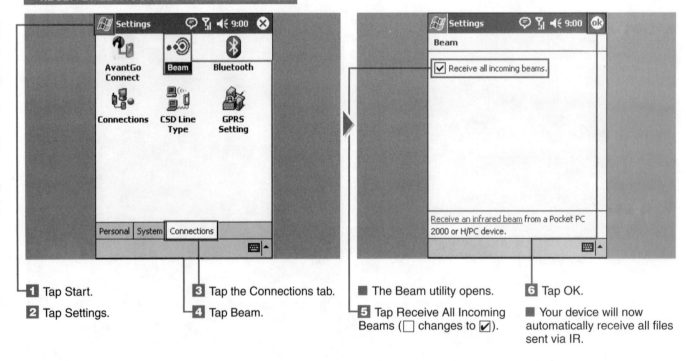

1 Tap Start.

2 Tap Settings.

3 Tap the Connections tab.

4 Tap Beam.

■ The Beam utility opens.

5 Tap Receive All Incoming Beams (☐ changes to ☑).

6 Tap OK.

■ Your device will now automatically receive all files sent via IR.

RECEIVE AN INFRARED BEAM MANUALLY

For added security and privacy, you can set your device to only manually receive IR file transfer requests. In order to receive a file from the IR port, you will manually set your device to receive the file. Your device will prompt you when the file transfer is complete.

I seem to be having trouble receiving a file from another device. Is there anything that I can do?

✔ In some cases, one brand of device may not transfer all files as easily as others. You can download and install one of the third-party tools such as PeaceMaker from Conduits (www.conduits.com) that are available to help bridge this device-to-device gap.

Can I beam files to and from my PC?

✔ Yes. Files can be transferred via IR beam to and from your PC the same way that they are transferred from device to device.

RECEIVE AN INFRARED BEAM MANUALLY

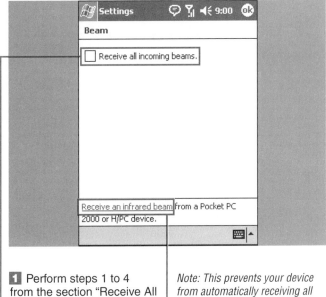

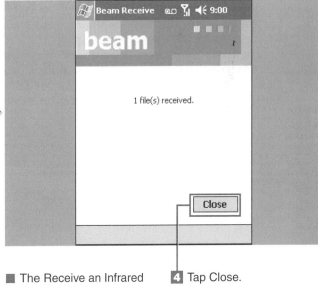

1 Perform steps 1 to 4 from the section "Receive All Incoming Infrared Beams" to launch the Beam utility.

2 If Receive All Incoming Beams is checked, tap the check box (☑ changes to ☐).

Note: This prevents your device from automatically receiving all file transfers.

3 Tap Receive an Infrared Beam.

■ The Receive an Infrared Beam screen appears, informing you that a file has been received.

4 Tap Close.

■ The received file is stored in My Documents.

UNDERSTANDING THE CONNECTIONS MANAGER

The Connections Manager was first used in Pocket PC 2002 devices and has gone through an update in Windows Mobile 2003 to allow for an easier setup of connections — especially for connections to corporate networks. Windows Mobile 2003 devices are becoming a regular part of the enterprise community, and it is important to make connections for users of multiple VPNs, 802.1x, and IPSec L2TP VPNs with 128-bit

SSL or with 128-bit CAPI encryption.

The Connections Manager enables you to connect to the Internet or corporate networks so that you can browse the Internet or intranet, send and receive e-mail and instant messages, and synchronize your device using ActiveSync. The Connections Manager has two groups of settings: My ISP and My Work Network. You can use My ISP

settings to connect to the Internet and My Work Network for private networks.

You can connect your device using these settings with a modem (connected to a landline or through a cellular phone), a wireless network (via an external card or integrated wireless radio on your device), or an Ethernet network card.

Accessing the Connections Manager

You can access the Connections Manager and other connection settings through the Connections display, which is found by tapping Start ⇨ Settings ⇨ Connections. Microsoft has placed all the connections-related setup utilities on the Connections tab. There is not a separate settings utility for My ISP or My Work Network because these are integrated into the Connections Manager.

Connections Manager Tasks

When you first launch the Connections Manager, the Tasks tab appears, and options to add a new modem connection for My ISP and My Work Network are shown with blue hyperlinks similar to what is found in Internet Explorer. Tapping the hyperlinks starts the connection wizards that take you through the configuration setup of the network connection that you want. You also have the option to add a new VPN server connection under the My Work Network heading. After at least one connection is set up, you will then see the option to manage any existing network connections on the main task management display.

Network Management

Using the Advanced tab of the Connections settings, you can access the Select Networks manager. Using the Network Management display, you can specify what connection programs that connect automatically to the Internet or private network will use when they are launched. For example, when you start Internet Explorer, your mobile device will automatically attempt to connect to the Internet using the connection you set up called My ISP. You do not have to go to a connection display to initiate a connection because Windows Mobile 2003 manages that for you.

Wireless Network Connections

Microsoft made connections with 802.11b WiFi networks easy to manage with the new Zero Configuration utility. If you have a device with an integrated WiFi radio or use an external WiFi card with Windows Mobile 2003 drivers, then as soon as you turn on the WiFi radio or place the card in the expansion slot, a Zero Configuration notification bubble will appear on your device. This notification bubble lists all wireless networks that are in range of your device and enables you to select and then connect to the network. Windows Mobile 2003 uses the default settings and attempts to connect you to the selected network. If the wireless network has advanced settings, you may be prompted to enter more advanced settings on your device, which you can do through the Connections Manager.

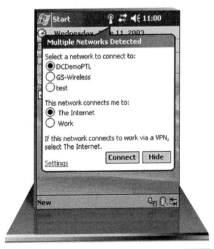

SET UP MODEM CONNECTIONS

Y ou can set up modem connections to either your My ISP or My Work Network using the Connections Manager. The modem connection settings are used to set up connections through an external dial-up modem, mobile cellular phone using a cable, Bluetooth or infrared connection, or a Bluetooth access point.

The external dial-up modem connection uses the Hayes

Compatible on COM1 settings by default. Connection with your cellular phone can be performed as a regular dial-up connection or as a 1xRTT CDMA or GPRS high-speed data connection. External modem, cellular dial-up, Bluetooth dial-up, and infrared dial-up connections can have a theoretical connection up to a speed of 56Kbps, with actual speeds at about 14.4 or 28.8Kbps. 1xRTT CDMA

connections have a theoretical maximum speed of 153Kbps. 1xEV-DO CDMA connections have a maximum data rate of 2.4Mbps, but this technology is just starting to appear in the United States. GPRS connections can have up to 150-170Kbps data speeds, but you can expect to see speeds of about 50Kbps; this is dependent on carrier infrastructure and support.

SET UP MODEM CONNECTIONS

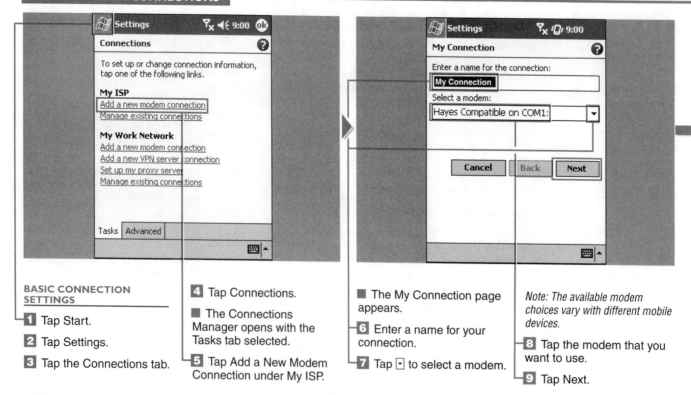

BASIC CONNECTION SETTINGS

1 Tap Start.

2 Tap Settings.

3 Tap the Connections tab.

4 Tap Connections.

■ The Connections Manager opens with the Tasks tab selected.

5 Tap Add a New Modem Connection under My ISP.

■ The My Connection page appears.

6 Enter a name for your connection.

7 Tap ⊡ to select a modem.

Note: The available modem choices vary with different mobile devices.

8 Tap the modem that you want to use.

9 Tap Next.

Can I connect to a Bluetooth modem plugged into a standard telephone line?

✔ Yes, set up your connections using the Bluetooth modem settings just as you would with a Bluetooth-enabled cellular phone. Check the manufacturer's documentation for any custom settings that you may have to use.

Do I have to be paired to a Bluetooth phone or access point prior to setting up my modem connetions?

✔ No, the Windows Mobile 2003 connection wizards enable you to select a new Bluetooth device and go through the pairing and bonding process.

What kind of data transfer speeds will I see with a Bluetooth connection?

✔ The wireless connection to a Bluetooth access point attached to a cable or DSL service is limited by the Bluetooth data protocol rate of 721Kbps and the distance you are from your access point.

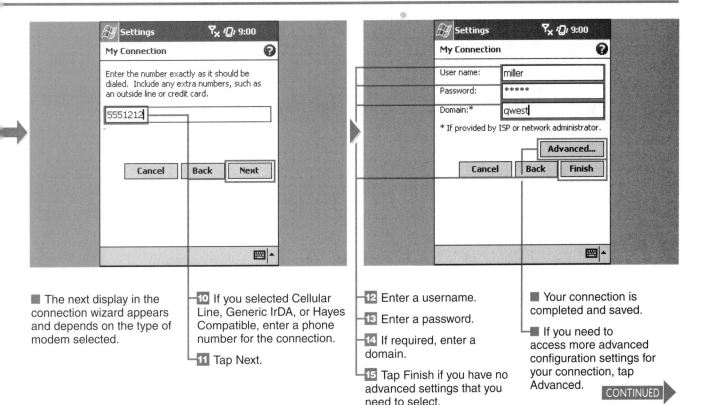

■ The next display in the connection wizard appears and depends on the type of modem selected.

🔟 If you selected Cellular Line, Generic IrDA, or Hayes Compatible, enter a phone number for the connection.

1️⃣1️⃣ Tap Next.

1️⃣2️⃣ Enter a username.

1️⃣3️⃣ Enter a password.

1️⃣4️⃣ If required, enter a domain.

1️⃣5️⃣ Tap Finish if you have no advanced settings that you need to select.

■ Your connection is completed and saved.

■ If you need to access more advanced configuration settings for your connection, tap Advanced.

CONTINUED

SET UP MODEM CONNECTIONS (CONTINUED)

Most of the time, you can successfully use a basic setup and never have to use the Advanced settings. However, you may need to configure the Advanced settings on your device to make a successful modem connection. The Advanced settings configuration screens vary between two and four tabbed screens, depending on the type of modem that you selected in the basic setup.

If you are setting up a dial-up modem, the Advanced settings require you to specify some general dialing options. These include dialing speed, delays that may be required, and special initialization strings that your service provider may require.

If you are setting up a GPRS connection on a Phone Edition device, there are only two tabbed setting screens, TCP/IP and Servers, where you can enter specific settings.

The other tabbed display that you may see are the Port settings. These are for special connection preferences and terminal settings.

SET UP MODEM CONNECTIONS (CONTINUED)

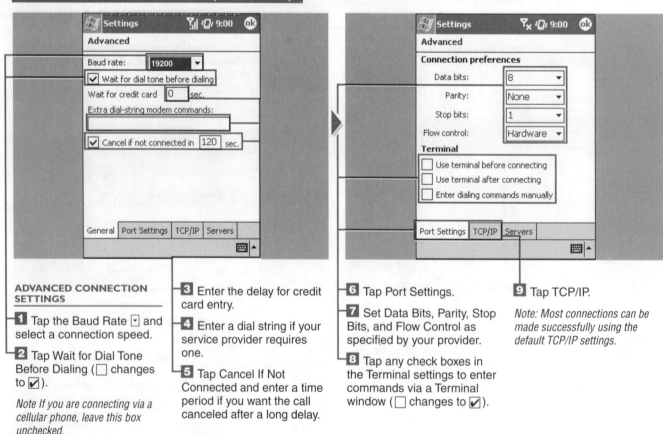

ADVANCED CONNECTION SETTINGS

1 Tap the Baud Rate ⊡ and select a connection speed.

2 Tap Wait for Dial Tone Before Dialing (☐ changes to ☑).

Note If you are connecting via a cellular phone, leave this box unchecked.

3 Enter the delay for credit card entry.

4 Enter a dial string if your service provider requires one.

5 Tap Cancel If Not Connected and enter a time period if you want the call canceled after a long delay.

6 Tap Port Settings.

7 Set Data Bits, Parity, Stop Bits, and Flow Control as specified by your provider.

8 Tap any check boxes in the Terminal settings to enter commands via a Terminal window (☐ changes to ☑).

9 Tap TCP/IP.

Note: Most connections can be made successfully using the default TCP/IP settings.

Do I have to enter Advanced settings for all my modem connections?

✔ No, most of the default settings work fine with modems. You should check with your system administrator or Internet service provider before entering Advanced settings.

Why would I want to use the check boxes for the Terminal settings?

✔ The Terminal settings enable you to connect to an online service or corporate server that requires TTY or VT-100 terminal emulation. For example, you may want to connect to other computers, telnet sites, or bulletin boards using the Terminal.

What do DNS and WINS mean, and what are the Alt settings for these under Use Specific Server Address?

✔ DNS stands for Domain Name Server and is a database that translates the domain name to a specific number IP (Internet protocol) address. WINS stands for Windows Internet Naming Service, which translates Windows computer names into IP addresses. The alternative (Alt) addresses may enable you to connect when the primary server is unavailable.

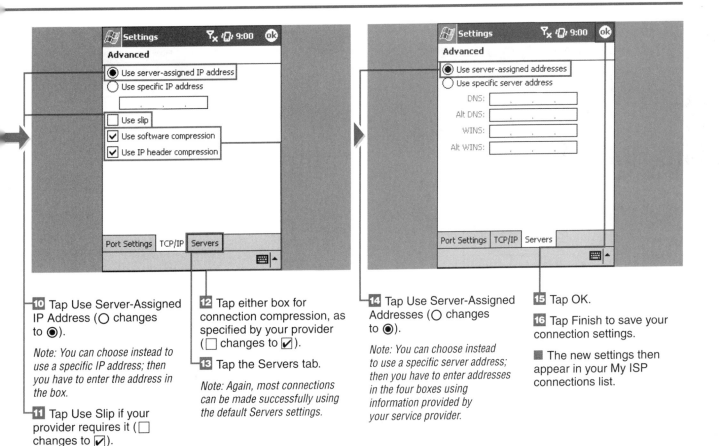

10 Tap Use Server-Assigned IP Address (○ changes to ◉).

Note: You can choose instead to use a specific IP address; then you have to enter the address in the box.

11 Tap Use Slip if your provider requires it (☐ changes to ☑).

12 Tap either box for connection compression, as specified by your provider (☐ changes to ☑).

13 Tap the Servers tab.

Note: Again, most connections can be made successfully using the default Servers settings.

14 Tap Use Server-Assigned Addresses (○ changes to ◉).

Note: You can choose instead to use a specific server address; then you have to enter addresses in the four boxes using information provided by your service provider.

15 Tap OK.

16 Tap Finish to save your connection settings.

■ The new settings then appear in your My ISP connections list.

SET UP VPN SERVER CONNECTIONS

If your company provides the functionality or you set up your home computer, you can make Virtual Private Network (VPN) connections using your device. A VPN connection enables you to securely connect to your servers or computer, so you can perform tasks while away from your desktop computer.

PPTP (Point to Point Tunneling Protocol) was supported in Pocket PC 2002, and Microsoft has added IPSec/L2TP (IP Security/Layer 2 Tunneling Protocol) in Windows Mobile 2003. This added protocol offers administrators more flexibility in selecting server-based VPN clients.

Network administrators can also configure multiple VPN connections on the server and allow you to select which VPN you want to connect with on your device.

SET UP VPN SERVER CONNECTIONS

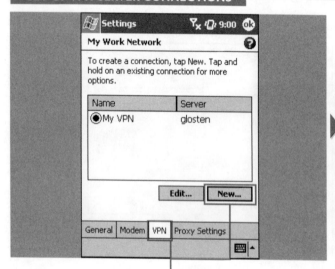

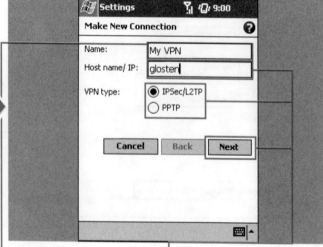

1 Tap Start ➪ Settings.

2 On the Connections tab, tap Connections.

3 Tap the Manage Existing Connections hyperlink under My Work Network.

4 Tap the VPN tab.

5 Tap New.

Note: Alternatively, you can tap the Add a New VPN Server Connection hyperlink from the main Connections display.

6 Enter a name for the connection.

Note: This is the name that will appear in your Connections list on your device and is not the name of the server.

7 Enter the VPN server name or IP address.

8 Select the type of authentication to use with your device and server (○ changes to ◉).

9 Tap Next.

What can I do with a VPN connection?

✔ A VPN connection enables you to access your network securely via the Internet to ensure that corporate security is maintained through your device connection. You can also synchronize your device using ActiveSync via a VPN connection.

I have a Novell server in my office; can I set up a VPN connection with my device?

✔ Yes, you can access Novell Groupwise from your device if your Groupwise is configured to use POP3 or IMAP via a VPN.

Why would I need to change the Advanced VPN settings?

✔ If the server you are connecting to does not use dynamically assigned addresses or you need to change DNS or WINS settings, you need to enter information into one or both of the Advanced Settings displays, accessed on the last page of the VPN settings by tapping the Advanced button. See the section "Set Up Modem Connections" for more information on the Advanced settings.

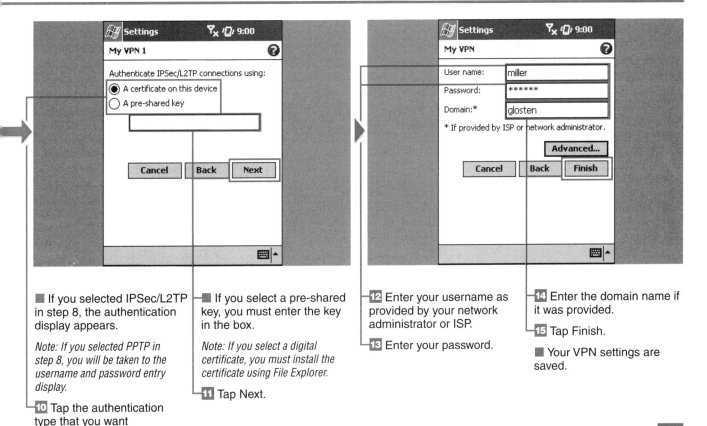

■ If you selected IPSec/L2TP in step 8, the authentication display appears.

Note: If you selected PPTP in step 8, you will be taken to the username and password entry display.

10 Tap the authentication type that you want (○ changes to ◉).

■ If you select a pre-shared key, you must enter the key in the box.

Note: If you select a digital certificate, you must install the certificate using File Explorer.

11 Tap Next.

12 Enter your username as provided by your network administrator or ISP.

13 Enter your password.

14 Enter the domain name if it was provided.

15 Tap Finish.

■ Your VPN settings are saved.

CONNECT TO THE INTERNET

A fter configuring the Advanced network connection settings (see the section "Set Up Modem Connections" for more information), you will be able to connect to the Internet by simply starting an application that uses an Internet connection, such as Internet Explorer. After you launch the application, your device attempts to make a connection and

pops up a notification bubble to inform you of the connection's status. After a connection is established, you can use other Internet applications such as the Inbox without having to make another connection.

You can also initiate a connection manually by using the Connection settings.

Why is my device requesting another username and password when I connect for the first time?

✔ The first time that you connect, you are prompted for your username and password. You can then tap the check box to remember the password, so the pop up will not appear for future connections.

CONNECT TO THE INTERNET

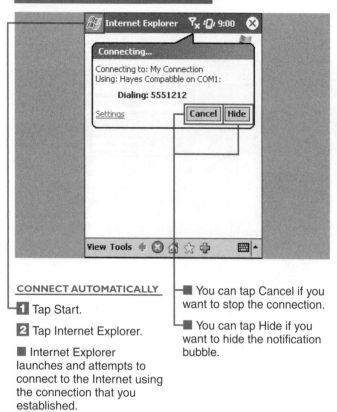

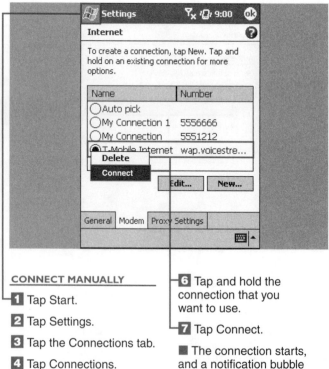

CONNECT AUTOMATICALLY

1 Tap Start.

2 Tap Internet Explorer.

■ Internet Explorer launches and attempts to connect to the Internet using the connection that you established.

■ You can tap Cancel if you want to stop the connection.

■ You can tap Hide if you want to hide the notification bubble.

CONNECT MANUALLY

1 Tap Start.

2 Tap Settings.

3 Tap the Connections tab.

4 Tap Connections.

5 Tap the Manage Existing Connections hyperlink.

6 Tap and hold the connection that you want to use.

7 Tap Connect.

■ The connection starts, and a notification bubble such as the one for the automatic-connection method appears.

CONNECT TO WORK

You can connect to either a modem or VPN connection for work-related connections. Windows Mobile 2003 will also connect automatically to a work network if the site that you are attempting to connect to does not have a period in its name. If there is a period in the name, the operating system attempts to use your My ISP Internet settings. This method can help network administrators ensure that corporate devices connect using My Work Network settings while you are operating in an enterprise environment.

Where can I find the settings I need for my work network?

✔ Your system administrator should be able to help you set up your work network by giving you the phone number, username, and password to use. You should also obtain VPN settings from your system administrator.

CONNECT TO WORK

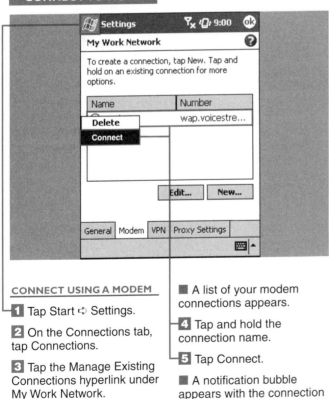

CONNECT USING A MODEM

◼1 Tap Start ➪ Settings.

◼2 On the Connections tab, tap Connections.

◼3 Tap the Manage Existing Connections hyperlink under My Work Network.

■ A list of your modem connections appears.

◼4 Tap and hold the connection name.

◼5 Tap Connect.

■ A notification bubble appears with the connection status.

CONNECT USING A VPN

◼1 Perform the previous steps 1 to 3.

■ A list of your modem connections appears.

◼2 Tap the VPN tab.

◼3 Tap and hold the VPN connection name.

◼4 Tap Connect.

■ A notification bubble appears with the connection status.

SET UP PROXY SERVER CONNECTIONS

If you need to operate your device behind a corporate firewall or want to improve the performance of Internet Explorer on your device, you can set up a proxy server connection.

A *proxy server* is a server that sits between your mobile device application and the server or Internet. It intercepts all requests

to the server or Internet and attempts to satisfy the request. Proxy servers allow direct Internet access from behind a firewall by opening a socket on the server that allows communications to flow on that particular socket.

Windows Mobile 2003 enables you to specify the proxy server and specific settings for HTTP, WAP,

Secure WAP, and Socks. Socks is a protocol that relays TCP sessions at a firewall host to allow application users transparent access across the firewall.

A server should be much faster than your mobile device at pulling down requests from the network or Internet and can speed the transfer of that information to your device.

SET UP PROXY SERVER CONNECTIONS

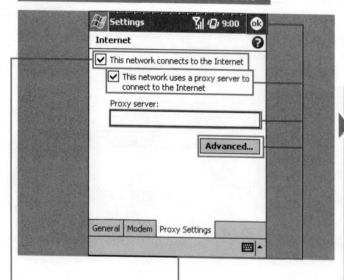

BASIC PROXY SETTINGS

1 Tap Start ➪ Settings.

2 On the Connections tab, tap Connections.

3 Tap the Set Up My Proxy Server hyperlink.

4 Tap This Network Connects to the Internet.

5 Tap the next check box.

6 Enter the name of the proxy server.

7 If the default settings satisfy your needs, tap OK.

■ If you need to change the port number or proxy server type, tap Advanced.

ADVANCED PROXY SETTINGS

■ The server configuration display appears.

8 Enter the server names and port IDs for each type that you want attached to this proxy server connection.

Note: Contact your administrator for details on these settings.

9 Tap Socks 4 to select this protocol.

10 Tap OK to save the Advanced settings.

11 Tap OK to save and exit the proxy server settings.

■ The main Connections display appears.

What information do I need to request to set up my proxy server?

✔ Ask your system administrator or ISP for the proxy server name, server type, port, type of Socks protocol used, and your username and password.

What is the difference between Socks 4 and Sock 5?

✔ Socks 5 improves upon Socks 4 by adding or improving strong authentication, authentication method negotiation, address resolution proxy, proxy for UDP-based application, and the Generic Security Service API.

Is there any way to automatically receive my proxy settings?

✔ Yes, if you are connected to your ISP or private network during synchronization and your system administrator configured the proxy to auto-configure, then your device will download proxy settings from your PC during synchronization.

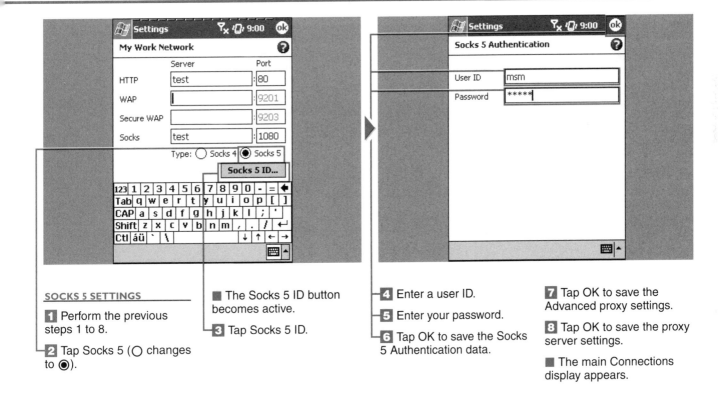

SOCKS 5 SETTINGS

1 Perform the previous steps 1 to 8.

2 Tap Socks 5 (○ changes to ◉).

■ The Socks 5 ID button becomes active.

3 Tap Socks 5 ID.

4 Enter a user ID.

5 Enter your password.

6 Tap OK to save the Socks 5 Authentication data.

7 Tap OK to save the Advanced proxy settings.

8 Tap OK to save the proxy server settings.

■ The main Connections display appears.

CHANGE THE CONNECTION NAME AND DELETE CONNECTION SETTINGS

You can change the name of your connections and delete connections that you no longer need on your device. Windows Mobile 2003 comes with "My ISP" and "My Work Network" as the titles attached to the default settings. You may want to change the names to match the ISP that you are using or your company name.

You can also set up multiple network connections on your device; when you do so, having names that can be easily distinguished from each other is helpful.

You may also find that you have connections that need to be deleted from your device because they are

no longer valid or needed. Microsoft made eliminating your connections simple in Windows Mobile 2003.

CHANGE THE CONNECTION NAME AND DELETE CONNECTION SETTINGS

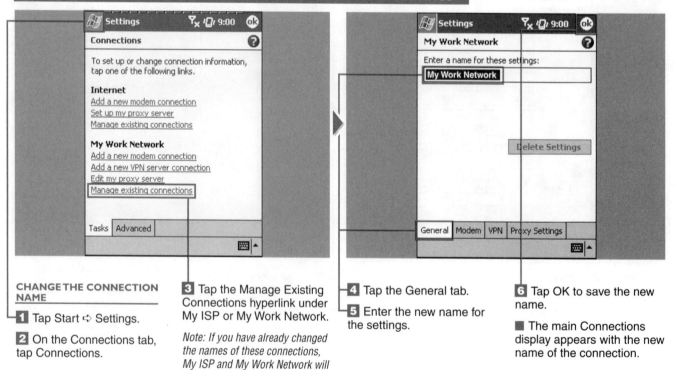

CHANGE THE CONNECTION NAME

1 Tap Start ➪ Settings.

2 On the Connections tab, tap Connections.

3 Tap the Manage Existing Connections hyperlink under My ISP or My Work Network.

Note: If you have already changed the names of these connections, My ISP and My Work Network will not be the current headings.

4 Tap the General tab.

5 Enter the new name for the settings.

6 Tap OK to save the new name.

■ The main Connections display appears with the new name of the connection.

Can I show more than two networks on my Connections display?

✔ No, only two networks can be shown on your Connections display. By default, one is for Internet connections, and the other is for private work connections.

If I delete a connection and then decide that I need to use it again, can I recover the previous settings?

✔ You may be able to recover your previous settings if you created a backup of your device with those settings. You can then perform a recovery using your backup application.

Can I hide the work network if I never use it on my device?

✔ No, but you do not have to use the network. If you do not use a work network, you can select another Internet network from the Advanced connection settings; in this manner, the work connection will be hidden from your view.

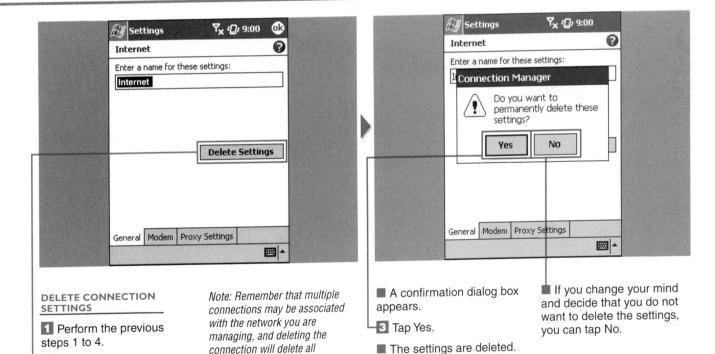

DELETE CONNECTION SETTINGS

1 Perform the previous steps 1 to 4.

2 Tap Delete Settings.

Note: Remember that multiple connections may be associated with the network you are managing, and deleting the connection will delete all individual connections.

■ A confirmation dialog box appears.

3 Tap Yes.

■ The settings are deleted.

■ If you change your mind and decide that you do not want to delete the settings, you can tap No.

SET UP OR MODIFY NETWORK CARD SETTINGS

You can use the Advanced Connections settings on your device to select what network your card or internal radio connects to, as well as the particular settings for that card or radio.

Microsoft includes a few network drivers on your device that you can use with your hardware or external card. The NE2000 Ethernet driver

enables you to connect to a network using an external Ethernet card. The three NDISWAN drivers are associated with VPN and asynchronous connections.

If you use a different network card, the manufacturer may include drivers that will be installed on your device and accessible when you configure your network

adapter. Configuration of your network adapter is required only if you need to enter specific IP addresses and name servers to access your network.

After setting up your network card, you can later go back and edit the settings using the same Advanced Connections configuration displays.

SET UP OR MODIFY NETWORK CARD SETTINGS

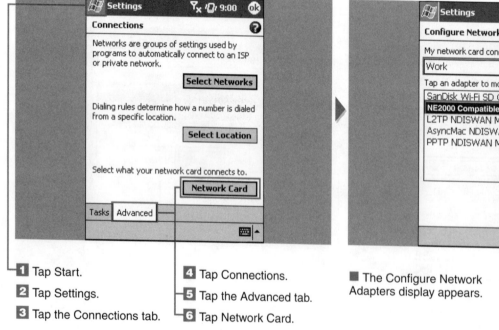

1 Tap Start.
2 Tap Settings.
3 Tap the Connections tab.
4 Tap Connections.
5 Tap the Advanced tab.
6 Tap Network Card.

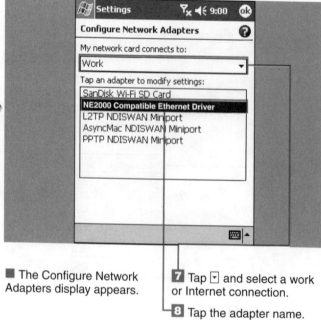

■ The Configure Network Adapters display appears.

7 Tap ⊡ and select a work or Internet connection.
8 Tap the adapter name.

MASTER IT

What do I do if I use the same network card to access both home and work networks?

✔ You need to select and change the network to which the card connects when prompted after inserting the network card. You can also set the network card to Work and tell the system that the work network also connects to the Internet. Then you can use both at the same time.

Are there different configuration windows for modifying an existing network card setup?

✔ No, you will edit the existing connection setting if you need to change the network card settings.

Is there another way to configure a network card, instead of using the Configure Network Adapters settings?

✔ Yes, if the network card is inserted or attached to your device, the Network Settings notification will appear automatically. If your network uses DHCP, you should not have to change the adapter settings for your card, and you should not change them without first checking with your system administrator.

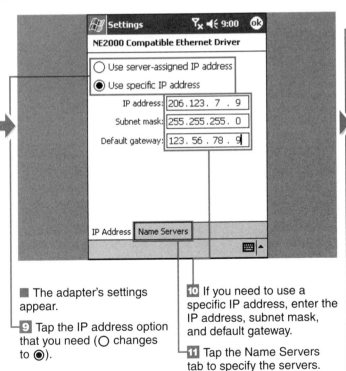

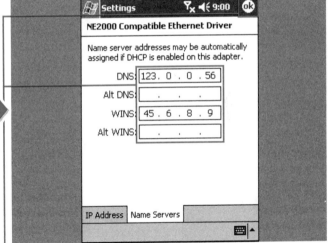

■ The adapter's settings appear.

▇9 Tap the IP address option that you need (○ changes to ◉).

▇10 If you need to use a specific IP address, enter the IP address, subnet mask, and default gateway.

▇11 Tap the Name Servers tab to specify the servers.

▇12 Enter the name server addresses needed for your network.

Note: If DHCP is enabled and your network provides DNS settings via DHCP, you do not need to enter any specific addresses.

▇13 Tap OK.

■ A pop-up window appears.

▇14 Tap OK to clear the notification.

▇15 Tap OK to close the Network Card Settings wizard.

■ The settings are saved and will be used the next time that you attempt to connect.

87

SET UP A WIRELESS NETWORK

In addition to connecting to a network via a wired connection, you can use a wireless, 802.11b, connection on your device with an integrated radio or external card. If your external card includes Windows Mobile 2003 drivers or you have an internal WiFi radio, then the

Zero Configuration enhancements can be used. If you need to set up advanced wireless network settings, there are a few configuration settings that must be completed.

Advanced wireless settings can be used to set up an ActiveSync connection through a wireless

router to your desktop computer, to set up an ad-hoc computer-to-computer connection, or to specify WEP encryption settings. You will need a WiFi access point or hotspot to connect with in order to use the wireless features on your device.

SET UP A WIRELESS NETWORK

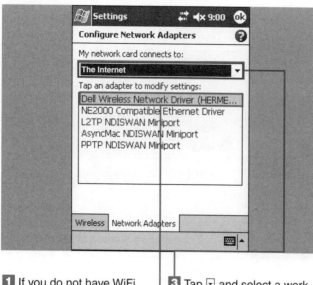

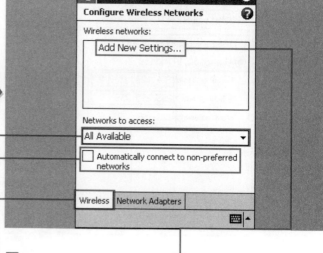

1 If you do not have WiFi integrated into your device, install the manufacturer's driver and insert the card into your device.

2 Perform steps 1 to 6 from the "Set Up or Modify Network Card Settings" section.

3 Tap ⊡ and select a work or Internet connection.

4 Tap the driver for your card.

Note: If you do not use DHCP, enter the IP address and name servers required for your wireless network.

5 Tap the Wireless tab.

6 Tap ⊡ and select the networks to access.

7 Tap Automatically Connect to Non-preferred Networks (☐ changes to ☑).

8 Tap Add New Settings.

■ The Configure Wireless Network display appears.

Are public WiFi hotspots free?

✔ There are some areas that provide free wireless access, but the majority of public facilities charge an hourly or monthly access fee. After you attempt to connect to a hotspot, a Web page will appear in Internet Explorer detailing service charges and sign-up information.

What kind of range will my WiFi radio or WiFi connection card have?

✔ The range of your WiFi connection depends on the Pocket PC hardware and the wireless router that you are attempting to connect with. WiFi range can reach 1,500 feet at 1 megabit speed and is dependent on your operating environment.

Should I enable WEP security on my mobile device, and what impact does it have on my connection?

✔ Enabling WEP security will help maintain the security of your data, but WEP can be hacked and is not failsafe. Enabling WEP security may have a slight effect on WiFi performance by reducing the connection speed and range, but this is dependent on the hardware being used.

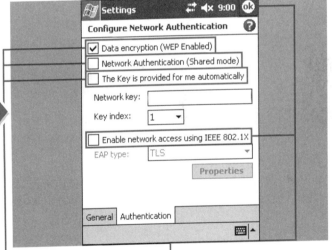

9 On the General tab, enter the SSID or network name.

10 Tap ⊡ and select the connection.

11 Tap the check box if you are setting up an ad-hoc connection (☐ changes to ☑).

Note: Ad-hoc connections are used to connect your device to a computer rather than a wireless router or hotspot.

12 Tap the Authentication tab.

13 To set up a secure network, tap Data Encryption.

14 Tap the second check box to enable network authentication.

15 Tap the third check box if the key is provided automatically from the server.

Note: If the key is not provided, you need to enter the key and key index.

16 If needed, tap Enable Network Access Using IEEE 802.1X.

17 Tap OK twice.

■ The wireless network is set up and ready to access.

SELECT NETWORKS

You can select the two networks that your device will use to attempt to make connections. Networks are groups of settings, as discussed in Chapter 10. The My ISP network is designed for Internet network connections, and the My Work Network settings are designed for private, work-related activities.

Your device automatically tries to connect to the networks that you select based on the application being used. Programs such as Internet Explorer or the Inbox attempt to connect to the My ISP settings and the Internet if you use the default settings. Programs such

as FTP or other server-related applications attempt to use the My Work Network settings.

If your company uses periods in its intranet URL, you need to set up Work URL exceptions. You can use an asterisk (*) wildcard to identify multiple areas of a particular URL.

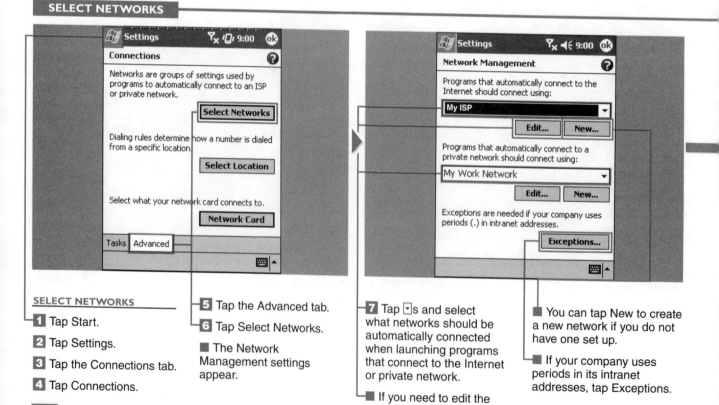

SELECT NETWORKS

SELECT NETWORKS

1 Tap Start.

2 Tap Settings.

3 Tap the Connections tab.

4 Tap Connections.

5 Tap the Advanced tab.

6 Tap Select Networks.

■ The Network Management settings appear.

7 Tap ⊡s and select what networks should be automatically connected when launching programs that connect to the Internet or private network.

■ If you need to edit the network, you can tap Edit.

■ You can tap New to create a new network if you do not have one set up.

■ If your company uses periods in its intranet addresses, tap Exceptions.

Do I need to change my network settings using the Advanced settings?

✔ No, most networks use DHCP, so the default settings should work without any editing or customization. If you have a problem, contact your network administrator or perform a soft reset.

What will happen if I do not enter any exceptions even though my company uses periods in its intranet addresses?

✔ Your device will attempt to connect to your company intranet via the Internet and will time out, looking unsuccessfully for the intranet location.

Can I change my networks without having to add new connections?

✔ Yes, the connections that you set up stay associated with the network that they were created under. You can quickly change networks and thus connections using the Network Management display. If you delete a network, all the connections associated with that network are also deleted.

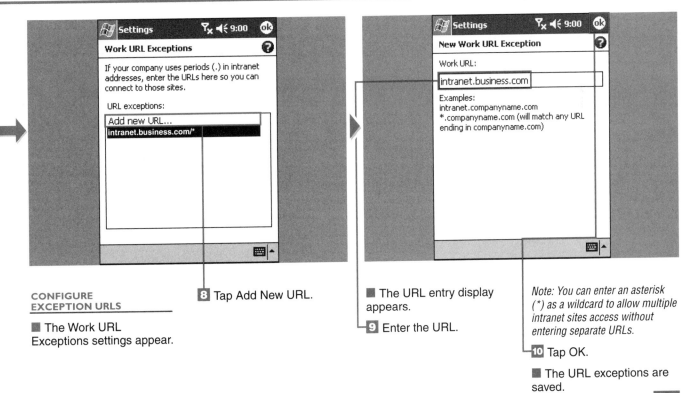

CONFIGURE EXCEPTION URLS

■ The Work URL Exceptions settings appear.

⑧ Tap Add New URL.

■ The URL entry display appears.

⑨ Enter the URL.

Note: You can enter an asterisk (*) as a wildcard to allow multiple intranet sites access without entering separate URLs.

⑩ Tap OK.

■ The URL exceptions are saved.

USING DIALING RULES

You can specify different dialing rules for several locations on your device to make connecting via a dial-up modem quicker and easier than manual entry. This is useful if your work settings require that you dial a 9 to place an outgoing call. Also, if you travel to the same location frequently, it is faster to have a rule for the specific area code rather

than create a new modem connection every time that you travel.

By default, Home, Mobile, and Work dialing locations are included on Windows Mobile 2003 devices. The Home location dials the local seven-digit number, the Mobile location dials a ten-digit number, and the Work location dials a

seven-digit number after the 9 prefix. You can modify these settings and add new ones if needed.

In addition to the codes shown in the Dialing Patterns settings, there are several more dialing codes that you can find in the Help file for dialing rules.

USING DIALING RULES

1 Perform steps 1 to 5 from the "Select Networks" section.

2 Tap Select Location.

3 Tap Use Dialing Rules to make the locations active (☐ changes to ☑).

■ A pop-up dialog box appears.

4 Tap OK.

5 Tap Home, Mobile, or Work (○ changes to ●).

Note: You can delete or connect to a location by tapping and holding the location name and selecting Delete or Connect from the menu that appears.

6 Tap New.

MASTER IT

Can I use all the dialing pattern codes found in the Help file?

✔ You can put the codes into your dialing patterns, but some modems may not respond to all the characters.

Can I use dialing rules to place a call using a credit card?

✔ Yes, you can use a dollar sign ($) to prompt the modem to wait for a credit card tone.

Is there a limit to the number of dialing locations that I can create?

✔ No, you can create locations for all the destinations to which you normally travel and save them on your device. If you add more than four locations, a scrollbar appears on the right side of the location name window on the Dialing Locations display.

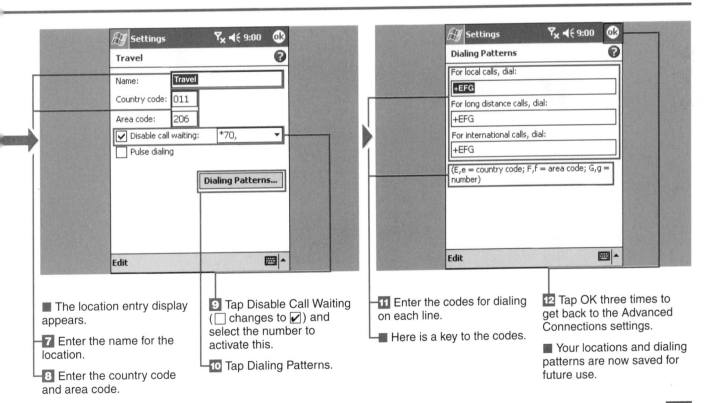

■ The location entry display appears.

7 Enter the name for the location.

8 Enter the country code and area code.

9 Tap Disable Call Waiting (☐ changes to ☑) and select the number to activate this.

10 Tap Dialing Patterns.

11 Enter the codes for dialing on each line.

■ Here is a key to the codes.

12 Tap OK three times to get back to the Advanced Connections settings.

■ Your locations and dialing patterns are now saved for future use.

SECTION IV

APPLICATIONS

SYNC FROM YOUR WINDOWS MOBILE DEVICE

Microsoft ActiveSync is used to connect your Windows Mobile 2003 device to your desktop computer and sync Contacts, Calendar, Tasks, Notes, Favorites, Folders, Inbox messages, and other data from third-party applications. Your device has an ActiveSync client installed as part of the Windows Mobile 2003 operating system and works with the desktop ActiveSync application. You can view more details and

download the latest version of the desktop version of ActiveSync by visiting the Microsoft Web site, www.microsoft.com/windowsmobile/ resources/downloads/pocketpc/ activesync37.mspx. You can also visit the CEWindows.NET site, www.cewindows.net/faqs/activesync 3.7.htm, for details on setting up and using the desktop client.

The type of information, how the information is synched, any rules that apply to the syncing operation,

the schedule, and other settings are controlled by the desktop ActiveSync application.

After you have established a partnership between your desktop and mobile device, you can sync data back and forth through a cradle docking station or cable connection. You have limited control — start and stop — of the syncing process using the ActiveSync client installed on your device.

SYNC FROM YOUR WINDOWS MOBILE DEVICE

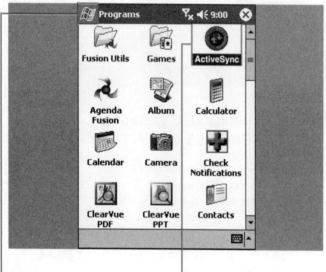

1 Tap Start.

2 Tap Programs.

3 Tap ActiveSync.

Note: You may also have ActiveSync located directly on your Start menu.

■ The mobile device ActiveSync client appears on your device.

■ The status of your connection appears under the partnership name.

■ The status of the connection is also shown with the ActiveSync icon.

How many computers can I sync with?

✔ ActiveSync enables you to create partnerships on two computers, such as work and home. You can use a third-party utility, such as ManyPartners, to sync to more computers.

Why won't my 32MB file sync to my storage card through ActiveSync?

✔ There is a limit of a 16MB file size in ActiveSync. To transfer a large file to your device, use a storage card reader.

After I stop a sync, can I start it again using the same connection?

✔ If you are connecting via infrared or Bluetooth, you can start the sync again by tapping Sync. However, if you connected via a cable connection, ActiveSync will attempt to connect using your Work settings and will not start the sync again. You need to disconnect the cable and reconnect to establish the connection again. Use caution when stopping a sync before it has completed because it may cause data corruption.

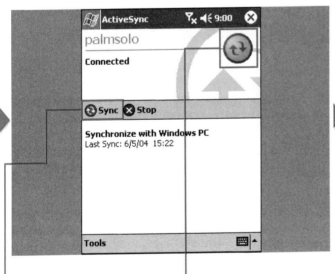

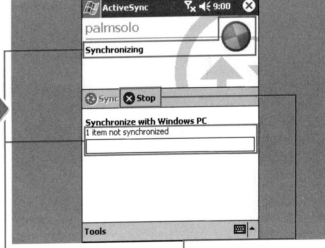

■4 Connect your device to your computer with a cable or cradle.

■5 After the status is shown as Connected, tap Sync.

■ The ActiveSync icon changes to a solid green color after a successful connection is made.

■ The connection status changes to Synchronizing, and the ActiveSync icon changes to a rotating green disc.

■ The number of items and status of syncing appear as a progress bar.

■ You can tap Stop to halt the syncing operation.

■ After your device has synched, the status changes back to Connected.

CONNECT VIA INFRARED OR BLUETOOTH

In addition to using a cable or cradle to sync to your PC, you can sync using wireless technology. If you have an infrared (IR) port or Bluetooth capability on your PC, you can use this to sync through ActiveSync on your device. If your PC does not have integrated infrared or Bluetooth, you can add an infrared port or Bluetooth to your PC via USB accessories.

Infrared syncing performs at about 12KB/second, Bluetooth at about 20KB/second, and USB at about 110KB/second. Although infrared syncing may not be as fast as other methods, you may find it useful when a cable or Bluetooth dongle is not available. Infrared is also included on all Windows Mobile 2003 devices, whereas you may have to add Bluetooth with an external card.

CONNECT VIA INFRARED OR BLUETOOTH

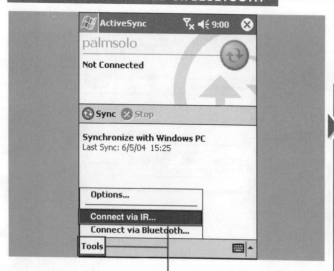 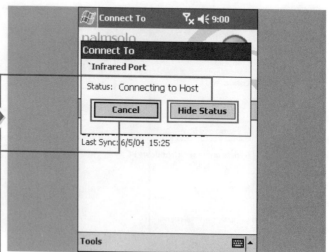

CONNECT VIA IR

1 Ensure that the Infrared port option is enabled on your desktop PC connection settings in ActiveSync.

Note: Also ensure that the Receive All Incoming Beams check box is selected; see Chapter 9.

2 Align your device's IR port with the IR receiver on your desktop or laptop.

3 Launch ActiveSync on your mobile device.

4 Tap Tools.

5 Tap Connect via IR.

■ A connection dialog box appears, showing the status of the connection.

■ You can hide the connection status dialog box by tapping Hide Status.

■ If you want to cancel the connection, you can tap Cancel.

■ After the connection is successfully made, syncing may begin, depending on your desktop ActiveSync settings.

6 If syncing does not start automatically, tap Sync to sync your device.

When would I want to use IR to sync instead of a cradle or cable?

✔ I suggest that you keep a cradle or cable on your home computer and use IR to sync to computers at work or on the road. Most laptops have IR ports.

Do I have to create an ActiveSync partnership prior to syncing via IR or Bluetooth?

✔ No, ActiveSync will walk you through the partnership wizard on your desktop if you use IR or Bluetooth to sync. You will have to have a Bluetooth bond prior to using Bluetooth to sync your device.

Can I sync using WiFi, and what kind of speeds can I expect?

✔ Yes, WiFi syncing is an option on your mobile device. You have to enter IP and DNS address information into your network card settings as discussed in Chapter 11. You also need to create a partnership through a cable or cradle prior to syncing via WiFi. After initating a WiFi connection with your desktop, you then launch ActiveSync and tap Sync to start the process. ActiveSync speeds via WiFi are faster than USB, at about 120KB/second.

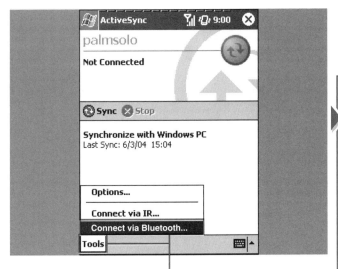

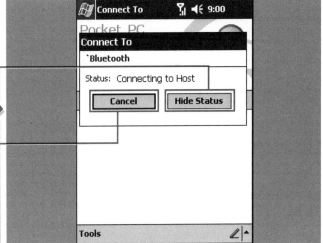

CONNECT VIA BLUETOOTH

1 Ensure that a Bluetooth partnership has been established and the COM port associated with Bluetooth is selected in ActiveSync on your desktop.

2 Turn on the Bluetooth radio on your mobile device.

3 Launch ActiveSync on your mobile device.

4 Tap Tools.

5 Tap Connect via Bluetooth.

■ A connection dialog box appears, showing the status of the connection.

■ You can hide the connection status dialog box by tapping Hide Status.

■ If you want to cancel the connection, you can tap Cancel.

■ After the connection is successfully made, syncing may begin, depending on your desktop ActiveSync settings.

6 If syncing does not start automatically, tap Sync to sync your device.

SET UP PC SYNCHRONIZATION OPTIONS

Microsoft ActiveSync enables you to create a partnership with two desktop computers when you set up partnerships. You can manage some of your PC synchronization settings using ActiveSync on your mobile device.

You can select what PC you want to sync with when syncing remotely to your PC. Remote syncing with your

PC can be conducted through a dial-up modem and is not a common practice. However, selecting the PC to sync with is required for syncing via a WiFi connection, which is a common practice.

You can also select to use the mobile schedule to sync with your PC and whether you want to sync with your PC during a manual sync. Mobile

schedule details are discussed in the section "Set Up Mobile Schedule Options." PC options include setting the speed to sync at when the device is cradled or connected via a cable and choosing to maintain a connection when syncing remotely or disconnecting after the sync is completed.

SET UP PC SYNCHRONIZATION OPTIONS

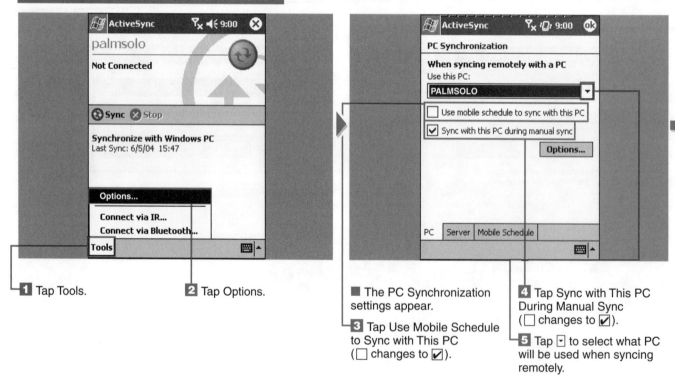

1 Tap Tools.

2 Tap Options.

■ The PC Synchronization settings appear.

3 Tap Use Mobile Schedule to Sync with This PC (☐ changes to ☑).

4 Tap Sync with This PC During Manual Sync (☐ changes to ☑).

5 Tap ▾ to select what PC will be used when syncing remotely.

Why would I need to change the syncing speed?

✔ If you are connecting remotely via a dial-up connection, you may need to change the speed to make a successful connection. Also, if you are connecting use a serial cable and are having any issues syncing with your desktop computer, you may want to try changing the speed of the connection from 115.2Kbps to 57.6Kbps or lower.

What can I do if the PC I want to sync with is not listed in the PC Synchronization settings?

✔ You have to perform a syncing operation with a cable or cradle for a valid PC name to appear in the list of available computers. You cannot add a PC name from your device.

Why would I want to maintain the connection after syncing remotely?

✔ You may want to perform other syncing functions without having to connect every time. Staying connected will also allow you to connect to the Internet if your network is set up to allow it. However, if you are syncing remotely via a dial-up connection, you may want to disconnect from the PC after syncing.

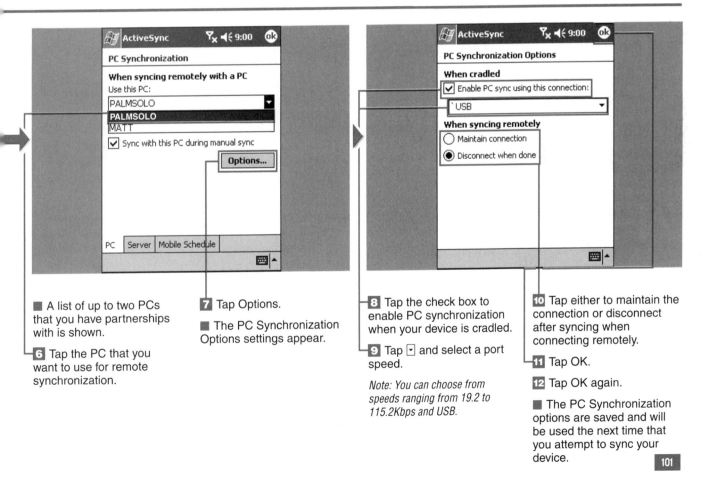

■ A list of up to two PCs that you have partnerships with is shown.

6 Tap the PC that you want to use for remote synchronization.

7 Tap Options.

■ The PC Synchronization Options settings appear.

8 Tap the check box to enable PC synchronization when your device is cradled.

9 Tap ⊡ and select a port speed.

Note: You can choose from speeds ranging from 19.2 to 115.2Kbps and USB.

10 Tap either to maintain the connection or disconnect after syncing when connecting remotely.

11 Tap OK.

12 Tap OK again.

■ The PC Synchronization options are saved and will be used the next time that you attempt to sync your device.

SET UP SERVER SYNCHRONIZATION OPTIONS

You can set up and synchronize your mobile device with a Microsoft Exchange Server that is running Exchange ActiveSync. Check with your system administrator to see if your company uses the required server setup to use the server sync option.

With server synchronization, you can sync your Calendar, Contacts, and Inbox directly with the server

from a remote location. You can set up rules so that your device automatically syncs with the server at preset time intervals ranging from five minutes to four hours. You can specify how conflicts are handled if they occur during synchronization. You can also enable logging of your sync sessions for troubleshooting and reference.

You can specify Calendar and Inbox server settings that will help you to manage the amount of data that is transferred to your mobile device. Calendar settings enable you to specify what appointments in the past are synched. All future appointments are synched by default. Inbox settings include selecting a time frame, message size, and attachment size to be synched.

SET UP SERVER SYNCHRONIZATION OPTIONS

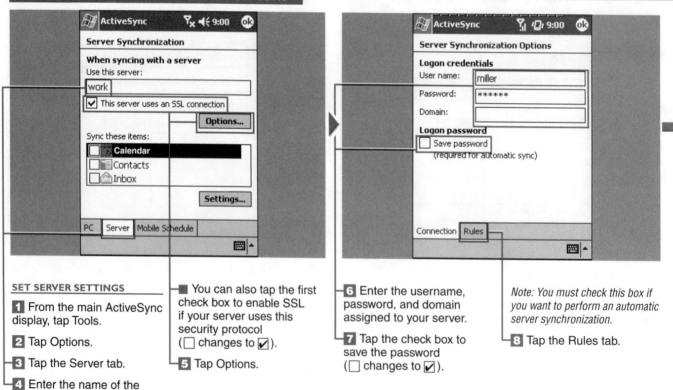

SET SERVER SETTINGS

1 From the main ActiveSync display, tap Tools.

2 Tap Options.

3 Tap the Server tab.

4 Enter the name of the Microsoft Exchange Server that you want to connect with.

■ You can also tap the first check box to enable SSL if your server uses this security protocol (☐ changes to ☑).

5 Tap Options.

6 Enter the username, password, and domain assigned to your server.

7 Tap the check box to save the password (☐ changes to ☑).

Note: You must check this box if you want to perform an automatic server synchronization.

8 Tap the Rules tab.

Can I establish settings for Contacts?

✔ No, there are no custom settings for Contacts. All Contacts in the default Contacts folder are synched if you select the Contacts check box on the Server Synchronization page.

Can I establish settings for the Calendar?

✔ Yes, to do so, tap Calendar on the main Server Synchronization page and then tap Settings. Tap ▼ and select how far back you want appointments to be synched — from all in your database to two weeks' worth.

Is there any other way to configure server synchronization settings?

✔ Yes, when you first create a partnership on your desktop PC, you can use the desktop version of ActiveSync to configure remote synchronization. You can also add, modify, or remove server synchronization settings by connecting your device and using the ActiveSync Options menu.

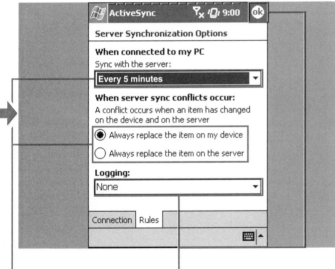

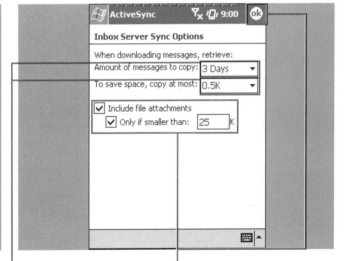

■ The Rules settings appear, and your login details are saved.

9 Tap ▼ and select how often your device will sync with the server when connected to the PC.

10 Tap one of the two options to resolve conflicts.

Note: You can choose to have the item on the server always replace the item on your device or vice versa.

11 Tap the Logging ▼ and select None, Brief, or Verbose.

12 Tap OK.

■ The server settings are saved.

SET INBOX SETTINGS

1 Perform the previous steps 1 to 3.

2 Tap Inbox.

3 Tap Settings.

4 Tap ▼ and select how many messages to copy.

5 Tap ▼ and select how much to save.

Note: You can choose from all to headers only, with 0.5K, 1K, and 5K options.

6 Tap Include File Attachments and set a size limit.

7 Tap OK twice.

■ Your settings are saved.

SET UP MOBILE SCHEDULE OPTIONS

I f you sync with a wireless connection, you can set up your mobile device to sync based on a time schedule that you choose. In the PC Synchronization settings, you are able to specify the options to use when syncing using the

mobile schedule. Mobile schedule options include specifying actions to take during peak and off-peak times, as well as what action to take when roaming. You can also choose to sync outgoing items as they are sent.

You can also specify what the Mobile Schedule options considers peak times; *peak times* are generally set as the times when you receive the most e-mail. Peak times settings include days of the week and peak hours.

SET UP MOBILE SCHEDULE OPTIONS

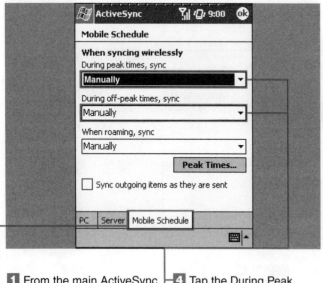

1 From the main ActiveSync display, tap Tools.

2 Tap Options.

3 Tap the Mobile Schedule tab.

■ The Mobile Schedule configuration display appears.

4 Tap the During Peak Times ⏷ and select how often you want to sync in peak times.

5 Tap the During Off-Peak Times ⏷.

6 Tap how often you want to sync in off-peak times.

Note: The options include Manually and intervals ranging from every five minutes to four hours.

Note: Short intervals consume a lot of battery life, so be careful with the interval time that you select.

How often should I set my device to sync?

✔ I recommend that you set your device to sync every 10 to 15 minutes during peak times. During off-peak times, you should probably set it to 60 minutes or 2 hours. Finally, when roaming, I suggest that you set it to the manual option.

What happens if my synchronization schedule is set to occur more frequently than my power-off timer?

✔ Your power-off timer is reset each time that you sync, but if it never reaches the power-off time, your device will always remain on, and your battery may become depleted.

Why does my device sometimes attempt to connect via ActiveSync seemingly on its own?

✔ You may have chosen to have your device sync using a mobile schedule. If you do not have an Exchange Server or do not want to use automatic syncing to your server, uncheck the Use Mobile Schedule to Sync with This PC option in the PC Synchronization settings; see the section "Set Up PC Synchronization Options" for more information.

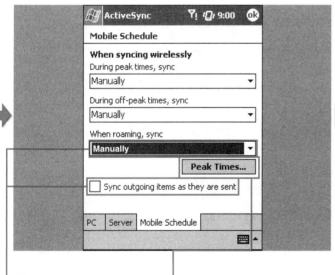

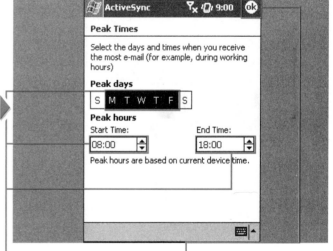

7 If you have a Phone Edition device, tap the When Roaming ⊡ and select Using Mobile Schedule or Manually.

8 Tap Sync Outgoing Items As They Are Sent (☐ changes to ✔).

Note: If this is not checked, outgoing items in your Inbox will be sent when the next scheduled synchronization occurs.

9 Tap Peak Times.

10 Tap the days of the week that you want set as peak days.

11 Tap ⊕ to set the start time.

12 Tap ⊕ to set the end time.

Note: You can also tap in the entry box and manually enter the times.

13 Tap OK twice to save your peak time and mobile schedule settings.

■ Your device is now configured to sync on a mobile schedule with your Microsoft Exchange Server.

DISPLAY THE CALENDAR AND APPOINTMENTS

The Calendar provides you with a complete list of your daily appointments. You can use the Calendar to view scheduled appointments, meetings, and other events. By default, the Calendar displays appointments that you have scheduled for the current day. You can also display your appointments for additional days. You can view your appointments by agenda, day, week, and month.

You can use the Agenda view to display a simplified list of all your appointments in an easy-to-read format. Upcoming appointments are displayed in bold, and previous days' appointments are displayed in gray. You can scroll through each day of appointments using the Agenda view.

You can view detailed appointment information in any view by simply tapping the appointment.

The Calendar also enables you to view all the days of the current month as well as the preceding and following months. The current day is displayed with a red pulsating outline in the Month view.

For your convenience, small blue arrows will indicate if there are more appointments above or below the current screen in the Day or Week views.

DISPLAY THE CALENDAR AND APPOINTMENTS

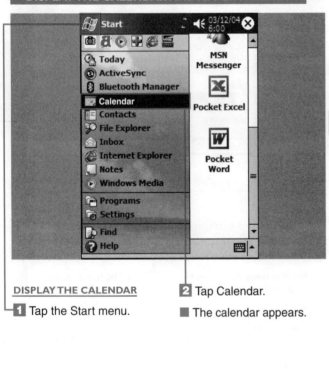

DISPLAY THE CALENDAR

■1 Tap the Start menu.

■2 Tap Calendar.

■ The calendar appears.

■3 Tap the Day View button.

■ A detail of the day's calendar entries is displayed.

■4 Tap the left or right arrows to change the day being viewed.

■5 Tap the appointment that you want to display.

■ You can tap the Return arrow to go back to the current day.

Note: If you tap the date, the current month is displayed in a pick so that you can easily change months.

Why do past appointments still appear in the calendar?

✔ Past appointments can provide useful historical information when you have to refer back to earlier appointment information or need to track time spent on completed projects. You can delete previous appointments when they are no longer needed: Simply tap and hold the appointment and select Delete Appointment.

What do the boxes in the Calendar Week view indicate?

✔ A box indicates that an appointment has been made for the time shown. You can tap the box, and the appointment summary will be displayed.

In the Month view, what do the small triangles and squares represent?

✔ An upward triangle represents a morning appointment, and a downward triangle represents an afternoon appointment. A solid square is displayed if you have both morning and evening appointments. A hollow square is displayed for an all-day event.

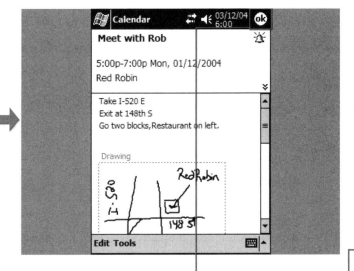

■ A detailed display of your appointment is now shown, including notes.

6 Tap OK to return your last Calendar view mode.

CHANGE THE CALENDAR'S VIEW

1 Tap the button representing how you want to view the Calendar (by agenda, day, week, month, or year).

■ The new view appears.

Note: In certain views, you see small blue up and down arrows. These indicate an appointment above or below the current screen. You can scroll up or down to view them.

CREATE A CALENDAR ENTRY

The Calendar application does more than synchronize your calendar from Microsoft Outlook, which is discussed in Chapter 12: You can create and edit entries while away from your PC.

You can create a new calendar entry and set specific details about that entry. When you create a new calendar entry, you can specify the subject of the appointment and its location. You can indicate a start time and an end time or indicate that the event is an all-day event. The appointment can be set to occur only once or reoccur following a preset pattern. Additionally, you can set an appointment reminder and assign the appointment to a category for easier viewing.

You can add text notes to your appointment entries or attach a voice note, which is a quick way to add a note that you do not have time to write down. Adding notes can help you organize your appointment by providing you with valuable information to refer to during your appointment.

CREATE A CALENDAR ENTRY

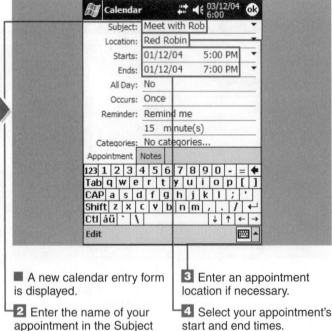

■1 In the Calendar, tap New.

■ A new calendar entry form is displayed.

■2 Enter the name of your appointment in the Subject field.

Note: Alternatively, you can select a preset subject from the Subject drop-down list.

■3 Enter an appointment location if necessary.

■4 Select your appointment's start and end times.

Do I have to keep entering the same meeting location for each appointment?

✔ No. The Calendar remembers locations you have used in the past. You can tap Location and select from the drop-down list of your previous locations.

Can I set an appointment to occur multiple times?

✔ Yes. Setting an appointment to occur on a schedule or at preset times throughout the year will free you from reentering the appointment every time. Tap Occur, and you can set the appointment to occur once, every week, every month, or every year or set a custom occurrence pattern.

Do I have to re-create the custom categories for my Calendar entries or can I select from ones I created in Tasks?

✔ The Calendar uses the same categories as Tasks and Contacts, so custom categories created in Tasks or Contacts are available in the Calendar, and vice versa. See "Select and Modify Calendar Categories" for more information on creating custom categories.

Can I add drawings to my appointment notes?

✔ Yes. You can draw by tapping the Pen icon on the Notes tab. This can be very useful for drawing a map.

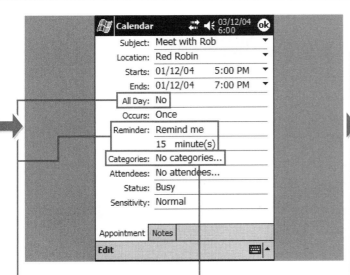

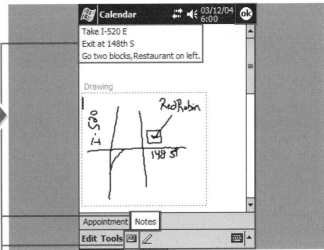

5 Tap All Day and select Yes or No to indicate whether this appointment is an all-day event.

6 Tap Reminder and set a reminder alarm for this appointment, if needed.

Note: You can specify your reminder time by minutes, hours, days, or weeks.

7 Tap Categories to assign an optional category.

Note: No Category is selected by default.

Note: You can also add attendees, set the meeting status, and assign a sensitivity level. The default settings work for most appointments.

8 Tap Notes.

■ You can enter text notes to further meeting details, such as directions or items to bring to your appointment.

■ You can add a voice note to your appointment.

Note: See Chapter 17 for more information on adding voice notes.

9 Tap OK.

■ Your appointment is saved.

EDIT A CALENDAR ENTRY

I n the Calendar, you can edit any previous, present, or future appointments that you have created. These changes are stored and will be synchronized with your desktop PC the next time you synchronize your device.

You can edit any part of your Calendar entries. This gives you a robust method to manage all

aspects of your appointments while away from your desktop PC.

You can add additional notes to your calendar entries while editing them. Adding notes can help to keep track of details from previous appointment entries or for future appointment entries.

After editing a note, is there a way to timestamp the change?

✔ Yes. On the Notes tab, you can tap and hold anywhere in the note, and a drop-down box appears. Select Insert Date to place the date next to your new entry.

EDIT A CALENDAR ENTRY

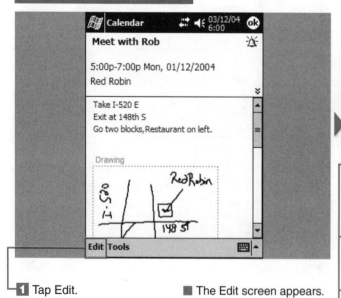

1 Tap Edit.

■ The Edit screen appears.

2 Make the appropriate edits to your appointment.

3 Tap Notes to make any changes or additions to your notes.

4 Tap OK to save your changes.

■ Your appointment and any changes are displayed in your calendar.

SET CALENDAR OPTIONS

You can set various options to change the way the Calendar displays your appointment data. For example, you can set the Calendar to show icons next to an appointment to visually indicate additional appointment information.

These icons can indicate whether your appointment has a reminder set, is recurring, or has a note attached. You can also display an icon indicating whether the appointment has a location set, you have requested attendees from your contacts, or the appointment is private.

You can change the way the Calendar displays the week, including how many days make up your week.

Why does the reminder alarm always default to 15 minutes?

✔ The default setting for a reminder is 15 minutes. You can change this to a new default by checking the box labeled Set Reminders for New Items and selecting a new default reminder time.

SET CALENDAR OPTIONS

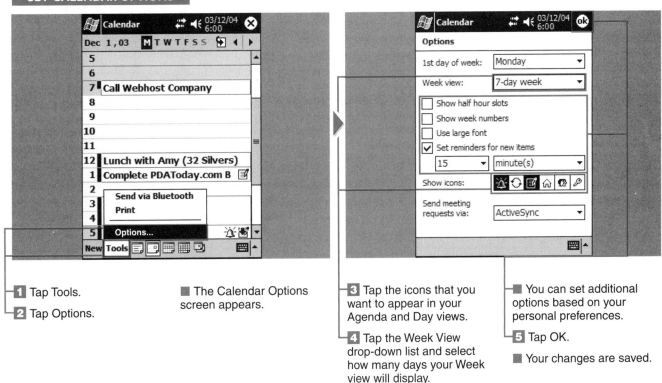

1 Tap Tools.

2 Tap Options.

■ The Calendar Options screen appears.

3 Tap the icons that you want to appear in your Agenda and Day views.

4 Tap the Week View drop-down list and select how many days your Week view will display.

■ You can set additional options based on your personal preferences.

5 Tap OK.

■ Your changes are saved.

SEND A CALENDAR ENTRY

In the Calendar, you can send an appointment entry to another Windows Mobile device via the built-in infrared port or — if your device is equipped with Bluetooth — via the Bluetooth radio. Sharing appointments with another Windows Mobile device is a quick and easy way to share your schedule with a colleague.

When sending an appointment to another device via Bluetooth, you need to make sure that the other device is able to receive a Bluetooth signal. Sometimes this setting is called *Discoverable mode*. Additionally, you will want to ensure that your Bluetooth radio is turned on. You can find more information about the Bluetooth

radio and Bluetooth manager in Chapter 8.

When sending an appointment to another device via infrared, you want to ensure that the device to which you are sending the appointment has the Beam utility set to receive all incoming beams. You can find more information about receiving infrared beams in Chapter 9.

SEND A CALENDAR ENTRY VIA BLUETOOTH

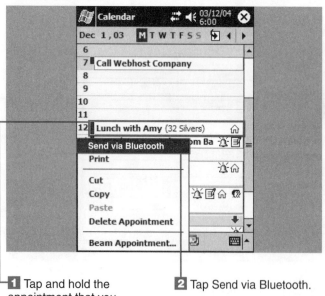

1 Tap and hold the appointment that you want to send.

■ A drop-down menu appears.

2 Tap Send via Bluetooth.

Note: These steps are HP iPAQ specific; other vendors may differ in their approach.

■ A list of available Bluetooth devices appears in your device's Bluetooth manager.

Note: Some Bluetooth managers look different than others.

3 Tap the device to which you want to send your appointment.

4 Tap OK to complete the transfer.

■ The device to which you sent your appointment receives a notification dialog box, asking the user if she wants to save your appointment to her calendar.

Is there a difference between Send via Bluetooth from the Tools menu and from the menu that you access by tapping and holding?

✔ No. Both of these locations enable you to send your appointment via Bluetooth.

When I try to send an appointment to the office next to me via Bluetooth, why does it connect only intermittently?

✔ Most Bluetooth radio-enabled devices beam information only about 10 meters (about 30 feet).

What can I do if my colleague's Windows Mobile device will not receive my infrared beam?

✔ Ensure that your colleague's device is set to receive all incoming beams. Additionally, you need to make sure that both IR ports are facing each other, nothing is between the two IR ports, and both devices are within the distance limit, which is usually several feet.

Can I send more than one appointment at a time?

✔ No. You need to select and send each appointment individually.

SEND A CALENDAR ENTRY VIA INFRARED

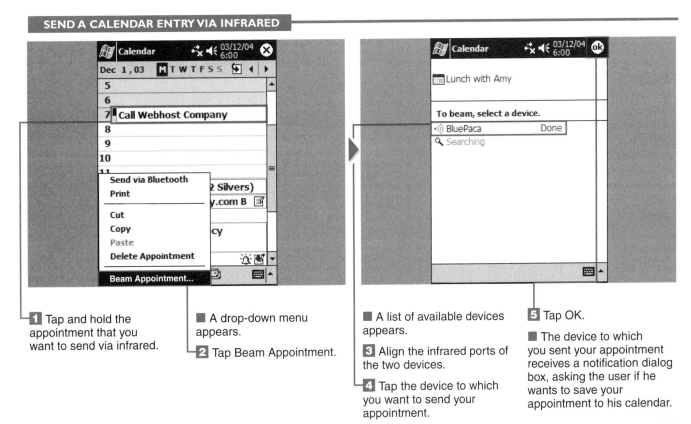

■ Tap and hold the appointment that you want to send via infrared.

■ A drop-down menu appears.

2 Tap Beam Appointment.

■ A list of available devices appears.

3 Align the infrared ports of the two devices.

4 Tap the device to which you want to send your appointment.

5 Tap OK.

■ The device to which you sent your appointment receives a notification dialog box, asking the user if he wants to save your appointment to his calendar.

SELECT AND MODIFY CALENDAR CATEGORIES

Y ou can use categories in the Calendar application to group appointments for quick filtering and sharing of your calendar. If you use Outlook on your desktop to sync with your mobile device, you can share an Outlook calendar with someone else and set up specific categories

for each person so that you can filter and view the appointments on your device.

Categories that you use with your Tasks and Contacts can be shared with your Calendar appointments. When you create an appointment, you can assign a category as

discussed in the section "Create a Calendar Entry." You can then select what categories you want to view. You can also add or delete categories within the Calendar application. However, you cannot rename or edit categories from within the Calendar.

SELECT AND MODIFY CALENDAR CATEGORIES

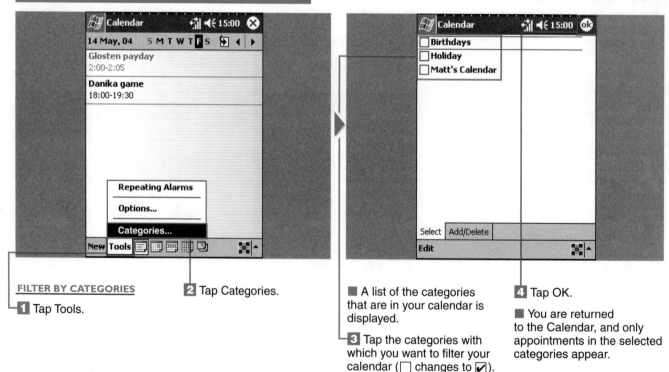

FILTER BY CATEGORIES

1 Tap Tools.

2 Tap Categories.

■ A list of the categories that are in your calendar is displayed.

3 Tap the categories with which you want to filter your calendar (☐ changes to ☑).

4 Tap OK.

■ You are returned to the Calendar, and only appointments in the selected categories appear.

After I delete a category, can I undo my deletion?

✔ No, there is no Undo function associated with category deletion, and a confirmation dialog box does not appear. To restore the category, you have to add it again.

If I delete a category in the Calendar application, is that category also deleted in Contacts and Tasks?

✔ No, the category still remains in those two applications, and any contacts or tasks associated with that category also remain.

After I select a category to view, my regular appointments are no longer visible. Where did they go?

✔ When you select a category to view, your calendar is filtered for that category. Only appointments that are assigned to that specific category appear. To show the rest of your calendar with no assigned category, you must uncheck the check boxes next to the categories on the Select tab.

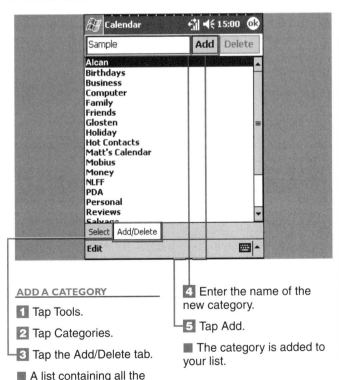

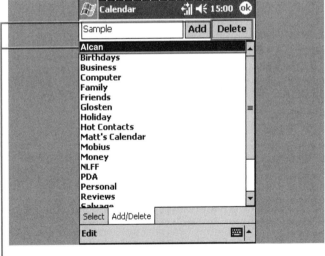

ADD A CATEGORY

1 Tap Tools.

2 Tap Categories.

3 Tap the Add/Delete tab.

■ A list containing all the categories in your Calendar, Contacts, and Tasks appears.

4 Enter the name of the new category.

5 Tap Add.

■ The category is added to your list.

DELETE A CATEGORY

1 On the Add/Delete tab, tap the category that you want to remove.

2 Tap Delete.

Note: No confirmation box appears, so use care when tapping Delete after selecting a category.

■ The category is removed from the list.

CREATE A NEW CONTACT

You can store all your personal and professional contacts on your Windows Mobile 2003 device. You can enter data into 28 fields for each contact, ranging from name and phone number to birth date, spouse's name, and children's names.

You can sync your device to your desktop or laptop computer and maintain a central database of all your contacts in Outlook. Windows Mobile 2003 devices use Pocket Outlook to store your contacts.

You can add as many contacts as you want until your device's available memory is full.

MASTER IT

My contact has multiple work numbers; can I add a custom field or change existing fields?

✔ No, the fields cannot be changed, and there are no custom fields available. You can add more details in Notes, which is discussed in the next section, "Add a Note to a Contact."

CREATE A NEW CONTACT

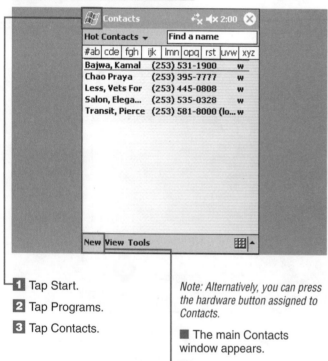

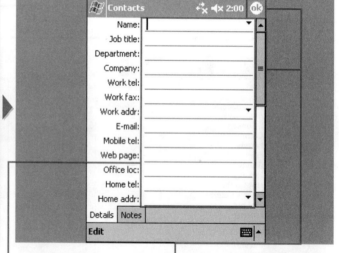

1 Tap Start.

2 Tap Programs.

3 Tap Contacts.

Note: Alternatively, you can press the hardware button assigned to Contacts.

■ The main Contacts window appears.

4 Tap New.

■ A blank contact entry window appears with the cursor on the Name line.

5 Enter information on each line that you want to fill out for the contact.

6 Tap the scrollbar to move down the field entry screen.

7 When all the fields are completed, tap OK.

■ The contact is saved, and the main contact list display appears.

ADD A NOTE TO A CONTACT

B ecause there may be information that you want to add to your contacts in addition to the default fields, Windows Mobile 2003 enables you to add notes to your contacts. You can add typed text, handwritten text, and even voice recordings on the Notes page.

Notes can be useful for adding more e-mail addresses, Web sites, company information, or personal information about a contact. You can hand write notes and then have your device convert them into text. Also, five different zoom levels are available in the Notes field.

Can I change the pen color?

✔ No, only black ink can be used for handwritten notes.

Can I use a voice recording, handwritten text, and typed text in the same note?

✔ Yes, all three can be used in the same note and alternated within the note.

ADD A NOTE TO A CONTACT

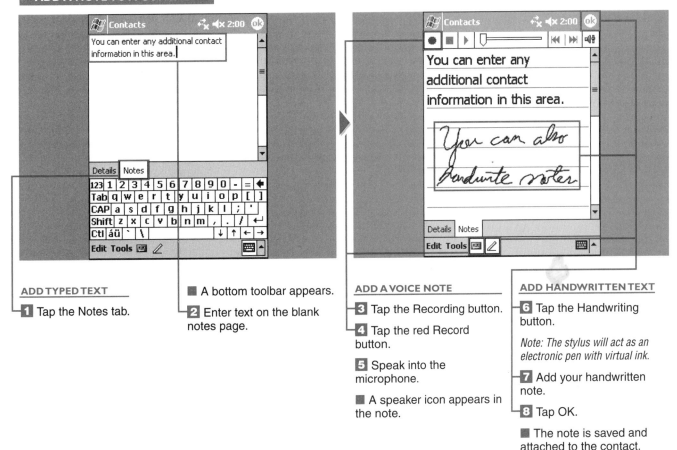

ADD TYPED TEXT

1 Tap the Notes tab.

2 Enter text on the blank notes page.

■ A bottom toolbar appears.

ADD A VOICE NOTE

3 Tap the Recording button.

4 Tap the red Record button.

5 Speak into the microphone.

■ A speaker icon appears in the note.

ADD HANDWRITTEN TEXT

6 Tap the Handwriting button.

Note: The stylus will act as an electronic pen with virtual ink.

7 Add your handwritten note.

8 Tap OK.

■ The note is saved and attached to the contact.

EDIT A CONTACT

Contact information may change, so with Pocket Outlook, you can edit a contact with a few simple taps on your device. Editing takes you back to the same field entry display that you used when you created the contact; you can change any information that you need to. Notes can also be edited by tapping the Notes tab at the bottom while in editing mode.

Can I access the Edit menu from the main Contacts display?

✔ No, you can edit a contact only after you have selected it and opened the viewing screen.

Can I undo changes I made to a contact?

✔ Yes, you can undo changes to the last contact that you worked on. To do so, select Undo from the Edit menu.

Is there a fast way to edit a large portion of the Notes field?

✔ Yes, you can tap Edit ➪ Select All and clear the Notes field for editing.

EDIT A CONTACT

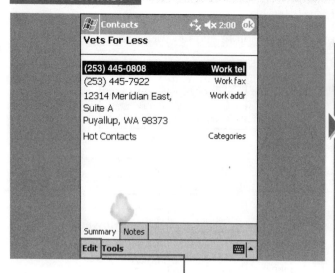

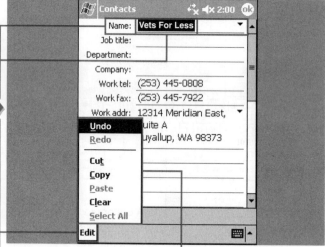

1 Tap the contact that you want to edit in the main Contacts view.

■ A display showing the data entered for the contact appears.

2 Tap Edit.

■ The contact field entry display appears with the name, or the first field with data, selected.

3 Tap the field that you want to change.

■ The text in that field is selected.

4 Enter the new text.

5 Tap Edit.

6 Tap a menu choice to perform that action.

■ You can tap the Notes tab to edit the Notes page.

■ The Notes window appears, in which you can make changes.

CHANGE THE CONTACTS VIEW

Y ou can view your list of contacts either by name or company. Instead of opening up individual contacts and viewing all the information, you can simply tap the letter to the right of a contact to view its home, work, and mobile number and e-mail address. In the Company view, you can also tap the company name to expand the selection and view all the contacts in the same company.

Can I change the number shown in the main contacts display?

✔ Yes, select the contact and then move your navigational pad left or right to change the primary number.

What is the number to the right of the company name?

✔ This number indicates how many contacts are filed with that company name.

CHANGE THE CONTACTS VIEW

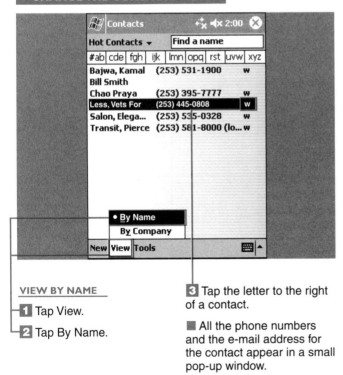

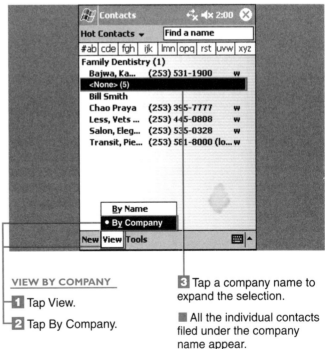

VIEW BY NAME

■1 Tap View.

■2 Tap By Name.

■3 Tap the letter to the right of a contact.

■ All the phone numbers and the e-mail address for the contact appear in a small pop-up window.

VIEW BY COMPANY

■1 Tap View.

■2 Tap By Company.

■3 Tap a company name to expand the selection.

■ All the individual contacts filed under the company name appear.

FIND A CONTACT

I f you have a large number of contacts, it can be tedious to find the one that you are looking for. With Windows Mobile 2003, you can quickly find a contact using one of four methods: You can use the Start menu, type a contact name in the Find a Name field until you see the one that you want displayed, filter your contacts with categories (see "Sort Your Contacts"), or view contacts by company as discussed in "Change the Contacts View."

Does entering a name in the Find a Name field look for company names as well as individual contact names?

✔ Yes, and as you enter letters, the number of contacts is filtered down. If you enter a company name, you will see the expanded version of the company.

What is the fastest way to find a contact?

✔ Entering a company name in the main Contacts display filters contacts faster than other methods.

FIND A CONTACT

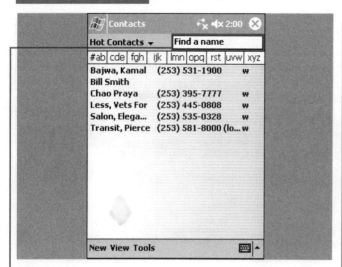

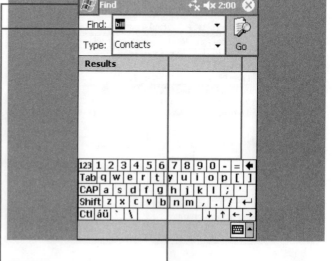

USING THE FIND A NAME FIELD

■1 Tap in the Find a Name field.

■2 Start typing the name of the contact that you are looking for.

■ The contact list starts filtering with the letters that you enter, until your choice is highlighted.

USING THE START MENU

■1 Tap Start.

■2 Tap Find.

■3 Enter the contact name that you want to find.

■4 Select Contacts from the Type drop-down list.

■5 Tap Go to start the search.

■ The Results list shows the contacts with the name that you entered.

SORT YOUR CONTACTS

You can sort or filter your contact list by category. Categories are synched with your desktop version of Outlook, so categories created on your desktop appear on your Windows Mobile 2003 device.

If you have hundreds of contacts, sorting can be important for

narrowing down the number of contacts that you will be scrolling or searching through. If a category is selected, entering letters in the Find box will result in searching only through contacts in that specific category.

Can I sort my contacts alphabetically?

✓ Yes, tap the ABC and so on tabs to quickly bring up contacts starting with that specific letter. Tapping twice brings up contacts starting with the second letter (for example, B), and tapping three times brings up contacts with the third letter.

SORT YOUR CONTACTS

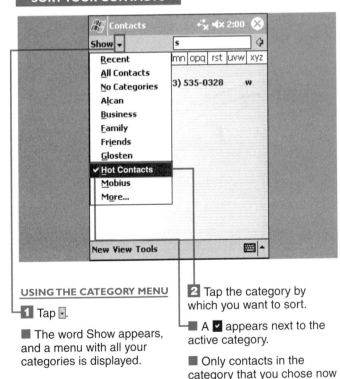

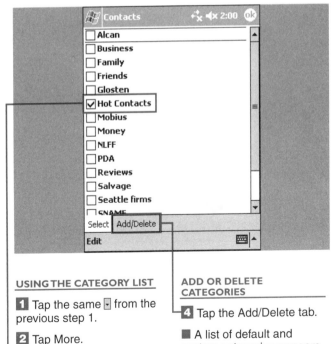

USING THE CATEGORY MENU

1 Tap ▾.

■ The word Show appears, and a menu with all your categories is displayed.

2 Tap the category by which you want to sort.

■ A ✓ appears next to the active category.

■ Only contacts in the category that you chose now appear in your Contacts view.

USING THE CATEGORY LIST

1 Tap the same ▾ from the previous step 1.

2 Tap More.

3 Tap the category by which you want to sort.

ADD OR DELETE CATEGORIES

4 Tap the Add/Delete tab.

■ A list of default and custom categories appears with Add and Delete buttons up top.

COPY, DELETE, AND BEAM CONTACTS

Y ou can copy or delete contacts from your device with a couple quick taps. If you have multiple people in the same company that have the same address, phone number, and so on, then it is much easier to just copy one and change the name on the copy than to enter the same

information several times for each contact. You may need to delete contacts if they leave jobs, move out of town, or simply no longer need to be in your contact list.

You can also beam contacts via infrared if you want to share information with fellow PDA

owners. Do not forget to align the infrared ports when beaming.

You can delete or beam a contact two different ways: by using the Tools menu from the Contacts list or by opening the contact and then using the Tools menu.

COPY, DELETE, AND BEAM CONTACTS

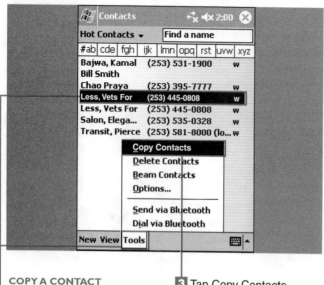

COPY A CONTACT

1 Select a contact without opening the editing window.

2 Tap Tools.

■ A menu with six items appears.

3 Tap Copy Contacts.

■ A copy of the contact appears in the list.

Note: Nothing is added to the copied contact title to differentiate it from the original contact.

DELETE A CONTACT

4 Perform steps 1 and 2.

5 Tap Delete Contacts.

■ A dialog pop-up box appears asking if you are sure that you want to delete the contact.

6 Tap Yes.

■ If you change your mind and do not want to delete the contact, you can tap No.

■ The dialog box closes, and you are returned to the original list.

Can I beam a contact to a Palm PDA?

✔ Yes, Windows Mobile 2003 supports the OBEX infrared system, which enables you to beam a contact without any third-party software or utility.

Can I beam a contact to Pocket PCs not running Windows Mobile 2003?

✔ Yes, you can beam to devices running previous versions of the Pocket PC operating system.

Can I beam my virtual business card to others?

✔ Yes, Windows Mobile 2003 supports vCard exchange.

Can I copy a contact to another category?

✔ No, when you copy a contact, an exact duplicate is made and placed in the list with the existing contact. You can then edit the duplicate contact to reflect the changes that you want.

Can I delete, copy, or beam multiple contacts?

✔ Yes, tap and drag your stylus over the contacts and then tap and hold the highlighted section to access the menu with these options. You can also tap the Tools menu after making your selection.

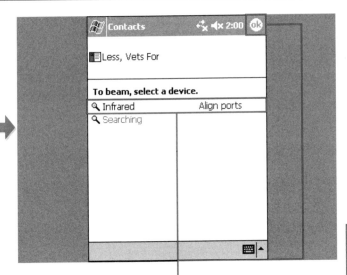

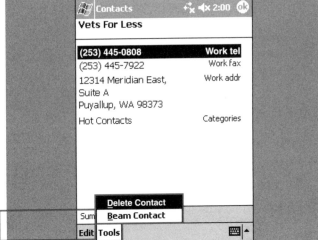

BEAM A CONTACT

7 Perform steps 1 and 2.

8 Tap Beam Contacts.

■ The infrared beaming utility appears.

9 Align the ports of the two devices.

10 Tap the device name to which you want to beam the contact.

11 Tap OK to close the beaming utility.

DELETE OR BEAM WITH THE CONTACT OPEN

1 In the Contacts list, tap a contact to go the individual view screen.

2 Tap Tools.

3 Tap Delete Contact or Beam Contact to perform that specific action.

■ The delete dialog box or beaming utility appears, depending on your selection.

■ If you are deleting a contact, tap Yes.

■ If you are beaming a contact, perform steps 9 to 11.

MODIFY VIEW SETTINGS

You can change how contacts are shown on your device in a couple ways. The Options settings enable you to show or hide the ABC tabs, show contact names only, and make the font bold for easier readability. The ABC tabs are helpful for quickly sorting your contacts. If you show only the contact names, the default primary number and e-mail address do not appear in the Contacts list.

You can also change the view in the main Contacts display to show your contact name or company name.

MASTER IT

Will my new primary number selection remain valid if I close Contacts and reopen them?

✔ Yes, changing the primary number in the main view saves the change.

Can an e-mail address be selected as the primary contact point?

✔ Yes. A lowercase *e* appears next to the name if e-mail is selected. A lowercase *h* stands for home, *m* for mobile, and *w* for work.

MODIFY VIEW SETTINGS

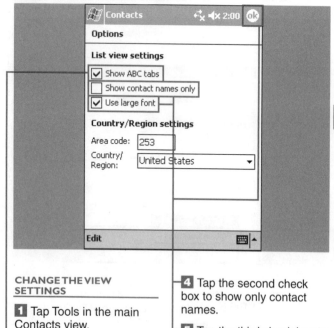

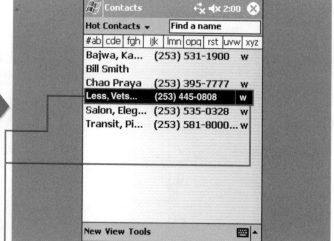

CHANGE THE VIEW SETTINGS

1 Tap Tools in the main Contacts view.

2 Tap Options.

3 Tap the first check box to show or hide ABC tabs.

4 Tap the second check box to show only contact names.

5 Tap the third check box to use a large font.

6 Tap OK.

■ The main Contacts window reappears with the selections that you made for viewing.

CHANGE THE PRIMARY NUMBER OR E-MAIL ADDRESS

7 Select a contact by tapping or using your directional pad.

8 Tap the letter.

■ A list of e-mail addresses and phone numbers appears.

9 Tap the number or e-mail address that you want to use as the primary contact listed on the one-line contact page.

■ The new selection appears in the Contacts List view.

MODIFY REGIONAL SETTINGS

You can change the default area code and country stored on your device. Because you can use your device to dial via Bluetooth, it is helpful to have your local area code be the default dialing code.

Several countries and regions are available for you to choose from in your Contacts regional settings. These settings can be quickly changed if you travel with your device.

Can I manually enter a different country or region?

✔ No, the Country/Region list is only for selecting what is on the device and does not allow you to enter text manually.

Do I have to change my settings when I travel?

✔ No, but if you do not change the area code, your phone may not dial correctly when you try to dial from your Contacts list.

MODIFY REGIONAL SETTINGS

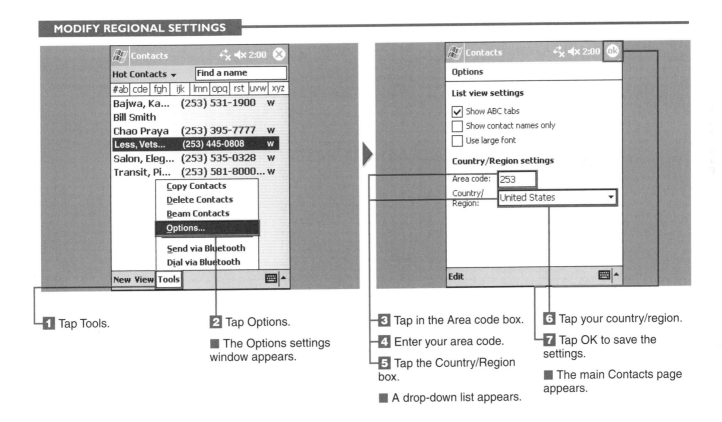

1 Tap Tools.

2 Tap Options.

■ The Options settings window appears.

3 Tap in the Area code box.

4 Enter your area code.

5 Tap the Country/Region box.

■ A drop-down list appears.

6 Tap your country/region.

7 Tap OK to save the settings.

■ The main Contacts page appears.

USING BLUETOOTH WITH CONTACTS

With certain models of Bluetooth wireless phones, you can dial a contact directly from within the Contacts application. You can also send contact information to other Bluetooth devices, phones, PDAs, and so on with a simple tap on your device. Bluetooth technology is designed to replace cables, so you do not need a serial cable to make a connection.

Sending via Bluetooth initiates the Bluetooth browser, which searches for and lists devices that have Bluetooth running in your local area. You can then send the contact information to the device that you choose.

Dialing via Bluetooth opens a new Bluetooth dialing window, the Bluetooth Assistant, which enables you to select the phone to use and

the number to dial before you actually dial the number. Your Windows Mobile 2003 device is used only for dialing the number, so after the call is made, your device will no longer be used for the connection. You may want to then use a Bluetooth headset with your Bluetooth phone for the call.

USING BLUETOOTH WITH CONTACTS

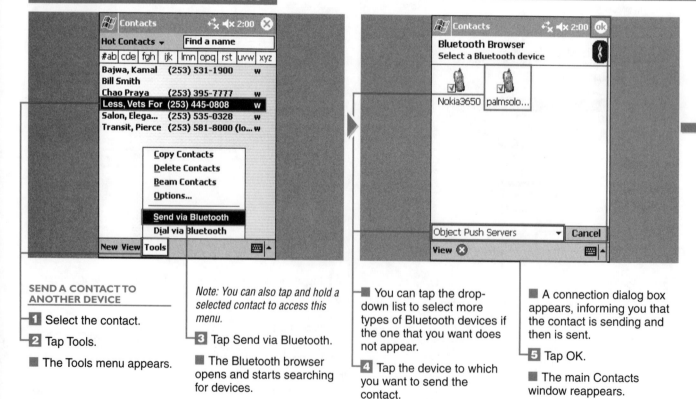

SEND A CONTACT TO ANOTHER DEVICE

1 Select the contact.

2 Tap Tools.

■ The Tools menu appears.

Note: You can also tap and hold a selected contact to access this menu.

3 Tap Send via Bluetooth.

■ The Bluetooth browser opens and starts searching for devices.

■ You can tap the drop-down list to select more types of Bluetooth devices if the one that you want does not appear.

4 Tap the device to which you want to send the contact.

■ A connection dialog box appears, informing you that the contact is sending and then is sent.

5 Tap OK.

■ The main Contacts window reappears.

MASTER IT

Can I send multiple contacts via Bluetooth?

✔ Yes, tap and drag over the list of contacts that you want to send, tap and hold the selection, and from the menu that appears, choose Send via Bluetooth. Sending contacts via Bluetooth is one way to keep multiple devices up-to-date with your latest contact information.

I cannot send a contact to the device that I want to via Bluetooth; what is wrong with the device?

✔ Some Bluetooth devices are not set up to receive contact information.

Can I dial or send via Bluetooth while viewing contact details?

✔ No, the send or dial functionality is accessible only from the main contact viewing screen.

Can I send my contact an e-mail via Bluetooth?

✔ Yes, but only if you have a data plan on your wireless phone and you have it set up for e-mail. Tap and hold a contact and then select the Send E-mail option. Windows Mobile 2003 then puts the contact's e-mail address into the To line of the Inbox, and the Inbox application handles sending the message via a Bluetooth connection.

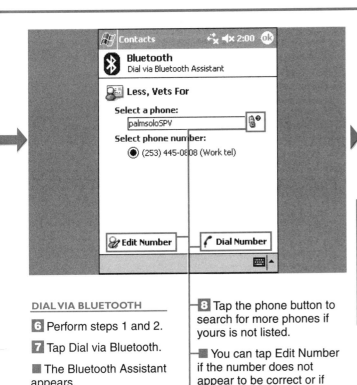

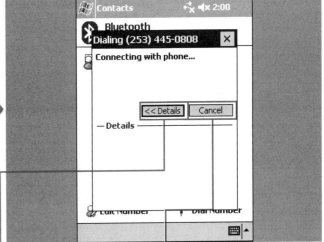

DIAL VIA BLUETOOTH

6 Perform steps 1 and 2.

7 Tap Dial via Bluetooth.

■ The Bluetooth Assistant appears.

8 Tap the phone button to search for more phones if yours is not listed.

■ You can tap Edit Number if the number does not appear to be correct or if an area or country code is required to dial.

9 Tap Dial Number.

■ A call status box appears.

10 Tap Details to view more specifics of the connection.

■ The Details area shows the connection status and then informs you that the number has been sent to be dialed.

11 Pick up your phone to talk with the person that your device dialed.

12 Tap Cancel on your device.

13 Tap OK.

■ The Bluetooth dialing window closes.

SET UP OR MODIFY AN E-MAIL ACCOUNT

Y ou can set up e-mail accounts on your mobile device that you can use to manage POP3 and IMAP4 accounts. An ActiveSync account is automatically set up on your device, and you can use the desktop ActiveSync client to specify if e-mail will be synched to this account on your mobile device. This account has been renamed to Outlook E-mail on Windows Mobile 2003 Second Edition devices.

You can also manage an SMS account that is configured to work with your wireless phone provider. Phone Edition devices have an SMS account loaded by default that cannot be deleted from the Inbox.

Multiple accounts can be added to your device, including a combination of POP3 and IMAP4 accounts. However, HTTP Web-based e-mail accounts such as

Hotmail cannot be used with the Inbox application.

You will need to have your e-mail address, username, password, account type, e-mail server name, SMTP (Simple Mail Transfer Protocol) host, and domain name, if used, available to set up each account. The SMTP host is used for outgoing mail configuration.

SET UP OR MODIFY AN E-MAIL ACCOUNT

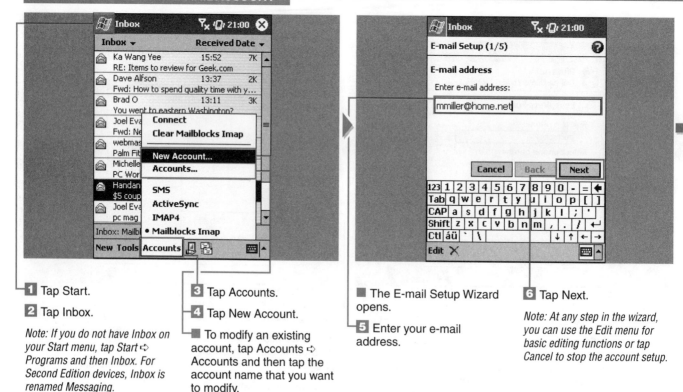

1 Tap Start.

2 Tap Inbox.

Note: If you do not have Inbox on your Start menu, tap Start ⇨ Programs and then Inbox. For Second Edition devices, Inbox is renamed Messaging.

3 Tap Accounts.

4 Tap New Account.

■ To modify an existing account, tap Accounts ⇨ Accounts and then tap the account name that you want to modify.

■ The E-mail Setup Wizard opens.

5 Enter your e-mail address.

6 Tap Next.

Note: At any step in the wizard, you can use the Edit menu for basic editing functions or tap Cancel to stop the account setup.

MASTER IT

Can I remove or delete the ActiveSync (or Outlook E-mail) account because I never use it for e-mail?

✔ No, this account is loaded by default and cannot be removed. This account is managed using the desktop version of ActiveSync, where you set up the folders that will be synched with your device.

Can I change an existing account type from POP3 to IMAP4?

✔ No, the account type and name cannot be changed on an existing account. To change the account type, you have to delete the account and create a new account, selecting IMAP4 as the type.

What is the red X at the bottom of the wizard pages?

✔ This is the Delete button. If you tap the X, a dialog box pops up, stating that the account will be deleted and all messages associated with that account will also be deleted. You can tap No to close the dialog box and continue the account setup.

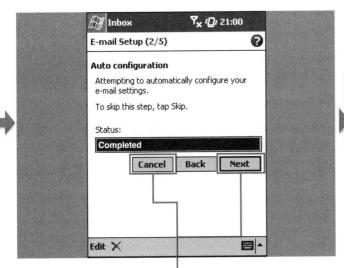

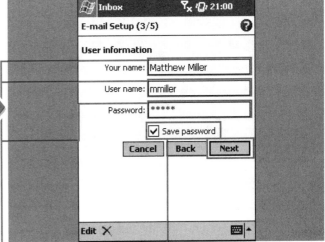

■ The Inbox attempts to make an Internet connection and configure basic account settings using the e-mail address that you entered.

Note: This step does not appear if you are editing an existing account.

■ The Inbox returns a status of Completed.

7 Tap Next.

■ You can tap Cancel if you do not want the Inbox to attempt to auto-configure your account.

■ The Inbox may fill in some of these fields during auto-configuration.

8 Enter your name as you want it to appear in e-mail headings.

9 Enter your account username.

10 Enter your password.

11 Tap Save Password (☐ changes to ☑).

Note: If this is not checked, you will be prompted for your password whenever you attempt to receive or send e-mail.

12 Tap Next.

Note: You can tap ? to get help with the wizard.

CONTINUED

SET UP OR MODIFY AN E-MAIL ACCOUNT (CONTINUED)

You can easily step through the Inbox e-mail account setup wizard when you create a new account or edit existing accounts. The wizard has five steps for new accounts and four steps for editing existing accounts. If your device is connected to the Internet, the Inbox's Auto Configuration feature will attempt to connect to your e-mail provider and download the settings. If the auto-configuration is successful, you can connect and begin downloading e-mail without completing the other steps in the wizard. The Auto Configuration page is not included when you are editing existing accounts.

The account name defaults to POP3 or IMAP4, but you can change this to match the name of your provider or to another name that you prefer. This name cannot be changed later, however, if you want to edit your account. The only way to change the account name at that point is to delete the account and create a new account.

SET UP OR MODIFY AN E-MAIL ACCOUNT (CONTINUED)

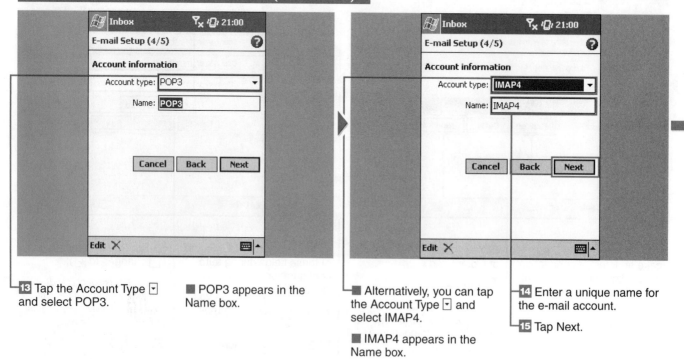

■13 Tap the Account Type ⏷ and select POP3.

■ POP3 appears in the Name box.

■ Alternatively, you can tap the Account Type ⏷ and select IMAP4.

■ IMAP4 appears in the Name box.

■14 Enter a unique name for the e-mail account.

■15 Tap Next.

How do I know if I have a POP3 or IMAP4 account, and which is the better alternative for the Inbox?

✔ Check with your e-mail provider for your account type and details. IMAP (Internet Message Access Protocol) accounts are particularly useful for mobile devices because the Inbox enables you to remotely manage your e-mail on the server and IMAP helps to avoid the duplication of e-mail on different mobile devices or platforms. IMAP also prevents you from accidentally deleting an e-mail on your device that you did not intend to delete from the server.

Can I add my Hotmail or Yahoo e-mail account to the Inbox?

✔ No, you cannot add any Web-based e-mail accounts to the Inbox application. If you pay for a premium Yahoo account, you can check e-mail using POP3 through the Inbox as well as checking e-mail via Internet Explorer. Microsoft will be adding a Pocket MSN client to the Windows Mobile 2003 platform in the near future that will allow access to Hotmail accounts.

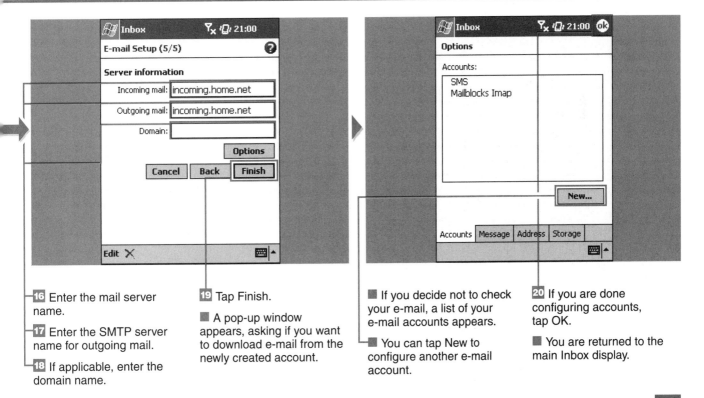

16 Enter the mail server name.

17 Enter the SMTP server name for outgoing mail.

18 If applicable, enter the domain name.

19 Tap Finish.

■ A pop-up window appears, asking if you want to download e-mail from the newly created account.

■ If you decide not to check your e-mail, a list of your e-mail accounts appears.

■ You can tap New to configure another e-mail account.

20 If you are done configuring accounts, tap OK.

■ You are returned to the main Inbox display.

SET UP ACCOUNT OPTIONS

After going through the steps of the new e-mail account wizard, you can access and set up advanced options for each of your e-mail accounts. These options are not required to receive e-mail, but they may be required to send e-mail if your e-mail provider requires authentication.

The advanced e-mail account settings enable you to configure your account to connect and check for e-mail messages at set time periods, select outgoing authentication, enable SSL connections, set how many days' worth of e-mails will be displayed, and select whether full copies or parts of messages will be downloaded.

Step 3 of 3 in the Options setup wizard differs slightly for POP3 and IMAP4. You can manage attachment sizes in the IMAP4 settings, but only the message size can be managed in the POP3 options. Steps 1 and 2 are the same for both types of accounts.

SET UP ACCOUNT OPTIONS

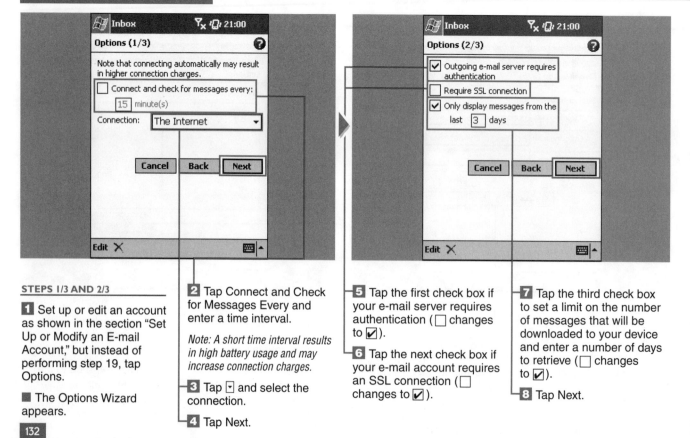

STEPS 1/3 AND 2/3

1 Set up or edit an account as shown in the section "Set Up or Modify an E-mail Account," but instead of performing step 19, tap Options.

■ The Options Wizard appears.

2 Tap Connect and Check for Messages Every and enter a time interval.

Note: A short time interval results in high battery usage and may increase connection charges.

3 Tap ⊡ and select the connection.

4 Tap Next.

5 Tap the first check box if your e-mail server requires authentication (☐ changes to ☑).

6 Tap the next check box if your e-mail account requires an SSL connection (☐ changes to ☑).

7 Tap the third check box to set a limit on the number of messages that will be downloaded to your device and enter a number of days to retrieve (☐ changes to ☑).

8 Tap Next.

How do I get attachments on my device with a POP3 account?

✔ You can download attachments in a POP3 e-mail account by tapping and holding the e-mail message and selecting to download the attachment.

Can I get full copies of messages at a later time without having to edit my advanced options?

✔ Yes, you can mark each message that you read for download and then download the entire message rather than just the header and a certain amount of the message.

What is the limit for e-mail message size and attachments that I can download?

✔ If you do not want to include the full copy of the messages, you can limit the download to 99KB. If you want to get the full copy, you can limit the attachment size to a maximum of 999KB.

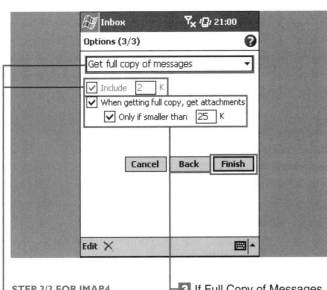

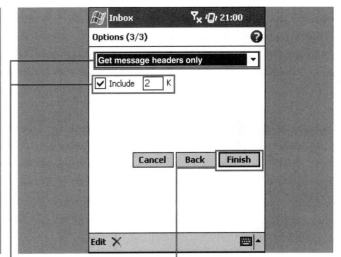

STEP 3/3 FOR IMAP4 ACCOUNTS

1 Tap ⊡ and select to retrieve full copies of messages or headers only.

2 If Headers Only is selected, tap Include and enter how many KB of the message you want to include.

3 If Full Copy of Messages is selected, tap the check boxes to retrieve attachments and set a size limit.

4 Tap Finish.

■ If the account is a new account, a pop-up box appears, asking if you want to download messages for the new account.

STEP 3/3 FOR POP3 ACCOUNTS

1 Tap ⊡ and select to retrieve full copies of messages or headers only.

2 If Headers Only is selected, tap Include and enter how many KB of the message you want to include.

Note: If you select Get Full Copy of Messages, there is no option to limit the size of the message.

3 Tap Finish.

■ If the account is new, a pop-up box appears, asking if you want to download messages for the new account.

SET UP MESSAGE PREFERENCES AND SIGNATURES

You can set up global message settings that apply to all e-mail accounts configured on your device. These global settings include reply formatting, keeping sent mail on your device, the action to take after a message is moved or deleted, and when to empty deleted items from your device.

The default setting is to not save sent mail on your device because this uses valuable storage memory. You can have the Inbox return to the message list, show the next message, or show the previous message when a message is moved or deleted. The Deleted Items folder can be emptied manually, immediately, or when connecting

to and disconnecting from your e-mail account.

You can also attach different signatures to each account and specify when the signature will be added to messages. Signatures can be added to ActiveSync and SMS accounts as well as POP3 and IMAP4 accounts.

SET UP MESSAGE PREFERENCES AND SIGNATURES

SET UP MESSAGE PREFERENCES

1 From the main Inbox view, tap Tools.

2 Tap Options.

3 Tap the Message tab.

4 Tap When Replying to include the body of the original when replying (☐ changes to ☑).

■ You can use the next two check boxes to specify how the original body appears in the reply.

■ You can tap Keep Copy to keep a copy of the sent mail on your device.

5 Tap the After Deleting or Moving a Message ⊡ and specify the action to take after a message is moved or deleted.

6 Tap the Empty Deleted Items ⊡ and specify when to empty the Deleted Items folder.

7 Tap Signatures to set up your e-mail signatures.

Can I use images in my signature?

✔ No, only text can be included in signatures. However, you can enter a URL of an image with http:// in the prefix that will show up as an active hyperlink in your e-mail signature.

If I deactivate my signature, will it still be there if I go back later and enable my signature with the same account?

✔ Yes. If you uncheck the Use Signature with This Account check box, you will see that the signature becomes grayed out. If you later go back and select the check box, the same signature will become active again.

Can I assign the same signature to multiple accounts?

✔ No, you cannot create one signature and then simply assign it to multiple accounts using the signature setup options. However, if you select all the text of a signature that you want to use repeatedly, you can tap and hold it and copy it to the Clipboard. Then select another e-mail account, tap and hold in the signature entry box, and select Paste.

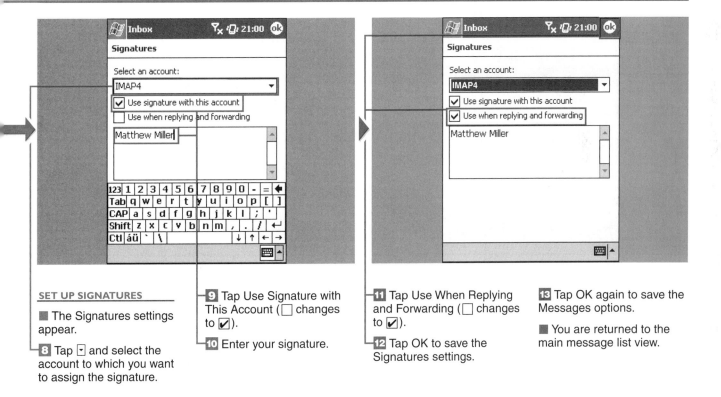

SET UP SIGNATURES

■ The Signatures settings appear.

⑧ Tap ⊡ and select the account to which you want to assign the signature.

⑨ Tap Use Signature with This Account (☐ changes to ☑).

⑩ Enter your signature.

⑪ Tap Use When Replying and Forwarding (☐ changes to ☑).

⑫ Tap OK to save the Signatures settings.

⑬ Tap OK again to save the Messages options.

■ You are returned to the main message list view.

SET ADDRESS PREFERENCES

You can specify where the Inbox will look for e-mail addresses when you are creating a new message. The default option is for the Inbox to look in all e-mail fields of your Contacts list, but you can specify None or one of the other e-mail fields in the Contacts database.

Another option to help you quickly fill out an e-mail message address

is to use Lightweight Directory Access Protocol (LDAP). LDAP works with Microsoft Exchange and other e-mail servers to verify names with an online address book. The Inbox adds your e-mail server's directory to the Address options tab, and you can tap the service's check box to enable it. Most ISPs and e-mail providers do not use LDAP, but it can be a valuable tool for corporate users who want to

check and verify that an e-mail address is correct before sending out a message.

You need to know the name of the server, your username, and password to set up the LDAP address preferences. You may also have to select to use authentication with the server.

SET ADDRESS PREFERENCES

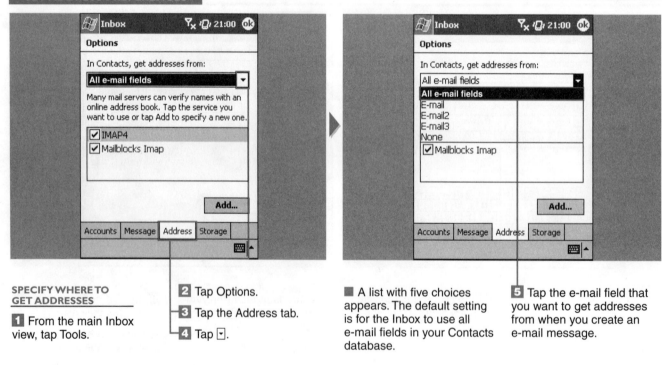

SPECIFY WHERE TO GET ADDRESSES

1 From the main Inbox view, tap Tools.

2 Tap Options.

3 Tap the Address tab.

4 Tap ▾.

■ A list with five choices appears. The default setting is for the Inbox to use all e-mail fields in your Contacts database.

5 Tap the e-mail field that you want to get addresses from when you create an e-mail message.

Why would I want or need to add another mail server to the mail servers list on the Address tab?

✔ Some mail servers do not support LDAP, and you may have a corporate server that you can use to verify e-mail addresses. If so, you can add that corporate server to the mail servers list.

Can I delete a mail server? If so, how do I do that?

✔ Yes, you can delete a mail server. To do so, tap and hold the mail server's name in the list on the Address tab of the Inbox Options. Then tap Delete on the menu that appears.

If I do not have a corporate server, do I need to change any options on the Address tab?

✔ No. If you create a new e-mail message, you will still be able to pull all e-mail addresses from your Contacts list without performing any configuration of the Address options, just using the default settings.

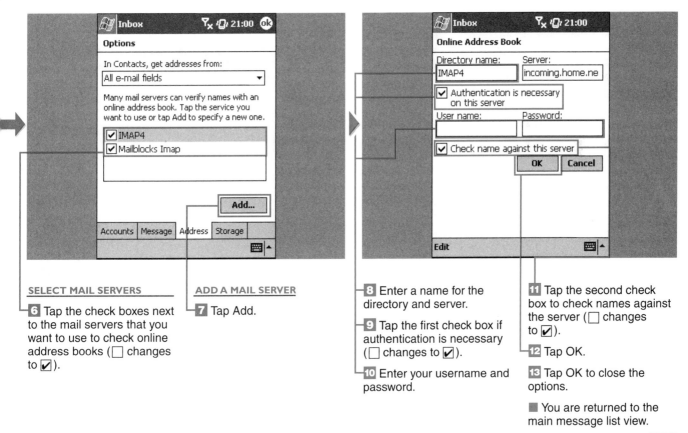

SELECT MAIL SERVERS

⑥ Tap the check boxes next to the mail servers that you want to use to check online address books (☐ changes to ☑).

ADD A MAIL SERVER

⑦ Tap Add.

⑧ Enter a name for the directory and server.

⑨ Tap the first check box if authentication is necessary (☐ changes to ☑).

⑩ Enter your username and password.

⑪ Tap the second check box to check names against the server (☐ changes to ☑).

⑫ Tap OK.

⑬ Tap OK to close the options.

■ You are returned to the main message list view.

SET ATTACHMENT OPTIONS AND VIEW THE INBOX STATUS

To save space on your device, you can set an option to store attachments on an external storage card. However, you cannot store your e-mail messages on an external card. The Inbox provides a summary of available main memory and storage card memory on your device, as well as the current size of attachments.

You can also view the current status of e-mail messages for each account on your device. The status lists the number of messages to be sent, copied, and deleted, as well as the attachments to be copied.

I have an HP iPAQ 2215 and see only a small amount of free space listed in the storage card area, even though I have an empty 256MB SD card in the slot. What is the problem?

✔ iPAQ 2215 devices have an issue with recognizing an external storage card. The free space you see available is the iPAQ File Store ROM area on your device. A Registry hack has been circulated online, but no official ROM update that fixes the issue has been released yet.

SET ATTACHMENT OPTIONS AND VIEW THE INBOX STATUS

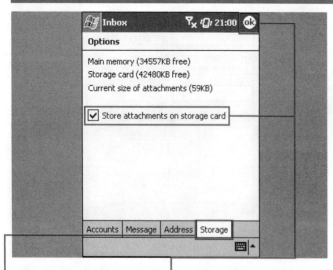

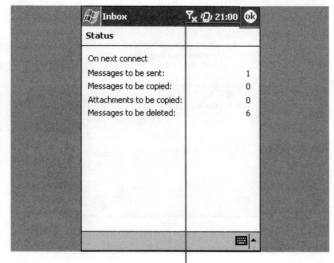

SET ATTACHMENT OPTIONS

1 From the main Inbox view, tap Tools.

2 Tap Options.

3 Tap the Storage tab.

4 Tap Store Attachments on Storage Card (☐ changes to ☑).

5 Tap OK to save the settings.

■ Existing attachments are moved to the storage card.

VIEW THE INBOX STATUS

1 From the main Inbox view, tap Tools.

2 Tap Status.

■ The status of messages and attachments appears.

3 When you are done viewing the statistics, tap OK.

■ The Status window closes, and the main message view appears.

CONNECT TO AN E-MAIL ACCOUNT AND CLEAR MESSAGES

You can connect to your e-mail account and check for new messages when you send out messages from your Outbox.

You can also choose to clear messages associated with a POP3 or IMAP4 account. All messages and folders that are linked to the account will be cleared, without deleting the messages from the server. The next time that you connect, the messages and folders will appear in the account. However, you cannot clear messages from your ActiveSync account.

Why would I want to clear messages from my device?

✔ You may want to change your account settings to download e-mail from a shorter time period; thus you can remove older messages from your device that you no longer need to view while recovering some available memory.

CONNECT TO AN E-MAIL ACCOUNT AND CLEAR MESSAGES

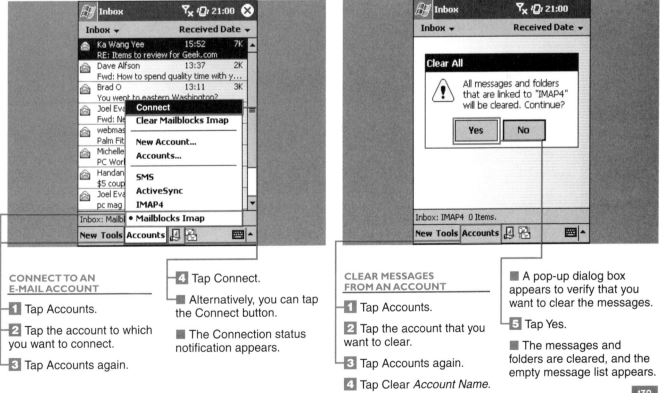

CONNECT TO AN E-MAIL ACCOUNT

1 Tap Accounts.

2 Tap the account to which you want to connect.

3 Tap Accounts again.

4 Tap Connect.

■ Alternatively, you can tap the Connect button.

■ The Connection status notification appears.

CLEAR MESSAGES FROM AN ACCOUNT

1 Tap Accounts.

2 Tap the account that you want to clear.

3 Tap Accounts again.

4 Tap Clear *Account Name*.

■ A pop-up dialog box appears to verify that you want to clear the messages.

5 Tap Yes.

■ The messages and folders are cleared, and the empty message list appears.

SWITCH BETWEEN E-MAIL ACCOUNTS

You can create and manage multiple e-mail accounts on your device, and you can switch between the different accounts a couple of ways.

In the folder view, you can switch between accounts and go to a specific e-mail folder. You can also use the Accounts menu to switch between accounts; this method takes you to the Inbox folder of each account.

How do I expand the e-mail account so that I can switch to a specific folder?

✔ Tap the + to the left of the account name to expand the folder list. Then tap the folder to which you want to switch.

Is there any other way to switch between accounts, aside from using the folder view or Accounts menu?

✔ Yes, if you press the left or right side of the navigational pad found on most Windows Mobile 2003 devices, you will be taken to the previous account's or next account's Inbox.

SWITCH BETWEEN E-MAIL ACCOUNTS

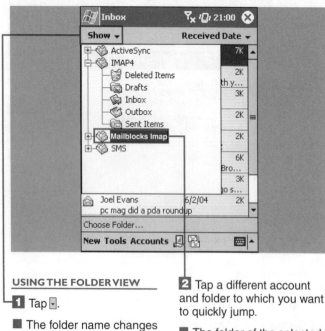

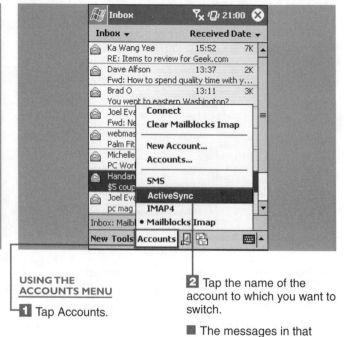

USING THE FOLDER VIEW

1 Tap ⊡.

■ The folder name changes to Show.

2 Tap a different account and folder to which you want to quickly jump.

■ The folder of the selected account appears on your display.

USING THE ACCOUNTS MENU

1 Tap Accounts.

2 Tap the name of the account to which you want to switch.

■ The messages in that account's Inbox appear.

MANAGE AND SORT MESSAGES

You can manage your messages a number of different ways. You can create a new message; delete a message; move a message to another folder; reply, reply to all, or forward a message; send and receive messages; mark a message as unread; or mark a message for download.

You can also sort messages by the sender, received date, or subject. You can change the sort order from descending to ascending and vice versa.

Can I move a message from one e-mail account to another e-mail account?

✔ No, you can only move messages within the same e-mail account. An illegal operation error appears if you attempt to place an e-mail in an invalid location.

Can I cancel a move after I select the Move option?

✔ No, there is no cancel option when moving a message. If you change your mind, you can move the message back to its old folder.

MANAGE AND SORT MESSAGES

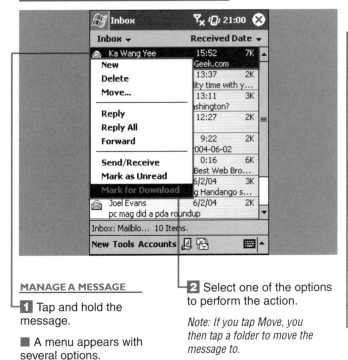

MANAGE A MESSAGE

■1 Tap and hold the message.

■ A menu appears with several options.

■2 Select one of the options to perform the action.

Note: If you tap Move, you then tap a folder to move the message to.

SORT MESSAGES

■1 Tap ▾.

■2 Tap one of the options.

REVERSE THE SORT ORDER

■3 Tap ▾ again.

■4 Tap the same option.

■ The order of the messages is reversed using the same criteria.

CREATE A NEW E-MAIL MESSAGE

You can create new e-mail messages on your device and send them via the ActiveSync conduit or another Internet connection. The standard To:, Cc:, Bcc:, and Subject lines are used to set up the header of your outgoing messages. You can manually enter an e-mail address or select a contact from your Contacts list.

You can use different input methods available on your device to create the e-mail body, and you can use a signature; see the section "Set Up Message Preferences and Signatures" for more information.

Several editing functions are available to you as you create your e-mail message, including the

standard Cut, Copy, Paste, Clear, and Select All options. You can conduct a spell check of your e-mail message before it is sent. Also, the message can be canceled or saved in the Drafts folder from the Edit menu.

CREATE A NEW E-MAIL MESSAGE

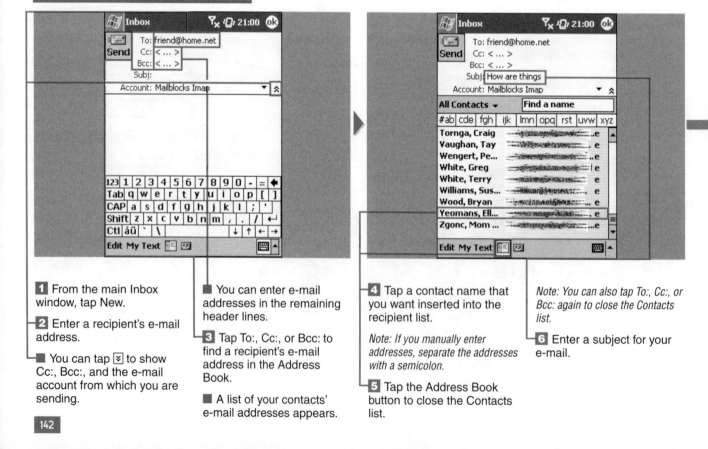

■1 From the main Inbox window, tap New.

■2 Enter a recipient's e-mail address.

■ You can tap ⊠ to show Cc:, Bcc:, and the e-mail account from which you are sending.

■ You can enter e-mail addresses in the remaining header lines.

■3 Tap To:, Cc:, or Bcc: to find a recipient's e-mail address in the Address Book.

■ A list of your contacts' e-mail addresses appears.

■4 Tap a contact name that you want inserted into the recipient list.

Note: If you manually enter addresses, separate the addresses with a semicolon.

■5 Tap the Address Book button to close the Contacts list.

Note: You can also tap To:, Cc:, or Bcc: again to close the Contacts list.

■6 Enter a subject for your e-mail.

Can I create HTML messages using the Inbox?

✔ No, the Inbox does not support sending or receiving HTML e-mail messages.

Can I send the same e-mail message from multiple accounts?

✔ No, you can select only one account from which to send a message.

Can I have my e-mail messages automatically spell checked before sending?

✔ No, you must manually initiate a spell check of your e-mail body using the Edit menu. The spell checker also does not check the e-mail header's spelling.

What is the Check Names option on the Edit menu used for?

✔ This option uses your LDAP server connection established in the Address options to check the recipients against the server's database for accuracy; see the section "Set Address Preferences" for more information.

Can I send SMS messages from my device?

✔ You can send SMS messages from a Pocket PC Phone Edition device, but you need a third-party application such as Simple SMS to send SMS via a Bluetooth or IR connection using your cell phone. Details on sending SMS messages with a Phone Edition device are covered in Chapter 28.

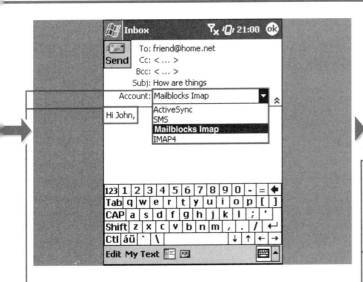

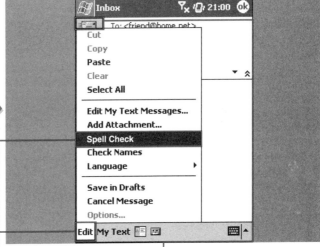

7 Tap ☑ and tap a new e-mail account to switch the account from which you are sending.

8 Enter the body of your e-mail message.

■ If the text of your message extends beyond the viewable area, scrollbars appear.

Note: You can hide Cc:, Bcc:, and the e-mail account if you want more viewable room to enter the e-mail body.

9 Tap Edit.

Note: You can tap one of the Editing functions to perform that action.

10 Tap Spell Check.

■ The first misspelled word is highlighted, and alternatives are offered that you can accept, ignore, or add to your dictionary.

11 Tap Send.

■ Your e-mail is sent the next time that your device is connected.

ADD AN ATTACHMENT TO YOUR E-MAIL

You can add files as attachments to your outgoing e-mail messages sent from your mobile device. The Inbox includes a simple utility to add an attachment, and the only limit on an attachment's size is the amount of available memory on your device.

There is no file compression utility included with Windows Mobile 2003, so each file has to be added as a separate attachment. You can use third-party compression utilities such as Resco Explorer 2003 and then attach the zipped file as a single e-mail attachment. You also cannot select multiple files in the attachment management window.

In the attachment management window, you can adjust the column widths so that you can view the entire filename, folder, date, size, type, and location. You tap and drag on the separation line found at the right side of the column heading to adjust the width.

ADD AN ATTACHMENT TO YOUR E-MAIL

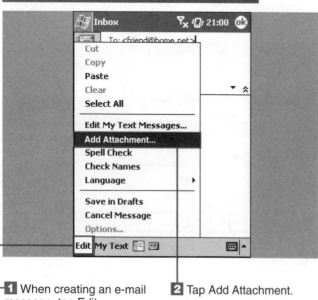

1 When creating an e-mail message, tap Edit.

Note: See the section "Create a New E-mail Message" for details on creating a message.

2 Tap Add Attachment.

■ The attachment management window opens.

3 Tap the Folder ▾ and select the folder to view.

4 Tap a heading to sort the list of files.

■ You can tap the scrollbar to view more file details.

5 Tap the file to add as an attachment.

■ You are returned to the e-mail message.

Note: You can repeat steps 1 to 5 to add multiple files to the e-mail message.

Will my recipient be able to read my Pocket Excel or Pocket Word document on his desktop computer if he does not have ActiveSync installed?

✔ Yes, Pocket Word documents are converted to `.doc` format and Pocket Excel documents to `.xls` when sent as an e-mail attachment.

Can I limit the types of files that the Inbox lists when attaching a file?

✔ No, the Inbox shows all files using the *.* search term. Only documents in the My Documents folders in RAM and on storage cards are used, so all files in Windows, Program Files, and so on are not shown.

Are there any restrictions on files that can be attached?

✔ Yes, OLE objects cannot be attached to e-mail messages.

Can I sort the available files so that I can find the document that I want to attach?

✔ Yes, tap the column header to sort the files using that criteria. Tapping a second time on the header reverses the order. An icon in the name also indicates if the file is on a storage card.

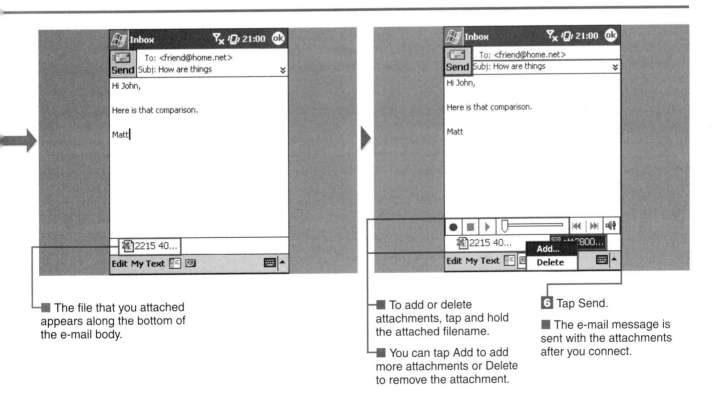

■ The file that you attached appears along the bottom of the e-mail body.

■ To add or delete attachments, tap and hold the attached filename.

■ You can tap Add to add more attachments or Delete to remove the attachment.

6 Tap Send.

■ The e-mail message is sent with the attachments after you connect.

SEND A VOICE MESSAGE

You can add recordings to your outgoing e-mail messages with a method that is similar to adding an e-mail attachment. The quality and size of the recordings is set using the Input settings on your device and cannot be changed within the Inbox application.

Voice messages are convenient to send when you are unable to spend the time writing out a full e-mail message using a text-entry method. The recipient receives the file as a .wav file, so it can be listened to on virtually any computer.

MASTER IT

Can I add multiple voice messages to my e-mail?
✔ Yes, the only limit on outgoing messages is the available memory on your device when you create the voice messages.

Is there any menu to add a voice message?
✔ No, you can only add voice messages by tapping the Record button.

SEND A VOICE MESSAGE

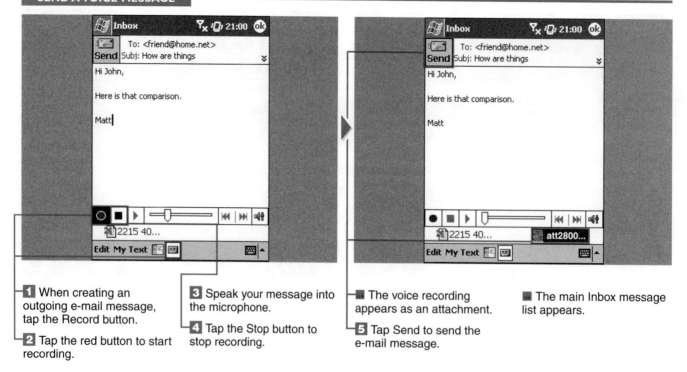

1 When creating an outgoing e-mail message, tap the Record button.

2 Tap the red button to start recording.

3 Speak your message into the microphone.

4 Tap the Stop button to stop recording.

■ The voice recording appears as an attachment.

5 Tap Send to send the e-mail message.

■ The main Inbox message list appears.

USE AND EDIT MY TEXT MESSAGES

My Text messages enable you to quickly add short statements to your e-mails with no text entry. Nine preset My Text messages are included on your device, and there is one blank slot for you to add your own message. You can also edit the existing messages and customize them to your needs. My Text messages can be fun statements or can be used to respond quickly to another person.

Can I add more My Text messages?
✔ No, only ten My Text messages are allowed on your device. They can be edited, but you cannot add or delete them from the system.

Is there another method to access the My Text Messages editing window, other than the Edit menu?
✔ Yes, from the main Inbox view, you can tap Tools ⇨ Edit My Text Messages.

USE AND EDIT MY TEXT MESSAGES

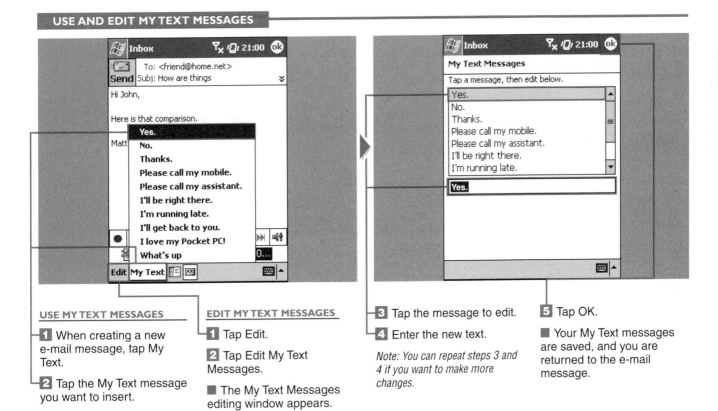

USE MY TEXT MESSAGES

1 When creating a new e-mail message, tap My Text.

2 Tap the My Text message you want to insert.

Note: You can insert multiple My Text messages by performing steps 1 and 2 repeatedly.

EDIT MY TEXT MESSAGES

1 Tap Edit.

2 Tap Edit My Text Messages.

■ The My Text Messages editing window appears.

3 Tap the message to edit.

4 Enter the new text.

Note: You can repeat steps 3 and 4 if you want to make more changes.

5 Tap OK.

■ Your My Text messages are saved, and you are returned to the e-mail message.

MANAGE FOLDERS

I f you use your mobile device regularly for sending and receiving e-mails, you may find that your Inbox is becoming unmanageable with so many messages. You can create and manage folders on your device to help organize your messages.

You cannot manage folders in your ActiveSync account on your device. Folders can be added using the desktop version of ActiveSync, and

you can specify the folders that will be synched to your mobile device during an ActiveSync connection.

You can add folders on your device for POP3 accounts, but these folders will reside only on your mobile device and will not be synched to your server. Folders created on your device in an IMAP4 account will be synched to your server along with any messages you place in those folders.

The power of an IMAP4 account can be seen when you select to sync a folder from your server to your device and all e-mails — up to the time period you specified in the Options setup wizard (see the section "Set Up Account Options") — in that folder are synched to your mobile device for use and reference while you are on the road.

MANAGE FOLDERS

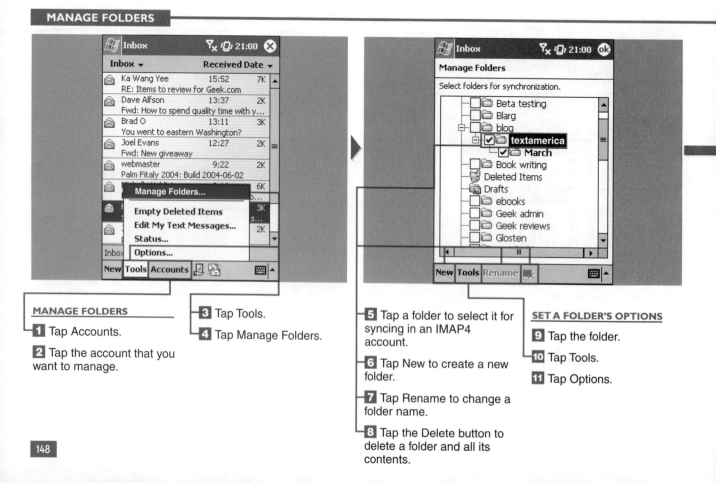

MANAGE FOLDERS

1 Tap Accounts.

2 Tap the account that you want to manage.

3 Tap Tools.

4 Tap Manage Folders.

5 Tap a folder to select it for syncing in an IMAP4 account.

6 Tap New to create a new folder.

7 Tap Rename to change a folder name.

8 Tap the Delete button to delete a folder and all its contents.

SET A FOLDER'S OPTIONS

9 Tap the folder.

10 Tap Tools.

11 Tap Options.

Why was my e-mail message deleted when I moved it into a different folder in my POP3 account?

✔ If you move an e-mail into another folder on your device, the link is broken between the messages on your device and server because folders are not synched to your server as they are with IMAP4 service.

Can I empty the Deleted Items folder of the ActiveSync account?

✔ No, this option is hidden from use on your device. You have to manually select all the messages in the Deleted Items folder and then tap and hold to select Delete.

What can I do with folders in a POP3 account?

✔ You can only create, rename, or delete local folders. There are no options or other settings available.

I cannot delete or rename folders in my IMAP4 account. Why not?

✔ Your device must be online and connected to change folders with IMAP because the folders are synched with your server and will appear on your server as well as your device.

Can I rename or delete any folder?

✔ No, you cannot rename or delete the Drafts, Outbox, Inbox, Deleted Items, or Sent Items folder.

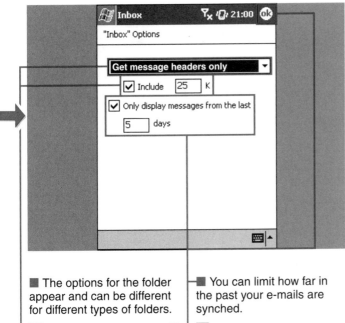

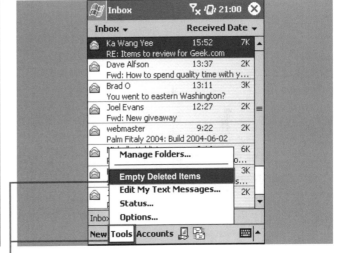

■ The options for the folder appear and can be different for different types of folders.

-12 For the Inbox folder, tap ⊡ and select headers only or full copies of messages.

■ If headers only is selected, you can specify how much of the message to include.

■ You can limit how far in the past your e-mails are synched.

-13 Tap OK twice.

■ Your folder settings are saved.

EMPTY THE DELETED ITEMS FOLDER

-1 Tap Tools.

-2 Tap Empty Deleted Items.

■ All the messages in your Deleted Items folder and on the server are deleted, and some memory is freed up on your device.

USING INTERNET EXPLORER

Y ou can browse the Internet from your Windows Mobile 2003 device using Pocket Internet Explorer. Although this version is more limited than the desktop version of Internet Explorer, it is quite capable of enabling you to view most Web sites.

This new version of Pocket Internet Explorer reformats

Web sites better than previous versions so that side-to-side scrolling is significantly reduced.

You can view Web sites via a wireless connection, via your cradle or cable and ActiveSync passthrough, and in an offline mode using pages synched with mobile favorites or services such as AvantGo or Mobipocket.

Can I open multiple browser windows?

✔ No, not in Pocket Internet Explorer. There are third-party add-ons that provide this capability in Internet Explorer.

Can I map hardware buttons to go back or forward?

✔ No, these options are not available in Pocket Internet Explorer.

USING INTERNET EXPLORER

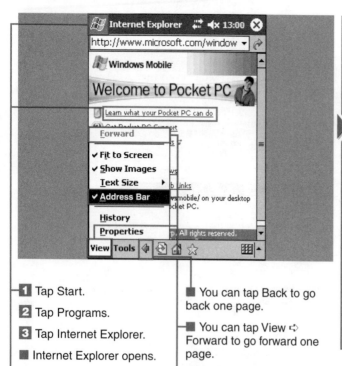

■1 Tap Start.

■2 Tap Programs.

■3 Tap Internet Explorer.

■ Internet Explorer opens.

■ You can tap a hyperlink to follow it to another site.

■ You can tap Back to go back one page.

■ You can tap View ⇨ Forward to go forward one page.

■4 Tap View.

■5 Tap Address Bar.

■ The Address Bar is toggled on.

■6 Tap the Address bar.

■7 Type the URL of the site that you want to visit.

■8 Tap the green arrow to load the URL.

■ The Web site loads.

■9 Tap and hold anywhere on the display to access other functions.

■ A pop-up menu appears. If text is selected, Copy is added to the list of functions.

■10 Tap the right scrollbar to move up and down the page.

Note: Some sites may also have a bottom left-and-right scrollbar. You can also use your navigation pad to move around the page if your device is so equipped.

VIEW PAGE HISTORY

You can save links to sites that you have visited and view those links in Internet Explorer's History file. Setting the number of days that the history shows is discussed in the section "Modify General and Advanced Settings."

The history can be viewed by page title or by URL and is organized so that the most recently visited page is at the top. There is no way to sort the history file.

Is there any way to see the full URL if it is longer than the display width?
✔ Not in the History view. You can copy and paste the URL in Notes or another text-editing program to view the full URL.

Can I delete history links individually?
✔ No, the History view screens are for viewinig history links only. You can clear the entire history in the General settings.

VIEW PAGE HISTORY

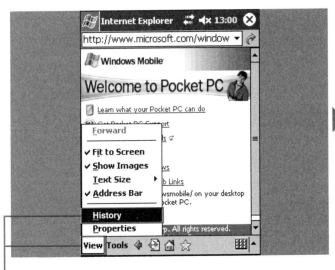

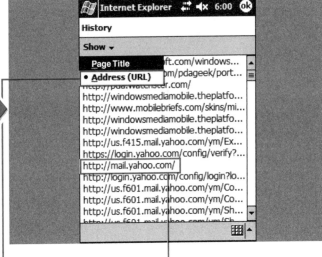

1 Tap View in Internet Explorer.

■ A pop-up menu appears.

2 Tap History.

■ The History file appears with the Page Title view automatically selected.

3 Tap Page Title.

■ "Page Title" changes to "Show," and a menu appears.

4 Tap Address (URL) to view the URL address of each site visited in your history.

5 Tap any URL in your history.

■ You are taken back to Internet Explorer and the page that you selected.

MODIFY THE VIEW SETTINGS

You can customize how Web sites are viewed on your mobile device using the View menu. You can have Web sites fitted to your screen so that only up and down scrolling is required, you can turn off images, you can change the text size, and you can view the URL Address bar.

Pocket Internet Explorer attempts to format pages so that they appear vertically by default. You can turn off this option and have pages shown in their full-screen format. This can be useful for sites such as MapQuest where you want to see the largest maps possible and they are not helpful when squeezed in the 240-pixel-wide area.

You can choose from five different sizes of text. You can also choose to have the URL Address bar shown at the top of the display and to hide or show images on the pages.

MODIFY THE VIEW SETTINGS

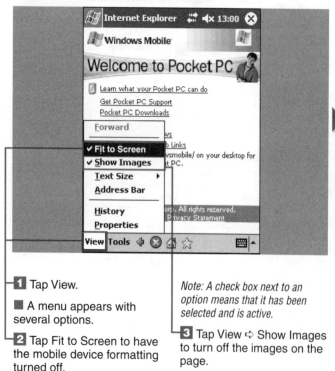

■1 Tap View.

■ A menu appears with several options.

■2 Tap Fit to Screen to have the mobile device formatting turned off.

Note: A check box next to an option means that it has been selected and is active.

■3 Tap View ➪ Show Images to turn off the images on the page.

■ The page refreshes, and the images are replaced by icons.

■4 Tap and hold on individual icons and select the Show Picture option.

■ The specific image appears while the remaining images remain icons.

Why would I want the Address bar shown?

✔ This is helpful when you want to enter a Web address manually or see the address of a site that you are visiting.

Why would I want to turn off images?

✔ If you are surfing via a Bluetooth connection and a Bluetooth phone or a Pocket PC Phone Edition device where data is metered, or the connection is slower than a WiFi connection, then turning off the images will speed page loading and save on data usage.

Why are some sites formatted well for my device's display?

✔ Web site owners can create mobile versions of their sites and add tags that automatically detect if you are surfing from a mobile device. These sites generally show up without having to perform side-to-side scrolling. You can also go directly to Windows Mobile–formatted sites. The Windows Mobile page has a link to several mobile-optimized sites.

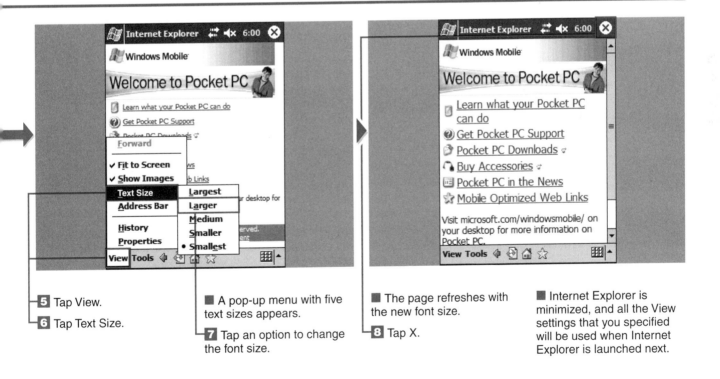

5 Tap View.

6 Tap Text Size.

■ A pop-up menu with five text sizes appears.

7 Tap an option to change the font size.

■ The page refreshes with the new font size.

8 Tap X.

■ Internet Explorer is minimized, and all the View settings that you specified will be used when Internet Explorer is launched next.

SEND A LINK VIA E-MAIL

People often find interesting sites that they would like to share with friends and family, so in Internet Explorer, you can send URL links to these sites via the Inbox application.

As previously discussed, you can view the URL by turning on the Address Bar view. You could go up to the Address bar, select the entire line of text, copy it, and then go into the Inbox and paste the URL into an e-mail. However, Microsoft has included a much shorter method for e-mailing URLs from your device — the Tools menu's Send Link via E-mail option.

Can I send multiple URLs in one e-mail?
✔ No, each time that you choose the Send Link via E-mail option, a new e-mail is generated with the URL in the body.

Can I send a URL to multiple people?
✔ Yes, see Chapter 15 for specifics on sending e-mail to more than one person.

SEND A LINK VIA E-MAIL

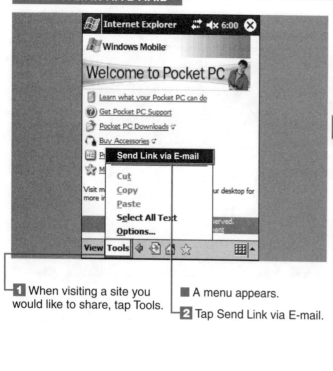

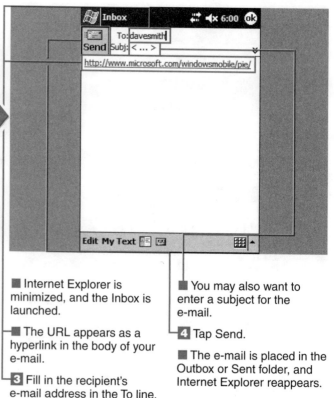

1 When visiting a site you would like to share, tap Tools.

■ A menu appears.

2 Tap Send Link via E-mail.

■ Internet Explorer is minimized, and the Inbox is launched.

■ The URL appears as a hyperlink in the body of your e-mail.

3 Fill in the recipient's e-mail address in the To line.

■ You may also want to enter a subject for the e-mail.

4 Tap Send.

■ The e-mail is placed in the Outbox or Sent folder, and Internet Explorer reappears.

MODIFY GENERAL AND ADVANCED SETTINGS

There are two Options screens in Internet Explorer that you can use to configure your General and Advanced browsing settings.

General settings enable you to set your home page, designate the number of days of history that will be stored on your

device, and delete temporary Internet files.

Advanced settings enable you to authorize cookies or clear cookies from your device, select a warning for nonsecure pages, and select the language that you want to use in Internet Explorer.

Why would I want to delete temporary Internet files?

✔ If you surf a lot on your mobile device, you will find that your temporary Internet files typically grow upwards of 1 to several megabytes in size. You will need to delete them occasionally to prevent maxing out your memory allocation.

MODIFY GENERAL AND ADVANCED SETTINGS

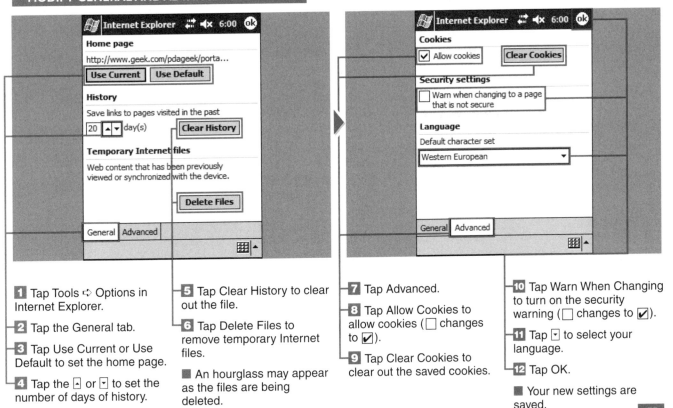

1 Tap Tools ➪ Options in Internet Explorer.

2 Tap the General tab.

3 Tap Use Current or Use Default to set the home page.

4 Tap the ⊡ or ⊡ to set the number of days of history.

5 Tap Clear History to clear out the file.

6 Tap Delete Files to remove temporary Internet files.

■ An hourglass may appear as the files are being deleted.

7 Tap Advanced.

8 Tap Allow Cookies to allow cookies (☐ changes to ☑).

9 Tap Clear Cookies to clear out the saved cookies.

10 Tap Warn When Changing to turn on the security warning (☐ changes to ☑).

11 Tap ⊡ to select your language.

12 Tap OK.

■ Your new settings are saved.

USING FAVORITES

To make navigating the Web a bit easier on your device, you can designate Web site links that you want to save for future access as favorites. These favorites are URL links like the favorites used in Internet Explorer on your desktop computer.

You can even simply copy over your existing Favorites folder from your Windows desktop and use that on

your mobile device. You can also place links to sites designed for mobile device displays in the Mobile Favorites subfolder on your desktop and use ActiveSync to sync these favorites to your device.

The star icon on the bottom toolbar in Internet Explorer is used to access your favorites. There is no menu selection to access your favorites.

You can add folders, rename favorites, and add or delete favorites, as well as open and launch favorites.

USING FAVORITES

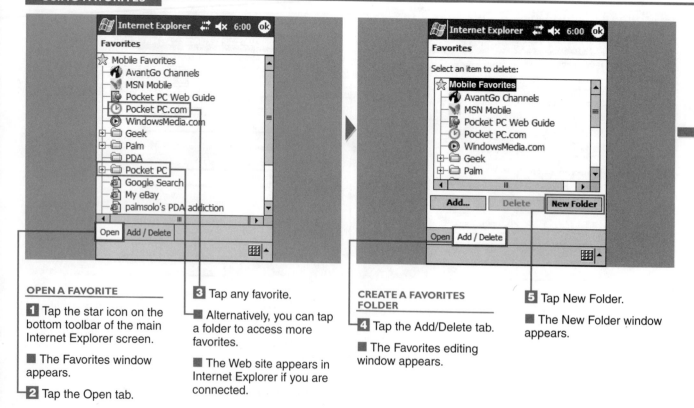

OPEN A FAVORITE

1 Tap the star icon on the bottom toolbar of the main Internet Explorer screen.

■ The Favorites window appears.

2 Tap the Open tab.

3 Tap any favorite.

■ Alternatively, you can tap a folder to access more favorites.

■ The Web site appears in Internet Explorer if you are connected.

CREATE A FAVORITES FOLDER

4 Tap the Add/Delete tab.

■ The Favorites editing window appears.

5 Tap New Folder.

■ The New Folder window appears.

Is there a limit to the number of favorites that I can have on my device?

✔ No, there is no limit — if there is available memory to store the favorites on your device.

Can I add subfolders in different levels on my mobile device?

✔ No, only one level of folders is allowed in Pocket Internet Explorer. If multiple-level folders are added on your desktop and then brought to your mobile device, the favorites will not appear in Pocket Internet Explorer.

Why are some of my favorites grayed out?

✔ You may not currently be connected, or the page may not be saved in your temporary Internet files. After you connect, the favorites should be enabled, returning to black text.

Is there another method for adding favorites, outside of the Add/Delete tab?

✔ Yes, if you tap and hold anywhere on the display, a pop-up menu appears. Tap Add to Favorites to go directly to the Add Favorite page.

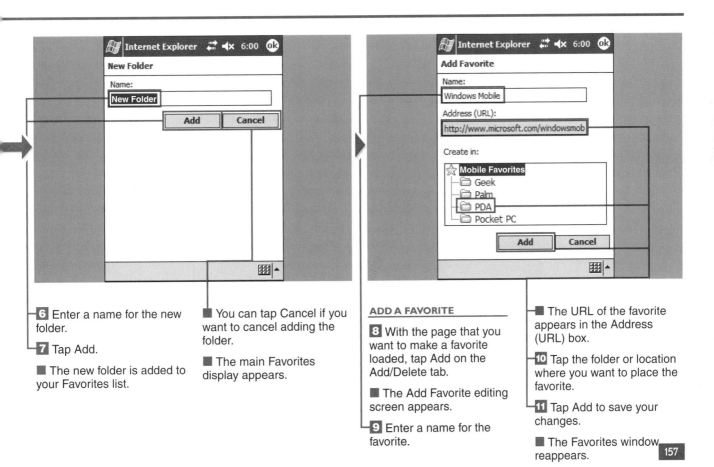

-6- Enter a name for the new folder.

-7- Tap Add.

■ The new folder is added to your Favorites list.

■ You can tap Cancel if you want to cancel adding the folder.

■ The main Favorites display appears.

ADD A FAVORITE

-8- With the page that you want to make a favorite loaded, tap Add on the Add/Delete tab.

■ The Add Favorite editing screen appears.

-9- Enter a name for the favorite.

■ The URL of the favorite appears in the Address (URL) box.

-10- Tap the folder or location where you want to place the favorite.

-11- Tap Add to save your changes.

■ The Favorites window reappears.

DOWNLOAD APPLICATIONS

Using Internet Explorer, you can download files and applications directly to your mobile device.

A few vendors have Web sites that are formatted for mobile devices and enable you to purchase or select trial versions of software and download them. The only limitation on downloading applications is the amount of memory available on your device.

You can select where the application or file is saved and if the file should be opened after downloading. The installation file will be a .cab file that will be deleted after installation, so you should save a copy to an external storage card for future use.

If I do not tap Change in the Download dialog box, where is the file downloaded?

✔ To the My Documents folder.

Can I open all files or applications that I download?

✔ No. You can open only files that can be used with applications loaded on your device. You may have to copy a file to your desktop to use it.

DOWNLOAD APPLICATIONS

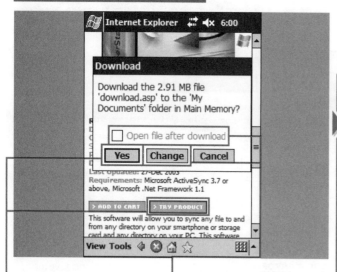

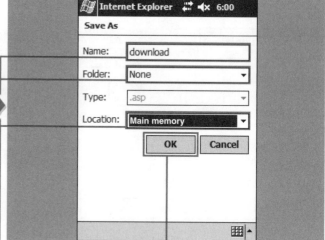

1 Tap a link in Internet Explorer that initiates a download of a file or product.

■ The Download dialog box appears.

2 Tap Yes.

3 Tap the check box to open the file after downloading (☐ changes to ☑).

4 Tap Change if you do not want the file downloaded to the default location.

■ The Save As screen appears.

5 Enter a name for the file or application.

6 Tap ⊡ and select the folder where the file will be saved.

7 Tap ⊡ and select the location.

Note: For example, you can choose to place the download on a storage card or in main memory.

8 Tap OK to start the download.

■ A download status window appears.

PREVIEW POCKET MSN

With your Windows Mobile 2003 device and Pocket MSN, you can access MSN Messenger, Hotmail e-mail accounts, Alerts, and the Mobile Web.

Pocket MSN is a Microsoft subscription service that was scheduled for launch in the fall of 2003, but it is still not available. The service appears in your Programs menu and launches a Pocket MSN Web site in Internet Explorer.

There are links on the Pocket MSN page to launch the four services, but they are not yet active on Windows Mobile 2003 devices.

Can I use MSN Messenger without the Pocket MSN service?

✔ Yes, Windows Mobile 2003 devices come with MSN Messenger loaded in the ROM. Go to Start ➪ Programs to find the MSN Messenger icon and launch the application.

What is the price for the Pocket MSN services?

✔ No pricing is yet available.

PREVIEW POCKET MSN

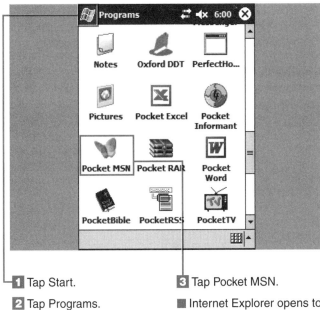

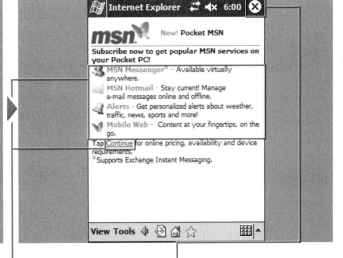

1 Tap Start.

2 Tap Programs.

■ All your installed programs appear.

3 Tap Pocket MSN.

■ Internet Explorer opens to the MSN page.

4 Tap one of the four choices to access MSN services.

Note: You can launch MSN Messenger, MSN Hotmail, Alerts, or the Mobile Web.

5 Tap Continue to view pricing and subscribe to the Pocket MSN service.

■ A page appears stating that the service is coming soon.

6 Tap X.

■ Pocket MSN and Internet Explorer close.

CREATE A NEW NOTE

You can create multiple-format notes using your Windows Mobile 2003 device. You can write notes in your own handwriting or using text via a text input method or an external keyboard, you can draw a picture, or you can record a voice note. Notes can also be a combination of any of these four options.

You can synchronize notes to your desktop, e-mail them to others, or beam them via infrared. Notes are saved in the .pwi format and can be opened in Outlook on your desktop PC.

How is my note titled by default?

✔ If you type a note, the first 20 letters on the top line are used for the note name. If you handwrite a note, it is named Note1, 2, 3, and so on if you are in the All Folders category. If you are in a specific category when you tap New, the note uses the category name and then a number, such as Business1.

CREATE A NEW NOTE

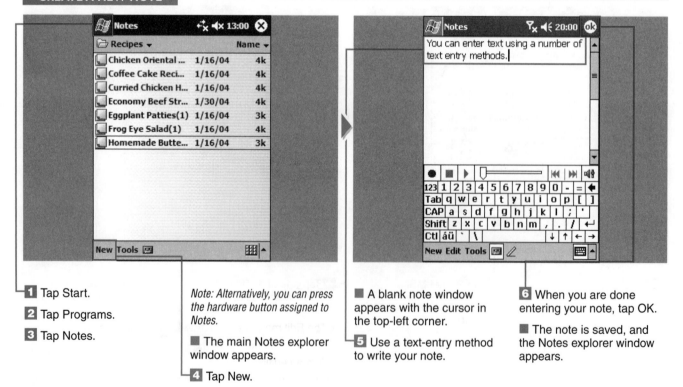

1 Tap Start.

2 Tap Programs.

3 Tap Notes.

Note: Alternatively, you can press the hardware button assigned to Notes.

■ The main Notes explorer window appears.

4 Tap New.

■ A blank note window appears with the cursor in the top-left corner.

5 Use a text-entry method to write your note.

6 When you are done entering your note, tap OK.

■ The note is saved, and the Notes explorer window appears.

EDIT A NOTE

After you have created a note, you can easily go back and make changes to it on your device. You can also edit the note in Outlook on your desktop, and the change will be synchronized to your device through ActiveSync.

You may want to edit a note if something changes in its status. For example, if you use the To Do

template and you complete a task, you will want to edit the note.

Editing a note is essentially the same as creating a new note, except that you open an existing note.

Can I add handwriting to a note that is all text?

✔ Yes, when you edit or create a note, you can use any of the four available methods (typed text, handwritten text, voice notes, and drawing) in combination within the note.

EDIT A NOTE

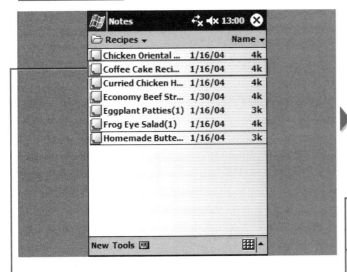

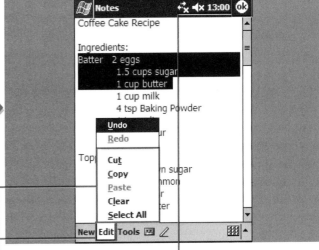

1 Tap once on the existing note in your list.

■ The note opens and appears on your display.

2 Make the changes using handwritten or typed text.

Note: The title of the note does not change even if you make changes to the first line.

3 Tap Edit to use the editing tools in your note.

■ The Edit menu items appear.

4 Tap an editing tool to use it in your note.

5 Tap OK.

■ The note is saved, and the main Notes explorer display appears.

RECORD A VOICE NOTE

You can use your Windows Mobile 2003 device to create a voice recording as either a standalone file or an embedded recording in an existing note. Microsoft has specified that all Windows Mobile devices include the capability to create voice recordings, and there is a dedicated button along the side of most devices. Pressing and holding this button starts the microphone and launches a new voice note.

Voice notes are useful when you are driving so that you can record thoughts and ideas without taking your eyes off the road.

Can I have more than one voice recording in a single note?
✔ Yes, but each voice note is indicated by a speaker icon with no title.

Can I edit a standalone voice note?
✔ No, if a voice note is created from the explorer view and is not embedded in an existing note, you can only listen to, copy, or delete the recording. You cannot add more voice recording to the end of the note or delete parts of the recording.

RECORD A VOICE NOTE

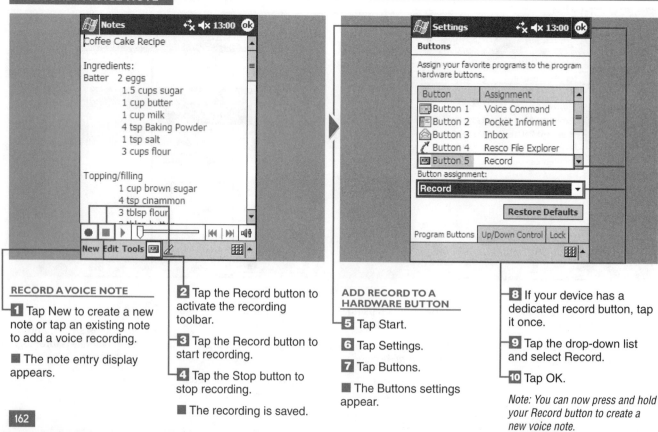

RECORD A VOICE NOTE

1 Tap New to create a new note or tap an existing note to add a voice recording.

■ The note entry display appears.

2 Tap the Record button to activate the recording toolbar.

3 Tap the Record button to start recording.

4 Tap the Stop button to stop recording.

■ The recording is saved.

ADD RECORD TO A HARDWARE BUTTON

5 Tap Start.

6 Tap Settings.

7 Tap Buttons.

■ The Buttons settings appear.

8 If your device has a dedicated record button, tap it once.

9 Tap the drop-down list and select Record.

10 Tap OK.

Note: You can now press and hold your Record button to create a new voice note.

SORT A NOTES LIST

Y ou can categorize your notes, or sort them, by name, date, size, or type. The default sorting is done by name. Tapping the Sort option once sorts by descending values, and tapping it again reverses the sort order. Sorting by type separates the voice recording notes from other notes.

By default, Notes shows you all folders. You can select a category, or folder, to help filter your notes for sorting.

Is there a limit to the number of categories I can use?

✔ No, there is no limit, and with many notes, more categories may help your organization.

Can I change the default sort option?

✔ No, Notes always launches with your notes sorted by name. If you exit Notes and then relaunch it, the folder you last had open is remembered, but Notes still defaults to sorting by name.

SORT A NOTES LIST

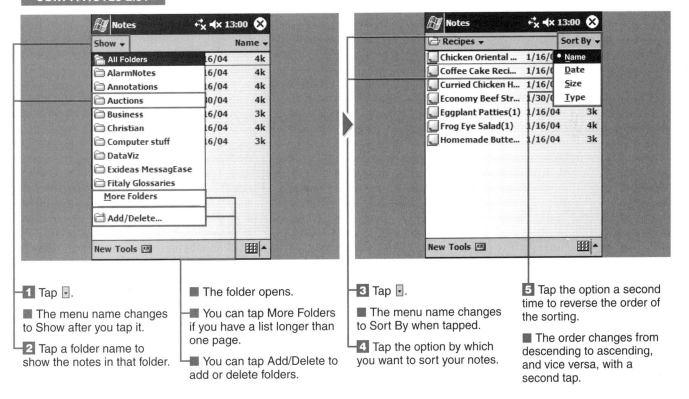

1 Tap ⬝.

■ The menu name changes to Show after you tap it.

2 Tap a folder name to show the notes in that folder.

■ The folder opens.

■ You can tap More Folders if you have a list longer than one page.

■ You can tap Add/Delete to add or delete folders.

3 Tap ⬝.

■ The menu name changes to Sort By when tapped.

4 Tap the option by which you want to sort your notes.

5 Tap the option a second time to reverse the order of the sorting.

■ The order changes from descending to ascending, and vice versa, with a second tap.

CREATE OR RECOGNIZE A HANDWRITTEN NOTE

Y ou can create handwritten notes on your device and even have them converted to typed text with the Recognize function in Windows Mobile 2003.

One of the most powerful aspects of the Windows Mobile 2003 platform is the capability to recognize each person's individual handwriting. Although accuracy

may not be 100 percent, there are some tips that you can follow to improve recognition. You can mix recognized text with handwriting and can handwrite in both cursive and print formats.

You can also choose to leave your notes in the handwritten format, which is handy for replacing the traditional yellow stickies that

many people use to jot down quick notes. You can also use your handwriting to draw objects, such as maps with directions.

Handwritten notes can also be beamed or e-mailed to other devices or people. You cannot set alarms for your handwritten notes, so you may want to create a To Do folder to store reminders.

CREATE OR RECOGNIZE A HANDWRITTEN NOTE

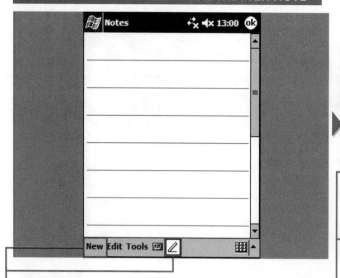

HANDWRITE A NOTE

1 Tap New from the main Notes explorer view.

2 Tap the Handwriting button if it is not selected automatically.

Note: The default input for notes can be changed to either handwriting or text; this is discussed in the section "Modify Notes Options."

3 Start writing your note on the display.

4 Tap the right scrollbar to add more text down the page.

■ The page may automatically move down if you extend a letter below the available display.

Can I scroll right and left when creating a handwritten note?

✔ No, Notes has only an up-and-down scrollbar. To write on the right side of the full note, you have to zoom out. However, zooming out makes handwriting recognition more difficult.

Can I change the pen size, color, or background color?

✔ No, Notes does not support these options. The pen is always black ink on a white background. There are third-party applications that do support changing the pen options.

How can I improve handwriting recognition of my notes?

✔ You can set the zoom level to 300 percent for more accurate recognition. Recognition does not work well below 150 percent zoom. You should also write on the lines. Place letters close together with a decent space between words so that the recognition engine can determine that there are separate words.

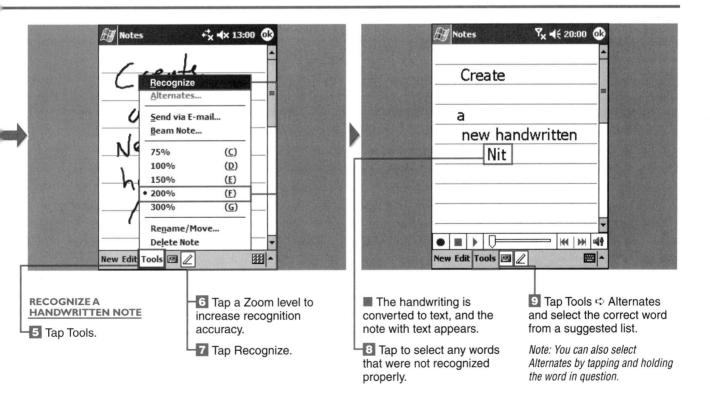

RECOGNIZE A HANDWRITTEN NOTE

5 Tap Tools.

6 Tap a Zoom level to increase recognition accuracy.

7 Tap Recognize.

■ The handwriting is converted to text, and the note with text appears.

8 Tap to select any words that were not recognized properly.

9 Tap Tools ➪ Alternates and select the correct word from a suggested list.

Note: You can also select Alternates by tapping and holding the word in question.

COPY OR DELETE A NOTE

You can copy or delete notes from your device with a couple quick taps. You can tap and hold a selected note from the main explorer window to access both the Copy and Delete functions. You can also delete a note after opening it.

If you have repetitive data in your notes, it can be handy to copy notes. You cannot copy and then paste a note in a different folder, though, because there is the Create a Copy function but no Paste function.

Can I copy multiple notes if I select multiple notes?

✔ No, the Copy function is disabled if multiple notes are selected. You can select and delete multiple notes, however.

Aside from tapping and holding a note to bring up a menu, how else can I delete a note?

✔ Open the note and then tap Tools ➪ Delete Note. A verification box appears to ensure that you mean to delete the note, in which you tap Yes.

COPY OR DELETE A NOTE

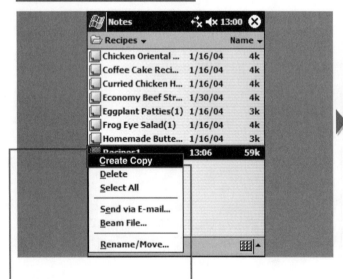

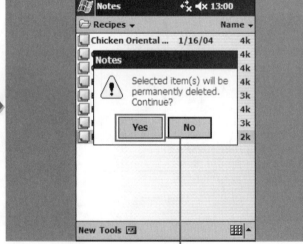

COPY A NOTE

1 Select the note.

2 Tap and hold the selected note.

■ A menu appears.

3 Tap Create Copy.

■ A duplicate note appears in the same folder with a (1) after it.

Note: You can rename the copy to avoid confusing the two notes.

DELETE A NOTE

4 Perform steps 1 and 2.

5 Tap Delete.

■ A dialog box appears to verify that you want to delete the note.

6 Tap Yes.

■ The note is deleted.

Note: If you tap No in the dialog box, you will be taken back to the Notes explorer view, and the note will not deleted.

RENAME OR MOVE A NOTE

Y ou can rename or move notes with a couple quick taps on your device. Notes are named by default, and if it is a text note, part of the first line is used to create the name. If the note is handwritten, a drawing, or a voice note, then a generic name related to the folder where the note originated is given to the note.

You can move notes to different folders or locations, such as different external storage cards or into the internal flash memory storage space.

What happens if I rename a note with the same name as an existing note?

✔ A warning box appears that states you must enter a different name for the note. There is no option to overwrite the existing note.

Can I access the Rename/Move function another way, instead of tapping and holding a note?

✔ Yes, open the note and then tap Tools ➪ Rename/Move.

RENAME OR MOVE A NOTE

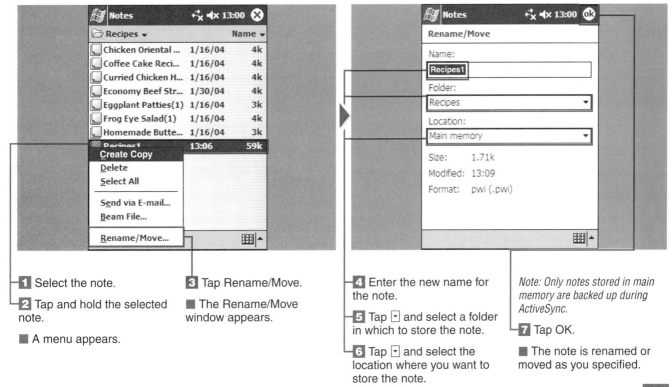

▬1 Select the note.

▬2 Tap and hold the selected note.

■ A menu appears.

▬3 Tap Rename/Move.

■ The Rename/Move window appears.

▬4 Enter the new name for the note.

▬5 Tap ▾ and select a folder in which to store the note.

▬6 Tap ▾ and select the location where you want to store the note.

Note: Only notes stored in main memory are backed up during ActiveSync.

▬7 Tap OK.

■ The note is renamed or moved as you specified.

SEND A NOTE VIA E-MAIL OR INFRARED

You can send notes to others via e-mail or beaming with infrared. Notes are saved as .pwi files, which others can open with Microsoft Word.

Notes containing handwritten text or drawings can also be opened with Word, and the content appears as a drawing. Notes with embedded

recordings can also be opened in Word, and the recording can be played right in Word.

Notes that are only recordings are sent as .wav-formatted files and can be listened to with Windows Media Player or other players capable of playing .wav files.

Can I beam notes to a Palm Powered device?

✔ No, Palm Powered devices cannot read .pwi formatted documents at this time. You can beam the file to a laptop or desktop with an infrared port and Windows XP.

SEND A NOTE VIA E-MAIL OR INFRARED

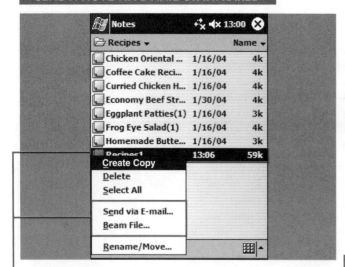

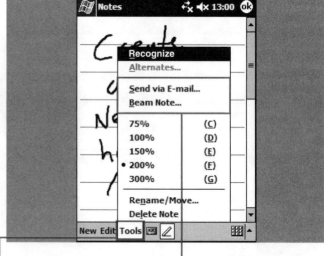

FROM THE NOTES EXPLORER VIEW

1 Select the note.

2 Tap and hold the note.

■ A menu appears.

3 Tap Send via E-mail or Beam File.

■ If you send via e-mail, the Inbox appears. Enter the e-mail address and subject. The note is sent as an attachment.

■ If you beam the file, the Infrared utility appears, and the device attempts to send to another device.

WITH THE NOTE OPEN

1 After opening the note, tap Tools.

2 Tap Send via E-mail or Beam Note.

■ The Inbox program or Infrared utility is launched as discussed earlier.

MODIFY NOTES OPTIONS

You can set up a couple options in the Notes application. You can specify the default note mode, a default template, where notes are saved, and the action that your record button performs.

There are two default entry modes, five templates to choose from, and two options for the Record button.

Even if you set the default modes in Options, you can always switch to another mode within notes that you create.

Can I use a template without setting it up in Options?

✔ No, if you use Blank Note as your template, there is no way to switch to another template in Notes without changing the template in Options.

Can I switch between writing and typing within a note?

✔ Yes, tap the Handwriting button to switch between writing and typing.

MODIFY NOTES OPTIONS

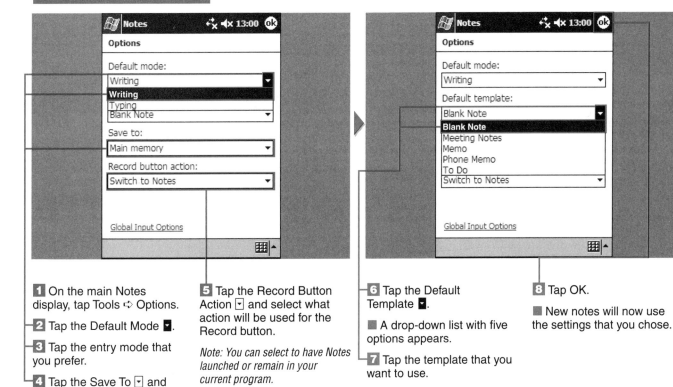

1 On the main Notes display, tap Tools ⇨ Options.

2 Tap the Default Mode ⏷.

3 Tap the entry mode that you prefer.

4 Tap the Save To ⏷ and select where you want notes stored.

5 Tap the Record Button Action ⏷ and select what action will be used for the Record button.

Note: You can select to have Notes launched or remain in your current program.

6 Tap the Default Template ⏷.

■ A drop-down list with five options appears.

7 Tap the template that you want to use.

8 Tap OK.

■ New notes will now use the settings that you chose.

PLAY MEDIA FILES

You can play audio and video files using the latest version of Windows Media Player 9 Series for Pocket PC. Files can be stored in RAM or on external storage cards, as well as streaming files from the Internet via Pocket Internet Explorer.

You can play Windows Media–formatted audio and video files or MP3 audio files. The following

types of files are supported: .asf, .wma, .wmv, and .mp3. All Windows Mobile 2003 devices include a headphone jack with stereo output because most devices have only a single internal speaker. Media files sound much better on headphones or external speakers, so these are the preferred ways to listen to media files.

Most media files consume a sizable amount of memory, but the files can be played off of external storage media with no lag in performance.

Note: Not all Windows Media Player files play; variable rate files do not play, nor do files that require a special codec to be installed on the Pocket PC.

PLAY MEDIA FILES

PLAY A MEDIA FILE

1 Tap Start.

2 Tap Windows Media.

■ The main Windows Media Player window appears.

3 Tap Playlist.

4 Tap the file that you want to load into the player.

5 Tap the Play button.

■ Windows Media Player plays the file.

■ The name of the file appears here.

■ The length of time the file has been playing appears here.

6 Tap the Stop button to stop playing the file.

■ The file goes back to the beginning, and Windows Media Player is in a ready state.

Can I view .mpeg video files in Windows Media Player?

✔ No, .mpeg, or .mpg, video files are not natively supported in Media Player. You can use the free desktop application Windows Movie Maker to convert .mpeg files into .wmv files or install a third-party application such as Pocket TV.

Can I listen to music downloaded from the Web with Apple iTunes?

✔ Not directly, because Apple uses the AAC file format. However, you can use iTunes to convert these files into .mp3 files and then play them on your Windows Mobile 2003 device. You also cannot play OGG files.

Can I turn off the display and listen to music files?

✔ Most Windows Mobile 2003 devices enable you to press and hold the On/Off button and either turn off the backlight or turn off the display to conserve battery life as you listen to music on your device.

Why is the file still playing after I close Windows Media Player?

✔ The X button minimizes the application, but it is still running in the background. If you do not stop the file or fully close the application, you can listen to music while you perform other tasks on the device.

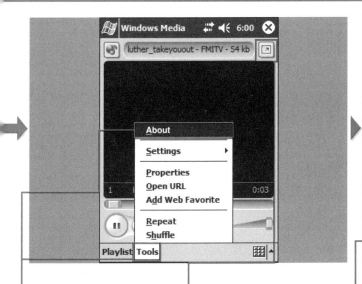

VIEW MEDIA PLAYER INFORMATION

7 Tap Tools.

8 Tap About.

■ The version of Media Player and licensing information appear.

SWITCH TO LANDSCAPE MODE

9 Tap the Rotate icon.

■ The Rotate icon is available only for video files.

■ The screen rotates to Landscape mode.

RETURN TO PORTRAIT MODE

10 Tap anywhere on the display.

■ Windows Media Player goes back to Portrait mode.

11 Tap X.

■ Windows Media Player is minimized. Files that are playing continue to play in the background until the application is closed or the file is stopped.

CREATE A PLAYLIST

You can organize your music for faster access using customizable playlists. The default playlists are Local Content and Web Favorites. The Local Content playlist shows you all the files that you have stored in internal memory and on external storage cards. The Web Favorites playlist stores URLs that you designate as

streaming media favorites. You cannot delete or rename the Local Content or Web Favorites playlists on your device.

You can create playlists for different artists or albums, different genres, or any other grouping that you want. You can then place songs and videos in the order that you want

to listen to or watch them in each individual playlist. Media files can be placed in multiple playlists for your convenience.

Icons appear in your playlists that indicate where the file is stored — in RAM, on an external card, or on the Internet.

CREATE A PLAYLIST

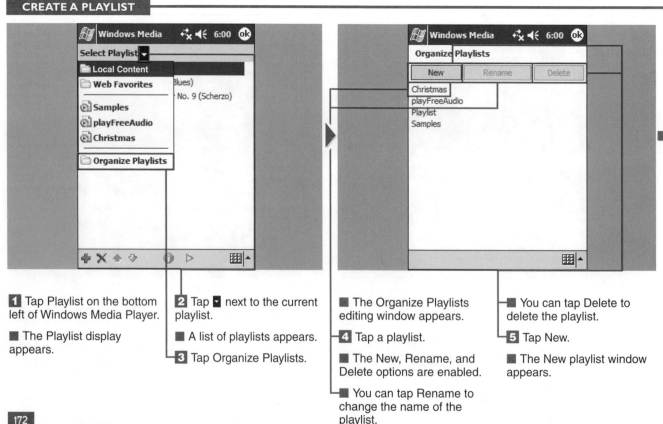

1 Tap Playlist on the bottom left of Windows Media Player.

■ The Playlist display appears.

2 Tap ▼ next to the current playlist.

■ A list of playlists appears.

3 Tap Organize Playlists.

■ The Organize Playlists editing window appears.

4 Tap a playlist.

■ The New, Rename, and Delete options are enabled.

■ You can tap Rename to change the name of the playlist.

■ You can tap Delete to delete the playlist.

5 Tap New.

■ The New playlist window appears.

If I delete a playlist, will my songs be deleted?

✔ No, the playlist is just a shortcut that links to songs; thus the songs will not be deleted.

What are the icons on the bottom of the main playlist display?

✔ The green ⊞ adds songs to existing playlists, ☒ deletes songs from the playlist, the blue up and down arrows enable you to reorder songs in the playlist, ⓞ shows the properties of the song, and the blue ▷ is used to start playing a selected song.

Can the same song be present in multiple playlists?

✔ Yes, it may be convenient to have the same song in artist, genre, and holiday playlists.

Can I create a new folder in which to place the playlist after selecting to add a new playlist?

✔ No, playlists can only be added to existing folders.

Where do the songs in the playlist go when I delete the playlist?

✔ The songs then appear in the Local Content folder.

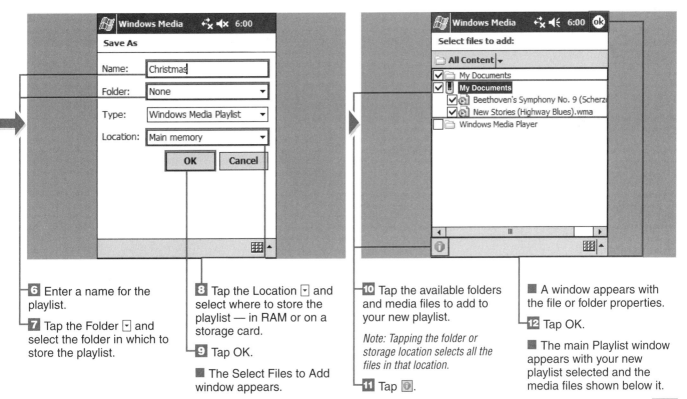

6 Enter a name for the playlist.

7 Tap the Folder ⏷ and select the folder in which to store the playlist.

8 Tap the Location ⏷ and select where to store the playlist — in RAM or on a storage card.

9 Tap OK.

■ The Select Files to Add window appears.

10 Tap the available folders and media files to add to your new playlist.

Note: Tapping the folder or storage location selects all the files in that location.

11 Tap ⓞ.

■ A window appears with the file or folder properties.

12 Tap OK.

■ The main Playlist window appears with your new playlist selected and the media files shown below it.

PLAY INTERNET MEDIA

You can find streaming audio and video files on the Internet, and you can play many of these files directly on your Windows Mobile 2003 device using Windows Media Player and Internet Explorer.

Your device must be connected to the Internet to play these media files. After connecting your device,

you can open a URL from within Windows Media Player, or you can surf to Web sites with media files using Internet Explorer. After you find a media file in Internet Explorer and tap it to open it, Windows Media Player launches and plays the streaming file.

What streaming rate does Windows Media Player support?

✔ Windows Media Player 9 supports streaming playback up to 300Kbps, provided that your connection supports this speed.

PLAY INTERNET MEDIA

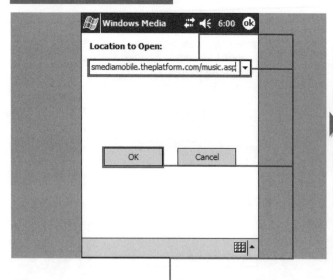

1 Tap Tools.

2 Tap Open URL.

■ The URL location page appears.

3 Enter the URL address for the media file that you want to open.

■ You can tap ⊡ to access previously viewed URLs.

4 Tap OK.

■ The media file begins playing in Windows Media Player.

5 Tap the Internet Explorer button.

■ The Windows Media site opens up in Internet Explorer, if you have an Internet connection.

6 Tap a video or audio file that you want to open.

■ Windows Media Player plays the audio or video file that you selected.

MODIFY AUDIO AND VIDEO SETTINGS

You can select a few audio and video preferences in Windows Media Player. You can choose to pause or play audio files when using other programs. You can also choose when to play a video in full-screen mode or shrink it to fit in the window, as well as rotate the full-screen mode 180 degrees.

Windows Media Player can be used to listen to music when you are using other applications because multitasking is supported in Windows Mobile 2003.

Why does my video still have a small playback screen even though I selected the full-screen mode?

✔ Windows Media Player shrinks large-size-formatted video down to 240 x 176 to fit in the skinned main Media Player window, but it will not increase the size for the full 240 x 320 display. A black border may be present around the video display.

MODIFY AUDIO AND VIDEO SETTINGS

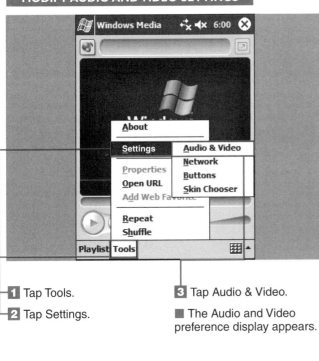

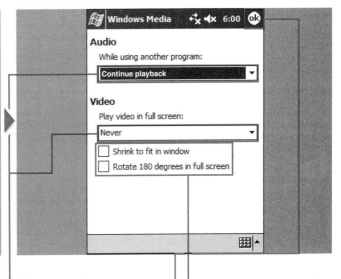

■1 Tap Tools.

■2 Tap Settings.

■3 Tap Audio & Video.

■ The Audio and Video preference display appears.

■4 Tap this ⯆ and select an audio option.

Note: Continue Playback enables you to listen to audio files while in another application. Pause Playback pauses the audio file when in another application.

■5 Tap this ⯆ and select Never, Only When Oversized, or Always for the full-screen option.

■ You can have video shrink to the window or rotate in full-screen mode.

■6 Tap OK.

■ The main Windows Media Player window appears.

MODIFY NETWORK SETTINGS

Y ou can select the connection speed that you use with Windows Media Player network files and what protocol you prefer to use to access network files.

You can select from four connection speeds — LAN, ISDN, 56Kbps, and 28.8Kbps — and three protocols — User Datagram Protocol (UDP),

Transmission Control Protocol (TCP), and Hypertext Transfer Protocol (HTTP). At least one protocol must be selected to play networked Windows Media files. All protocols are selected by default. Network settings should be checked and set up prior to attempting to listen to or view network media files.

What protocol is recommended for most users?

✔ Unless you have a specific network with which you want to connect, you can select all three protocols of the Network settings. This enables you to connect via Bluetooth and a cell phone, the USB port and ActiveSync, and WiFi and a network.

MODIFY NETWORK SETTINGS

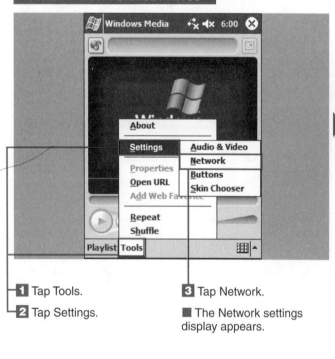

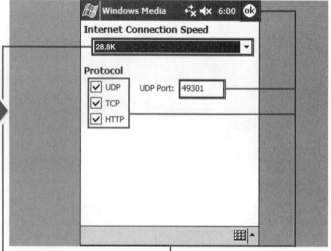

1 Tap Tools.

2 Tap Settings.

3 Tap Network.

■ The Network settings display appears.

4 Tap the Internet Connection Speed ⊡.

5 Select one of the speed options.

Note: If you are connecting via a wireless GPRS connection, a speed of 28.8K is recommended.

6 Tap one, two, or three of the protocol options.

7 If you selected the UDP protocol, enter a port.

8 Tap OK.

■ The network settings are established, and the main Windows Media Player display appears.

SET UP HARDWARE BUTTON MAPPING

I f you want to control your Media Player without using your stylus, you can select hardware buttons to perform the same functionality. Hardware button mapping is particularly useful if you listen to music files and turn off your display to help conserve battery life. You can still select different songs, pause playback, and perform other functions without a stylus.

The number of functions that you can map depends on how many buttons your particular device is designed to support.

How many functions are available to map to a hardware button?

✔ Window Media Player enables you to select from 11 functions, including Play, Pause, Next Track, Mute, and Full Screen Toggle.

Can my directional pad be used for button mapping?

✔ Yes, the four directions and the center action button can be mapped on some devices.

SET UP HARDWARE BUTTON MAPPING

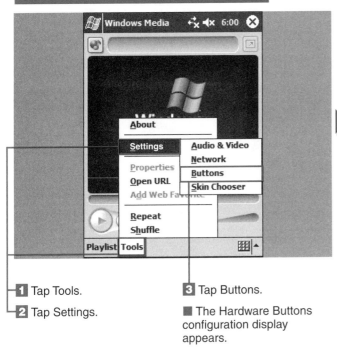

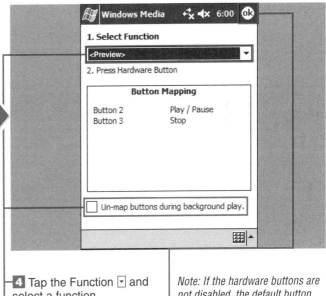

1 Tap Tools.

2 Tap Settings.

3 Tap Buttons.

■ The Hardware Buttons configuration display appears.

4 Tap the Function ⊡ and select a function.

5 Press the hardware button you want to map to that function.

6 Tap the check box to disable the hardware buttons when Windows Media Player is playing in the background.

Note: If the hardware buttons are not disabled, the default button options for other applications will not work.

7 Tap OK.

■ The hardware button mapping is saved.

SELECT A MEDIA PLAYER SKIN

To make your Windows Media Player more functional and personal, you can change the skin on your device. *Skins* serve as the user interface in Windows Media Player.

A couple of default skins are loaded on your device, and you can find many more on the Internet. You can also create your own custom skins and place them on your device.

Skins are stored as .skn files on your device and can vary from 1KB to 70KB, depending on their complexity.

Are there any special requirements for storing skins on my device?
✔ Yes, all the files associated with a particular skin must be in the same folder. However, these skin folders can be placed anywhere on your device for use.

Where can I find some skins?
✔ Microsoft's Windows Mobile site (www.microsoft.com/windowsmobile) has several skins to choose from and download for free.

SELECT A MEDIA PLAYER SKIN

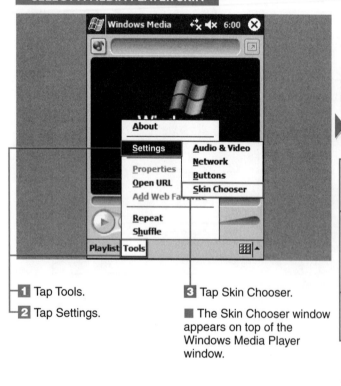

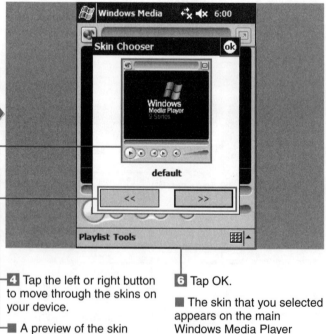

1 Tap Tools.

2 Tap Settings.

3 Tap Skin Chooser.

■ The Skin Chooser window appears on top of the Windows Media Player window.

4 Tap the left or right button to move through the skins on your device.

■ A preview of the skin appears here.

5 Stop tapping the left or right button when you find the skin that you want to use.

6 Tap OK.

■ The skin that you selected appears on the main Windows Media Player display.

USING THE MEDIA PLAYER TOOLBAR

Hardware buttons can be mapped to operate Windows Media Player, but you can also choose to use your stylus and the toolbar along the bottom of the Media Player display.

There are five buttons and two sliders that you can operate with your stylus. There are also two

buttons at the top of the display that link to Internet Explorer and full-screen viewing in Windows Media Player.

The toolbar controls enable you to navigate around a file but not to maneuver between files or operate multiple files.

If I tap the Stop button and then the Play button, will the file start where I stopped it?

✔ No, stopping the file takes it back to the beginning; thus the file would start all over again.

USING THE MEDIA PLAYER TOOLBAR

1 Tap the Play button to play the file.

■ The Play button turns into a Pause button.

2 Tap the Stop button to stop the file.

3 Tap the Rewind or Fast Forward button to skip to the beginning or end of the current file.

Note: Skipping to the beginning also takes you back to the previous file if one was played recently.

Note: If you tap the Rewind or Fast Forward button while a file is playing, it goes back or forward.

4 Tap the speaker on or off.

5 Tap and slide the Volume slider to decrease or increase the volume.

6 Tap and slide the playback progress slider to maneuver within the file.

■ The status and location within the file appear here.

CHAPTER 7

START A NEW GAME OF JAWBREAKER

Microsoft has included a new game in Windows Mobile 2003 called *Jawbreaker*. Jawbreaker follows in a long line of puzzle games that have become very popular on the PC and handheld devices.

You can start a new game of Jawbreaker to test your puzzle-solving skills in a fast and arcade-style of game play.

The objective of Jawbreaker is to line up like-colored jawbreakers in horizontal and vertical rows. The larger the number of like-colored jawbreakers you line up, the greater the score you get for "popping" that grouping. *Popping* means tapping a selected grouping so that the jawbreakers disappear. When you pop a grouping, you will notice that

the surrounding jawbreakers fall into the place of the jawbreaker grouping that you eliminated.

You continue popping jawbreakers until all possible groupings have been eliminated. The goal is to get to as close to no jawbreakers left as you can.

START A NEW GAME OF JAWBREAKER

1 Tap Start.

2 Tap Programs.

3 Tap Games.

■ The Games folder opens.

4 Tap Jawbreaker.

■ Jawbreaker launches.

5 Tap Game.

6 Tap New Game.

■ A new game screen is created.

Can I save my current game of Jawbreaker and finish it later?

✔ No, the current game cannot be saved. However, you can go on to another task or program, leaving Jawbreaker minimized, which will allow you to resume where you left off as long as the program has not been manually stopped.

Is there a two-player mode for Jawbreaker?

✔ No, there is no two-player mode for this game. Many people keep track of their statistics and compare them with friends, though.

Can I change my mind if I do not want to pop the group of jawbreakers that I have selected?

✔ Yes. You can single tap another jawbreaker that is not selected to deselect the first grouping.

Can I change my mind after popping a group of jawbreakers?

✔ Yes. You can tap the Undo button to restore the last eliminated group of jawbreakers.

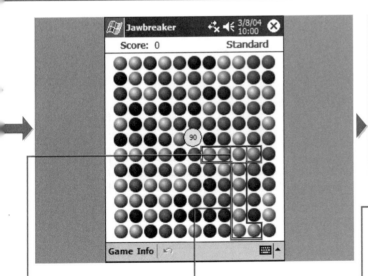

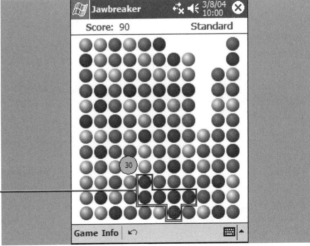

7 Tap a jawbreaker that is next to other same-colored jawbreakers.

■ The group of like-colored jawbreakers becomes highlighted.

8 Tap the selected grouping of jawbreakers again to pop that grouping.

■ The jawbreakers above the eliminated grouping fall into the empty space.

9 Repeat steps 7 and 8 until the game has ended — when there are no more possible groupings.

■ When you clear the screen of all possible jawbreaker groupings, you will proceed on to the next level.

SET JAWBREAKER OPTIONS AND ACCESS STATISTICS

The Jawbreaker game comes equipped with a variety of options. You can select to play sounds during game play, confirm the end of the game, display decimal averages, display bursts, and play in Guest mode.

You can also select alternative styles of game play. The forms of game play are Standard, Continuous, Shifter, and MegaShift. These different game styles change how the jawbreakers fill the screen during game play and can provide an added level of complexity to Jawbreaker, keeping the game fresh and challenging.

You can also change the jawbreaker set from colored to grayscale jawbreakers. This can add another level of challenge to the game because it replaces colored jawbreakers with grayscale jawbreakers containing shapes and patterns.

Jawbreaker keeps statistics of your previously played games. It tracks the number of games played of all four versions of the game. It also tracks the average score of the games played and the high score achieved for each game style.

SET JAWBREAKER OPTIONS AND ACCESS STATISTICS

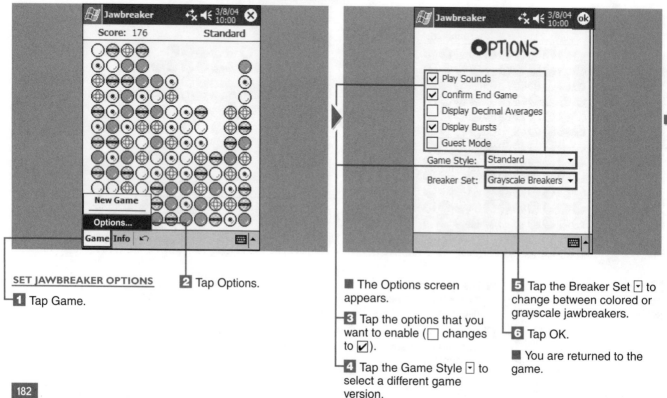

SET JAWBREAKER OPTIONS

1 Tap Game.

2 Tap Options.

■ The Options screen appears.

3 Tap the options that you want to enable (☐ changes to ☑).

4 Tap the Game Style ⊡ to select a different game version.

5 Tap the Breaker Set ⊡ to change between colored or grayscale jawbreakers.

6 Tap OK.

■ You are returned to the game.

What do the decimal averages mean?

✔ *Games* indicates the total number of games that you have played. *Average* is the aggregate average score of all games played under that style. *High* indicates the highest score that you achieved in that game style.

I want to play Jawbreaker on my PC. Can I move the application to my desktop computer?

✔ This version of the game was designed for the Pocket PC and therefore cannot be moved to the PC; however, there are versions of Jawbreaker for the PC available.

Is there a way to let another person play Jawbreaker and not affect my game statistics?

✔ Yes. You can place a check in the Guest Mode box; the statistics for games played while this box is checked are not added to the Statisics page.

Can I reset my game statistics and start them over?

✔ Yes. Simply tap Reset on the statistics screen to reset them all to zero.

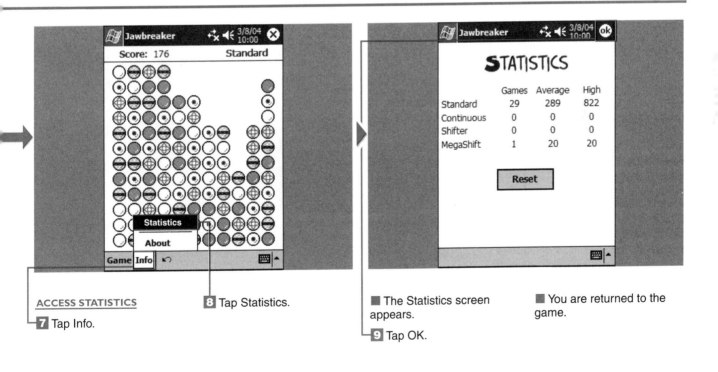

ACCESS STATISTICS

7 Tap Info.

8 Tap Statistics.

■ The Statistics screen appears.

9 Tap OK.

■ You are returned to the game.

START A NEW GAME OF SOLITAIRE

The Solitaire game has changed little since its early days on the PC with the introduction of Windows 3.1. Microsoft has included Solitaire in all editions of the Windows operating systems to date, including Windows Mobile 2003.

You can start a new game of Solitaire to be dealt a fresh deck of cards. You will see the deck of cards in the upper-left corner and the seven columns of cards with the top card displayed. You will also notice a place for four additional cards in the top-right corner of the screen.

You place cards in descending order from king to two and alternate between red and black in the columns of seven cards. You can move a king to an empty column, and aces can be dragged to the top row of four cards.

To win the game, build up your top row of four cards from ace to king all in the same suits.

START A NEW GAME OF SOLITAIRE

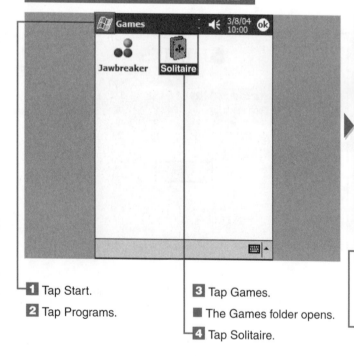

■ Tap Start.

■ Tap Programs.

■ Tap Games.

■ The Games folder opens.

■ Tap Solitaire.

■ The Solitaire game is launched.

■ Tap New.

■ A new game is started, and a new deck of cards is dealt.

Is there a two-player option for Solitaire, like Double Solitaire?

✔ No. Solitaire by definition is a single-player game. However, many people keep track of their scores and compare them with other Solitaire enthusiasts to see who can complete a game in the quickest amount of time.

Can I save my current game and finish it later?

✔ No, the current game cannot be saved. However, you can go on to another task or program, leaving Solitaire minimized, which allows you to resume where you left off as long as the program has not been manually stopped.

Can I undo a mistake or card that I just played?

✔ Yes. If you just played a card and are having second thoughts, you can undo that move by tapping the Undo button before making your next move. Note, however, that you will lose any points that you earned for the card prior to selecting Undo. Also, you can undo only one move.

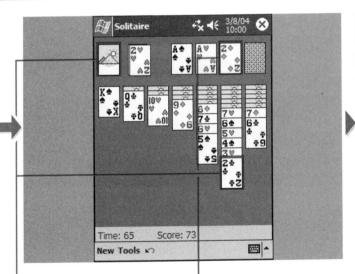

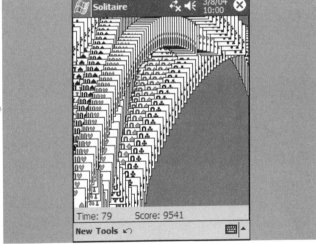

6 Tap the deck of cards to reveal the top card.

7 Drag alternating red and black cards to the appropriate stack in descending order.

8 Drag cards to the upper row in ascending order.

Note: You do not have to use the card from the upper deck; the cards will be cycled through as you continue to tap the deck.

9 Repeat steps 6 to 8 until you can no longer move cards.

■ You win the game when you have aligned all the suits from ace to king in the top four card slots.

■ Solitaire "celebrates" your win by bouncing the four stacks away.

SET SOLITAIRE OPTIONS

Playing the same variation of Solitaire can become repetitive over time. With Solitaire on the Windows Mobile device, you can change many of the options to make the game more challenging and visually appealing.

You can set the game type to one-card draw or three-card draw. You can set the scoring options to Standard, Vegas, or None.

Other options that you can set include timing the game, displaying the game status, and whether or not to keep a cumulative score while playing with the Vegas-scoring

rules. With the Vegas-scoring rules, you earn money for each card that you place from the top deck.

To add more visual appeal to the game, you can select the design for the back of the card deck from six included designs. Some card backs are animated, so keep a sharp eye out for added visual tricks.

SET SOLITAIRE OPTIONS

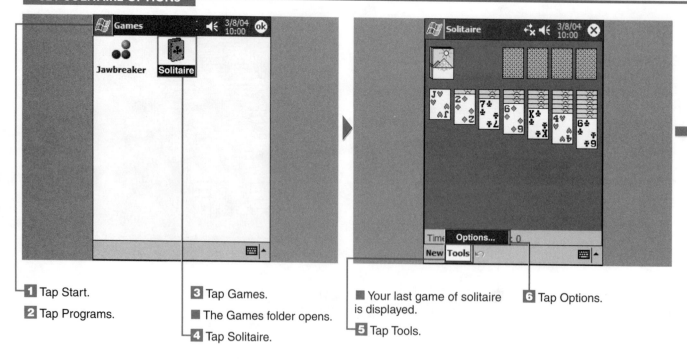

1 Tap Start.

2 Tap Programs.

3 Tap Games.

■ The Games folder opens.

4 Tap Solitaire.

■ Your last game of solitaire is displayed.

5 Tap Tools.

6 Tap Options.

Is there a way to ensure that I get dealt a winning deck?

✓ Yes. First bring up the soft keyboard and tap Ctrl and then Shift. Make sure that they are both highlighted. Then tap New. The deck that you are dealt is a winning deck. Now you can amaze your friends with how fast you can complete a game of Solitaire.

How do I activate the Keep Cumulative Score check box?

✓ First you must select Vegas scoring from the Scoring drop-down list. Then the Keep Cumulative Score option becomes available, and you will be able to keep a running score from game to game.

How are points awarded in the Vegas style of scoring?

✓ You start with a 52-dollar ante at the beginning of each game. You want to win more than your wager. To do so, you get 5 dollars for each card that you move to a suit stack. Unlike regular Solitaire scoring, there is no time penalty. You can select the Keep a Cumulative Score check box in Options to have the game track your dollars won or lost.

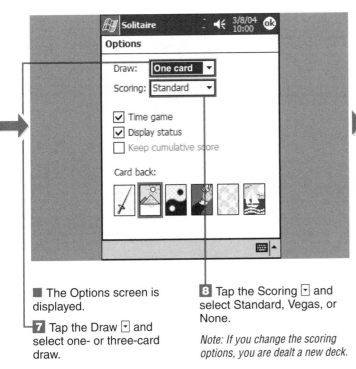

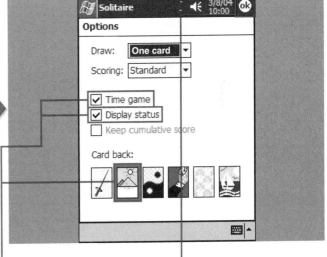

■ The Options screen is displayed.

7 Tap the Draw ⊡ and select one- or three-card draw.

8 Tap the Scoring ⊡ and select Standard, Vegas, or None.

Note: If you change the scoring options, you are dealt a new deck.

9 Tap a deck to select a new card back.

10 Tap Time Game to keep time during the game (☐ changes to ☑).

11 Tap Display Status to display the game status (☐ changes to ☑).

12 Tap OK.

■ Your changes are saved, and you are returned to the game.

Note: Some changes may cause your game to be redealt.

USING BASIC CALCULATOR FUNCTIONS

You can perform basic calculations using Windows Mobile 2003's calculator. The calculator enables you to add, subtract, multiply, divide, calculate a percentage, and calculate a fraction.

You can enter numbers using the calculator buttons, input panel, or attached keyboard. Numbers can be copied and pasted into the calculation line. You can also clear the last digit entered by using the arrow adjacent to the entry box.

MASTER IT

How do I get a fraction of a number?

✔ Enter a number and then tap the 1/x calculator button.

How many digits can fit on the entry line?

✔ The longest number can contain nine digits, but after eight decimal places, an *e* for exponential digits appears.

USING BASIC CALCULATOR FUNCTIONS

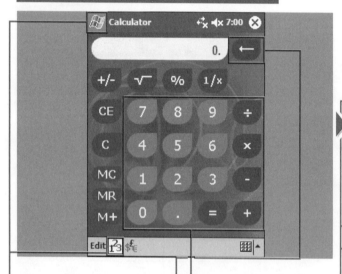

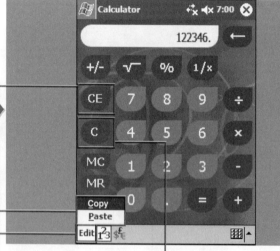

1 Tap Start.

2 Tap Programs.

3 Tap Calculator.

■ The calculator appears.

4 Tap the 123 button to use the calculator if the currency converter appears.

5 Tap numbers and functions to perform calculations.

■ You can tap the Backspace button to delete the previous digit in a multiple-digit entry.

6 Tap Edit.

7 Tap Copy or Paste to copy or paste digits in the entry line.

8 Tap CE to clear the displayed number.

■ Previous numbers entered in the calculation remain.

9 Tap C to clear the current calculation.

■ Any previously entered numbers in the calculation are removed.

USING THE MEMORY FUNCTIONS

I f you will be performing calculations that use the same number over and over or you have a long calculation, then you can use memory functions to temporarily store numbers in the calculator.

The calculator has the capability to store a single number for future recall. The number can be displayed or cleared using the buttons on the calculator. Multiple numbers cannot be placed into the calculator memory.

What happens if I tap M+ when another number is already stored in memory?

✔ The number is added to the number in memory, so the new number in memory will be the total of the two numbers. If you keep entering numbers and tapping M+ without using the MC function, the numbers continue to be added with the total in memory.

USING THE MEMORY FUNCTIONS

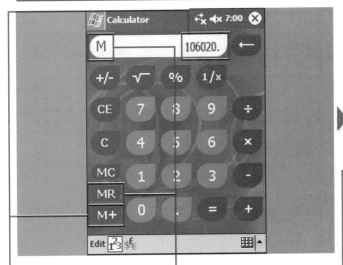

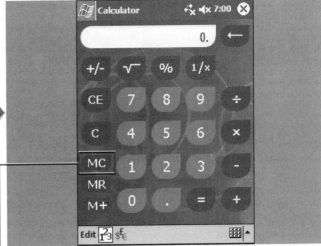

1 Enter a number in the entry line.

2 Tap the M+ button to store the number.

3 After entering another number and a function, tap MR to use the number stored in memory.

■ A capital *M* appears here when there is a number stored in memory.

4 Tap MC to clear out the memory.

■ The capital *M* in the entry line is cleared from the display, indicating that there is no number stored in memory.

USING THE CURRENCY CALCULATOR

In addition to using the calculator to perform basic math calculations, you can use the calculator as a currency calculator. This handy feature has several functions to convert between any two currencies that you choose. You can quickly calculate a currency conversion with a couple taps on your device.

You can copy the currency value from either line of the display and then paste it into other documents on your device. Numbers can also be pasted into the top conversion line.

Different currencies appear in the drop-down lists for countries that you have selected and that have established currency rates. The process of setting up currencies is discussed in the section "Enable Currencies and Modify Conversion Rates."

There are 176 currencies to select from in the Windows Mobile 2003 operating system by default. You can also choose to add custom currencies, which is discussed in the section "Add or Remove Currencies."

USING THE CURRENCY CALCULATOR

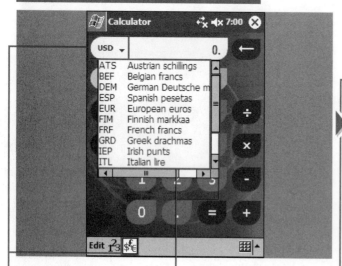

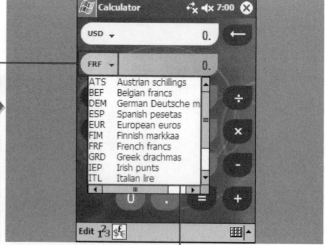

1 Tap the Currency Converter button.

■ The currency conversion display appears.

2 Tap the top currency symbol's ⊡.

■ A drop-down list with all the active currencies appears.

■ You can tap the right scrollbar to move through the available currencies.

3 Tap the currency that you want to convert from.

4 Tap the bottom currency symbol's ⊡.

■ A drop-down list with all the active currencies appears.

5 Tap the currency that you want to convert to.

Can I perform calculations in the currency converter?

✔ Yes, you will find the basic calculator under the currency conversion lines, which enables you to add, subtract, multiply, and divide values in the top conversion line.

Can I perform multiple currency conversions without entering another value on the top line?

✔ Yes, if you have a currency that you want to convert into multiple currencies, then after you enter the value in the top line, you simply tap different currencies in the bottom line's drop-down list.

Is there a fast way to perform conversions for different multiples of the top line value?

✔ Yes, if you want to convert multiples of a number such as 3 (that is, 3, 6, 9, and so on), you simply enter 3, tap the multipication symbol, and then repeatedly tap the equals sign. This same process can be used for addition, subtraction, and division.

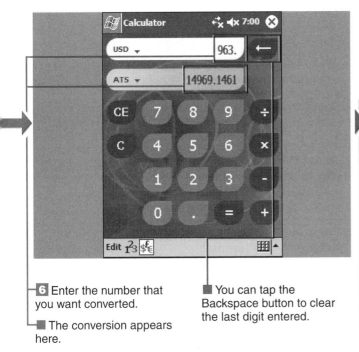

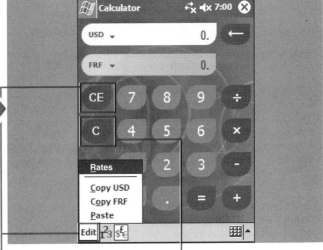

■6 Enter the number that you want converted.

■ The conversion appears here.

■ You can tap the Backspace button to clear the last digit entered.

■ You can tap CE to clear the displayed number.

■ You can tap Edit to open the Edit menu.

■7 Tap C to clear the calculation.

■ The calculation is removed, and the converter is ready to perform another conversion.

ENABLE CURRENCIES AND MODIFY CONVERSION RATES

There are 176 default currencies on your Windows Mobile 2003 device, and you can enable or disable as many as you want available to conduct currency conversions using the converter. The currencies that are enabled appear in both of the drop-down lists in the currency converter.

The first step in enabling a currency is establishing what currency you are using as your *baseline currency* — the one that you plan to convert from. You can use only base currencies that you have enabled in the rate-editing process.

You must manually enter conversion rates on your device. There is no mechanism for automatically

downloading the current conversion rates from the Internet. After currencies are enabled and the initial exchange rates are set, you need to update them manually with new currency values as well.

By default, the rates that are enabled on new Windows Mobile 2003 devices are based on the Euro.

ENABLE CURRENCIES AND MODIFY CONVERSION RATES

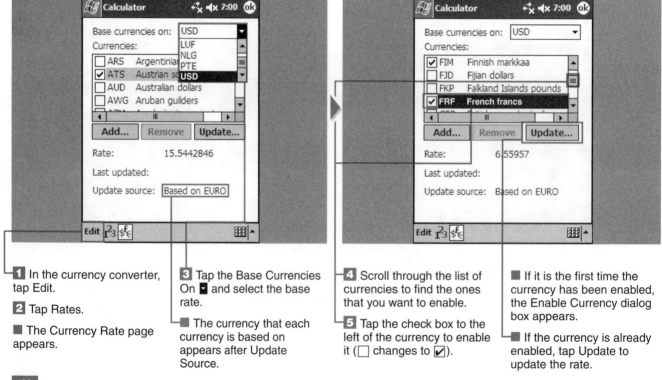

1 In the currency converter, tap Edit.

2 Tap Rates.

■ The Currency Rate page appears.

3 Tap the Base Currencies On ▼ and select the base rate.

■ The currency that each currency is based on appears after Update Source.

4 Scroll through the list of currencies to find the ones that you want to enable.

5 Tap the check box to the left of the currency to enable it (☐ changes to ☑).

■ If it is the first time the currency has been enabled, the Enable Currency dialog box appears.

■ If the currency is already enabled, tap Update to update the rate.

If I change the base currency, will I have to edit all the currency conversion rates again?

✔ No, all currencies that have been enabled automatically convert to the new base currency after you select it from the Base Currencies On drop-down list. Many currencies are based on the Euro and are tied to the Euro by a fixed rate that cannot be changed.

Can I base my currencies on any of the currencies in the list?

✔ Yes, if the currency has been enabled. You cannot use a currency that is disabled as a base currency.

Why do I get an error message when I tap OK in the rate entry screen?

✔ If you do not enter a rate in the rate entry screen and tap OK to close the window, an error message appears stating that the rate must be greater than zero. If you do not want to enter a rate at this time, tap No to close the error message. Tap Yes if you accidentally entered a number less than zero and make the correction.

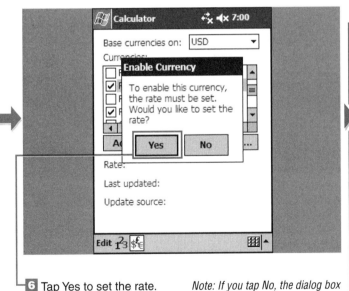

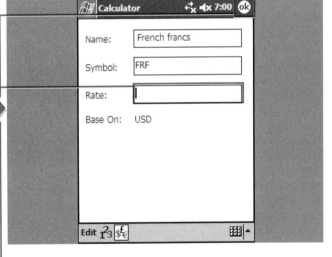

─**6** Tap Yes to set the rate.

Note: If you tap No, the dialog box closes, and you are returned to the editing screen.

─**7** Enter the currency conversion rate for the selected currency.

─**8** Tap OK.

■ The Currency Rate entry display closes, and the rate is established for that currency.

ADD OR REMOVE CURRENCIES

You cannot remove any of the 176 currencies that are loaded on your device, although they can be enabled or disabled as detailed in the section "Enable Currencies and Modify Conversion Rates." You will see that the Remove option is grayed out for the default currencies.

However, you can add and remove other currencies that may not be included on the default list. When you add a new currency, you must enter a name, currency symbol, and rate for the currency.

The currency name can be 60 characters long, and the currency symbol must be three letters with no numbers. The currency symbol defaults to all capital letters for the three characters that you enter and must be unique compared to the other symbols on your device.

There is no limit on the number that you enter for the conversion rate, except that it must be greater than zero.

ADD OR REMOVE CURRENCIES

ADD A CURRENCY

1 On the Currency Rate page, tap the Base Currencies On 🔽.

2 Tap the base currency that you want to use for your new currency.

3 Tap Add.

■ The new currency editing screen appears.

4 Enter a name for the new currency.

5 Enter a three-letter symbol for the currency.

6 Enter a rate based on the base currency that you selected.

7 Tap OK.

■ The entry screen closes, and the new currency appears in the currency list.

Does a custom currency have to be enabled to remove it from the list?

✔ No, you can select the currency by using your directional pad or scrollbar and then remove it by tapping the Delete button without enabling the currency.

Is there a limit to the number of currencies that I can add?

✔ No, the only limit would be due to using all possible three-letter combinations for the currency symbols, with the default 176 currencies and your custom currencies.

Can I have my custom currencies appear at the top or bottom of the full currency list?

✔ The currency list is organized alphabetically using the three-letter symbols. If you want your custom currencies at the beginning or end of the list, you can start the symbols with A or Z.

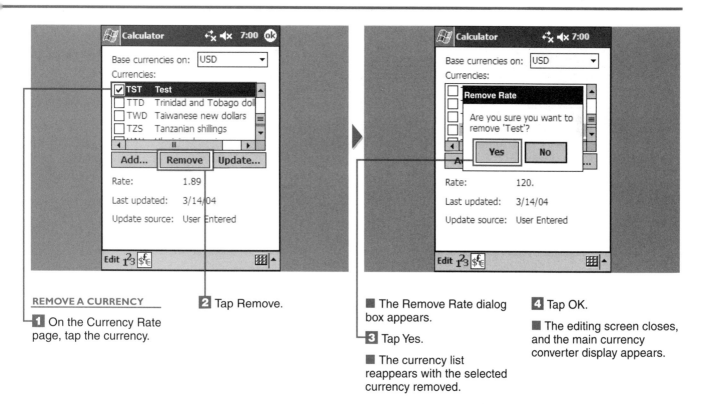

REMOVE A CURRENCY

1 On the Currency Rate page, tap the currency.

2 Tap Remove.

■ The Remove Rate dialog box appears.

3 Tap Yes.

■ The currency list reappears with the selected currency removed.

4 Tap OK.

■ The editing screen closes, and the main currency converter display appears.

USING FILE EXPLORER

Your Windows Mobile 2003 device uses a file system similar to a Windows desktop computer called *File Explorer.* With File Explorer, you can open, cut, copy, paste, move, sort, send via e-mail, beam, delete, and rename files. You can also create or delete folders.

Windows Mobile 2003 devices have external storage capacity, and File Explorer has icons and pull-down lists to quickly switch between the internal file system or the file structure on an external storage card.

You can select multiple files or folders to move, delete, copy, and paste. You cannot delete, move, or copy files in the device's ROM using File Explorer, however.

File Explorer shows the last date of modification and the size of individual files but does not show the size of folders. File Explorer also does not use a tree view like the one you may be familiar with in Windows Explorer. File Explorer opens each folder that you tap rather than expanding it for viewing.

USING FILE EXPLORER

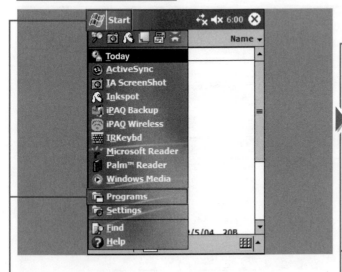

OPEN FILE EXPLORER

1 Tap Start.

2 Tap Programs.

3 Tap File Explorer.

■ The main File Explorer window appears.

Note: You may also have another shortcut to launch File Explorer on your device.

VIEW FILES AND FOLDERS

4 Tap ▾.

■ The menu's name changes to Show, and a drop-down list appears listing any folders in the hierarchy.

5 Tap the Memory icon.

■ A File Explorer window showing files and folders saved in RAM appears.

6 Tap the Storage Card icon.

■ A File Explorer window showing files and folders on the external storage card appears.

What do the rectangular icons on a folder mean?

✔ The icons indicate that the folder is on an external storage card. Many Windows Mobile devices also have available storage in the ROM of the device that shows up as an external storage card in File Explorer. The HP iPAQ ROM area is known as the iPAQ File Store.

Can I send files via Bluetooth from File Explorer?

✔ No, you can send files only via e-mail and the Inbox application or beam them via the infrared port on the device. Third-party vendors support sending files via Bluetooth.

Can I view file extensions, such as .txt, .doc, and .exe, in File Explorer?

✔ No, File Explorer shows the file type as icons. For example, an .html file has an Internet Explorer icon before its filename.

Can I change the application associated with different files or documents?

✔ No, file associations are automatic in File Explorer. Third-party file explorer applications are available with many more options and functions.

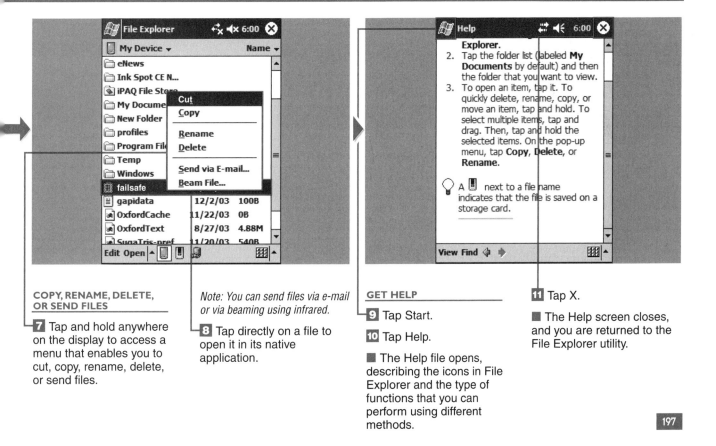

COPY, RENAME, DELETE, OR SEND FILES

7 Tap and hold anywhere on the display to access a menu that enables you to cut, copy, rename, delete, or send files.

Note: You can send files via e-mail or via beaming using infrared.

8 Tap directly on a file to open it in its native application.

GET HELP

9 Tap Start.

10 Tap Help.

■ The Help file opens, describing the icons in File Explorer and the type of functions that you can perform using different methods.

11 Tap X.

■ The Help screen closes, and you are returned to the File Explorer utility.

CREATE A NEW FOLDER

You can create an unlimited number of folders to organize and file your data. The Windows, My Documents, Program Files, iPAQ File Store (or other accessible ROM file), and Temp folders are preloaded on your device. The Storage Card(s) folder is automatically created when an external storage card is inserted into your device. The Windows folder cannot be deleted because it is a system folder and contains items found in the ROM. Some applications also add folders to your device when they are installed.

Can I have folders within folders?

✔ Yes, you can create a hierarchy of folders. For example, by default, there are a few levels of folders in the Windows directory installed on your device.

CREATE A NEW FOLDER

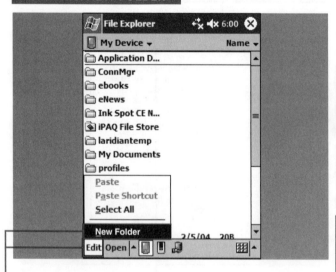

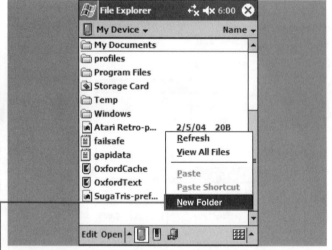

USING THE EDIT MENU

1 In File Explorer, tap Edit.

2 Tap New Folder.

■ A folder named New Folder appears and is selected automatically.

3 Type a name for the new folder.

■ The new folder is created.

USING A CONTEXTUAL MENU

1 Tap and hold anywhere in the window.

■ A pop-up menu appears.

2 Tap New Folder.

■ A folder named New Folder appears and is selected automatically.

3 Type a name for the new folder.

■ The folder with the new name is selected.

Note: After you open and close File Explorer again, the new folder will be sorted with the other folders.

SORT A FILE LIST

Y ou can have your folders and files sorted on your display using four different methods: You can sort them by name, date, size, or type. By default, files and folders are sorted by name in alphabetical order. Sorting files and folders can help you to quickly find a file, see when it was last modified, see how much memory it is consuming, and group files by their types.

How does File Explorer sort folders?

✔ The folders are always grouped together and are either above or below all the files. The folders are always sorted by their name if you select Name, Type, or Size, and their order changes only if you select Date.

Is there any other way to access the sort function, aside from using the Sort By menu?

✔ No, a tap-and-hold option for sorting is not available.

SORT A FILE LIST

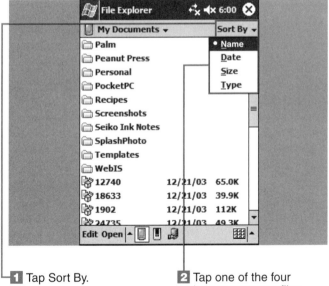

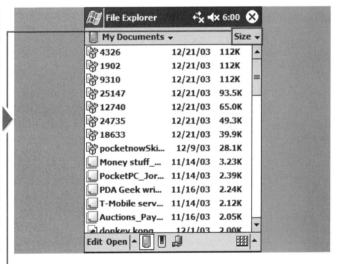

1 Tap Sort By.

■ A menu appears with Name, Date, Size, and Type.

2 Tap one of the four options to sort your files and folders.

■ The files and folders are sorted by the method that you selected.

3 Tap the current menu name.

■ The menu appears again.

4 Tap the same option that you chose in step 2.

■ The files and folders are sorted in reverse order.

OPEN A NETWORK PATH

With a connected device, you can access folders and files on a remote network. You can get connected either wirelessly or via your cable or cradle. This functionality can be useful for storing files on a network computer with larger storage capacity than a Windows Mobile 2003 device. The external network

folders can also be useful for storing backups of applications and data.

You can cut, copy, rename, and delete files and folders on the remote network. You cannot open files directly on a remote network using File Explorer standard functions, however. Third-party file

explorers do enable you to open files on a remote network, making them more functional as an external storage option.

You can set up multiple network paths using File Explorer in case you have access to multiple networks via your connected device.

OPEN A NETWORK PATH

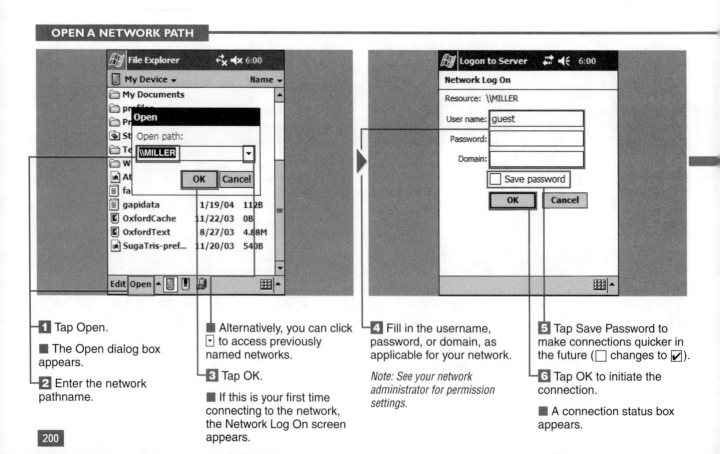

1 Tap Open.

■ The Open dialog box appears.

2 Enter the network pathname.

■ Alternatively, you can click ⊡ to access previously named networks.

3 Tap OK.

■ If this is your first time connecting to the network, the Network Log On screen appears.

4 Fill in the username, password, or domain, as applicable for your network.

Note: See your network administrator for permission settings.

5 Tap Save Password to make connections quicker in the future (☐ changes to ☑).

6 Tap OK to initiate the connection.

■ A connection status box appears.

Can I open files that are stored on a network?

✔ Yes, but files cannot be opened directly by tapping them in File Explorer. You must tap the file and select Copy. Then go to a location on your local device, such as the My Documents folder, tap and hold, and select Paste Shortcut. A shortcut directly to the file on the network is created. Tapping this shortcut opens the file stored on the network. This is useful for large-sized movies or songs that you do not have the capacity to store on your device.

Can I access files stored on a network from within other applications?

✔ Windows Mobile 2003 applications such as Microsoft Reader or Windows Media Player will not access files stored on a remote network, although these files can be opened individually using the method described previously.

Can I use a network image file on my device?

✔ Yes, if you tap and hold on a `.gif` or `.jpg` image file, you can select to have the image be used as your Today wallpaper.

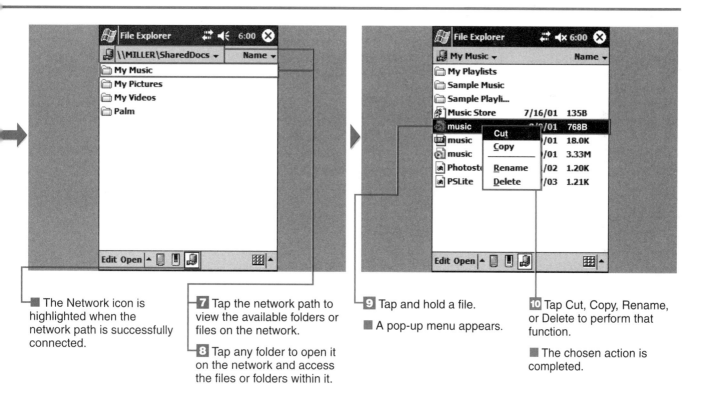

■ The Network icon is highlighted when the network path is successfully connected.

7 Tap the network path to view the available folders or files on the network.

8 Tap any folder to open it on the network and access the files or folders within it.

9 Tap and hold a file.

■ A pop-up menu appears.

10 Tap Cut, Copy, Rename, or Delete to perform that function.

■ The chosen action is completed.

SET AN IMAGE AS THE TODAY WALLPAPER

There are many ways to customize the look and feel of your mobile device. Chapter 2 shows you how to customize your Today screen with different background images or themes, but File Explorer makes it even easier to designate a photo for your Today background image. You

can select to set an image as the Today wallpaper with a couple of simple taps in File Explorer.

The image should be sized to fit the device's display, generally 268 x 240 pixels. If you select an image sized larger than this, the top-left 268 x 240 piece of the image will appear on the Today screen.

If you decide that you do not like your new Today wallpaper, however, you cannot remove it within File Explorer. You need to open up the Today settings to undo the new wallpaper.

SET AN IMAGE AS THE TODAY WALLPAPER

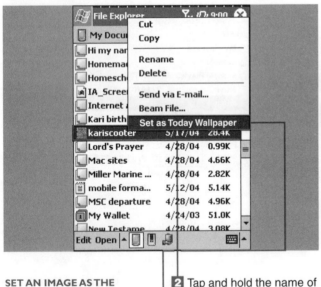

SET AN IMAGE AS THE TODAY WALLPAPER

1 Navigate to the folder with the image that you want to use as the Today wallpaper.

2 Tap and hold the name of the image file.

3 Tap Set as Today Wallpaper.

■ The Today screen appears with the new image in the background.

Can I use any common type of image file as the Today wallpaper?

✔ Yes, the image can be a `.jpg`, `.bmp`, `.tiff`, or `.gif` file. The tap-and-hold option to set the image as the Today wallpaper does not appear for other image file types.

Why does my image appear lighter as wallpaper than it actually is?

✔ When you set an image as the Today wallpaper, it is automatically adjusted to be less opaque so that text on the Today screen is visible.

Can I adjust the transparency level so that my image is not so washed out?

✔ Yes. The default setting in File Explorer washes out the image, but there are alternative ways to get an image on the Today screen. If your device has the Pictures application discussed in Chapter 23, you can adjust the transparency level there.

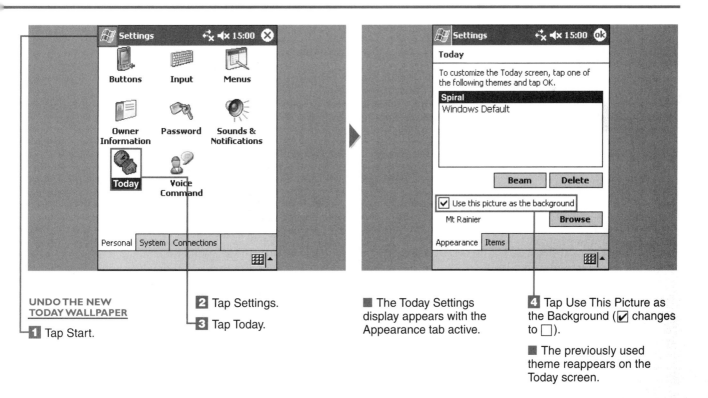

UNDO THE NEW TODAY WALLPAPER

1 Tap Start.

2 Tap Settings.

3 Tap Today.

■ The Today Settings display appears with the Appearance tab active.

4 Tap Use This Picture as the Background (☑ changes to ☐).

■ The previously used theme reappears on the Today screen.

ACTIVATE MICROSOFT READER

You can use Microsoft Reader on your device to read the hundreds of available public domain eBooks or eBooks that you create yourself using tools Microsoft provides for free. If you want to read new novels or premium titles with digital rights management (DRM) that you purchase online, then you have to first activate Reader. Publishers use DRM to manage the rights to read their books.

Activation requires you to sign in to a free Microsoft Passport account on your PC while your device is connected through ActiveSync. After you tap the Start button on the Web site, a permission code is placed on your device, and Reader is activated. You have to perform activation only once for your device.

Do I have to pay to activate my device?

✔ No, activation is free. Microsoft Reader is also free and can be installed on your desktop or laptop, and you can use the same books on those devices as your Pocket PC.

ACTIVATE MICROSOFT READER

1 Tap Start.

2 Tap Microsoft Reader.

■ The main Reader splash screen appears.

3 Check to see if Reader is activated on your device.

4 Make sure that your Pocket PC is connected to your PC (via the cradle or USB).

5 Visit http://das.microsoft. com/activate to activate Reader on your PC.

6 Follow the instructions.

7 After activation, launch Microsoft Reader again by tapping Start ➪ Microsoft Reader.

8 Check the splash screen to ensure that Reader is activated.

9 Tap X.

■ Reader is minimized, and you are taken back to the last active application.

SHOP AND GET HELP

From many places online, you can download free eBooks or purchase premium titles. Microsoft Reader can help you find these sites. You can shop directly from your connected device using Reader and Internet Explorer.

Microsoft Reader also has an extensive Help file that you can use

to answer common questions. The Help file includes topics such as how to move around in an eBook and how to listen to an audio book. The Help file supplements the material found in this book and is always with you on your device.

Can I purchase any format of eBook to use with Reader?

✔ No, eBooks formatted for Microsoft Reader have an .lit extension. There are other formats on various sites that are not compatible with Reader.

Do eBooks cost more than hard copies?

✔ Generally, eBooks cost about the same or a bit less than hard copies.

SHOP AND GET HELP

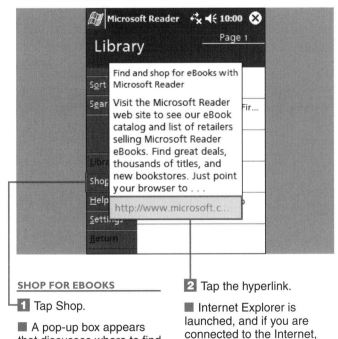

SHOP FOR EBOOKS

1 Tap Shop.

■ A pop-up box appears that discusses where to find and shop for eBooks.

2 Tap the hyperlink.

■ Internet Explorer is launched, and if you are connected to the Internet, you are taken to a Microsoft site that details where to find eBooks.

GET HELP

1 Tap Help.

2 Enter a word or phrase.

Note: You can also press the navigational pad to go to the next page to see the Help table of contents and browse through the Help file.

3 Tap Search.

■ The search term is highlighted in the Help document.

Note: Tapping and holding the term enables you to find the first, next, or previous term.

READA BOOK

With Microsoft Reader installed on your device, you can read eBooks that you download, purchase, or create yourself. Microsoft offers information on sites where you can find free public domain books, where you can make purchases, and where you can find the free tool to help you create your own electronic books.

A couple of powerful features available in Reader are the capability to find text quickly and instantly look up words with two simple screen taps. This makes searching through books easy.

You can place hyperlinks within eBooks that automatically launch Internet Explorer or move around inside the eBook, depending on how you create the links. EBooks

can be read in low light and dark conditions with your device because the screen has its own backlight.

It is very easy to navigate through eBooks as well. Rather than bend over a paper page or use a paper bookmark, you can use virtual bookmarks that can be quickly placed in your eBooks for fast navigation.

READ A BOOK

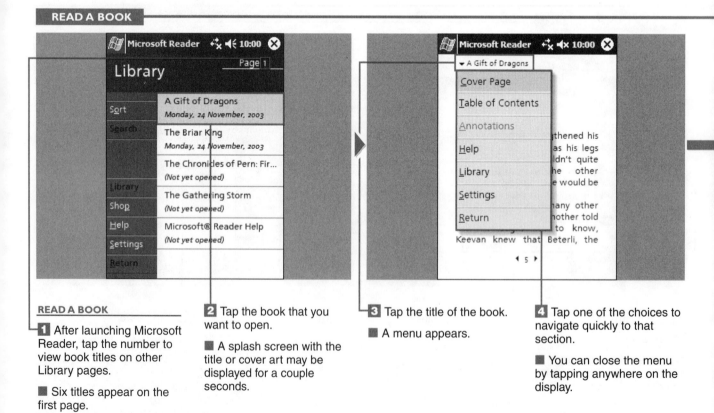

READ A BOOK

1 After launching Microsoft Reader, tap the number to view book titles on other Library pages.

■ Six titles appear on the first page.

2 Tap the book that you want to open.

■ A splash screen with the title or cover art may be displayed for a couple seconds.

3 Tap the title of the book.

■ A menu appears.

4 Tap one of the choices to navigate quickly to that section.

■ You can close the menu by tapping anywhere on the display.

Is there any other way to navigate around books besides tapping the arrows or the Riffle Control bar?

✔ Yes, you can use your navigation pad or the scroll button on your device to quickly move through the pages.

If I turn off my device while reading a book, where will it be when I turn it back on?

✔ If you just turn off the power, the book will be in the same place as when your device was powered off. If you fully exit from Reader, the book will open from the beginning again. You can use bookmarks to save your place in the book.

Is there any way to get back to where I was last reading, without using a bookmark?

✔ Yes, if you tap and hold on a book title in the Library view, you can select to go to the most recent page.

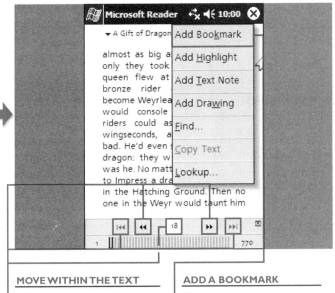

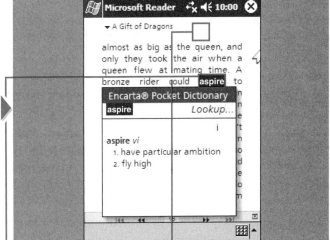

MOVE WITHIN THE TEXT

5 Tap the arrows to move one page forward or back.

■ You can tap here to move ahead or back one chapter.

■ You can tap and hold the page number to activate the riffle controls.

ADD A BOOKMARK

6 Tap and hold on the display to activate a menu.

7 Tap Add Bookmark.

■ A bookmark is placed at your current location in the text.

LOOK UP A WORD

8 Highlight a word and tap and hold it.

■ A menu appears.

9 Tap Lookup.

■ If a dictionary is loaded on your device, the definition appears in a text box.

10 Tap an empty area to close the text box.

■ You can continue reading using your stylus or navigation button.

LISTEN TO AN AUDIO BOOK

In addition to reading eBooks with Microsoft Reader, you can listen to audio books. Audio books are great for commuting, travel, or relaxing in your favorite chair.

You can use an FM transmitter or cassette adapter in your vehicle to listen to audio books over your vehicle audio system. You can also turn off the display on most devices to save battery power for longer listening time between charges.

You can use audio books that you purchase from Audible.com with Microsoft Reader after downloading and installing the Audible Manager software on your device. Audio books in other formats are not supported by Microsoft Reader.

A slightly different control interface is used with audio books, but they show up in the library in the same list as your eBooks.

LISTEN TO AN AUDIO BOOK

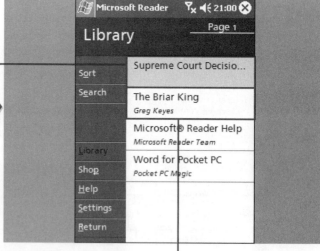

1 Purchase an audio book from Audible.com.

2 Load the Audible Manager on your desktop and device.

Note: Follow the instructions at Audible.com to load the Audible Manager.

3 Tap Start.

4 Tap Microsoft Reader.

■ The splash screen appears for a couple seconds, and then the library appears.

5 Tap an audio book in your library list.

■ You can tap and hold on a title for more options, such as deleting a book or viewing information about it.

Instead of using the Play button and such, are there other ways to move around an audio book?

✔ Yes, you can tap anywhere along the Riffle Control slide bar and go to that spot in the audio book. You can also use your device's navigation pad to move around the book.

What formats of Audible.com does Reader support?

✔ Microsoft Reader plays format 1, 2, or 3 Audible.com books. Format 4 books are not supported. MP3 audio books also will not play in Microsoft Reader, although they can be played in Windows Media Player 9.

Can I buy audio books anywhere besides Audible.com and play them with Reader?

✔ No, only Audible.com audio books are supported by Microsoft Reader.

What kind of audio books can I buy at Audible.com for Reader?

✔ You can select from over 18,000 books, magazines, newspapers, and radio programs. Purchases are stored online in your virtual library and can be downloaded to your device whenever you want. There are also some free audio titles available.

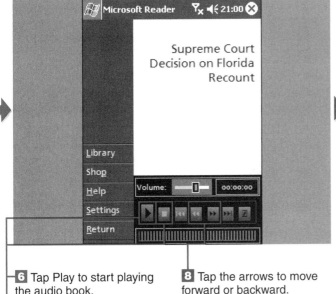

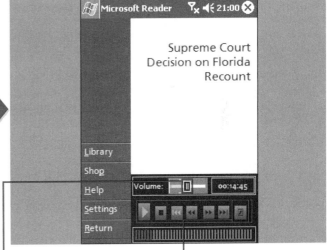

6 Tap Play to start playing the audio book.

■ The Play button grays out when activated.

7 Tap Pause to pause the audio book.

8 Tap the arrows to move forward or backward.

Note: The double arrows move in ten-second increments, and the double arrows with lines move to the next or previous section.

9 Tap the Volume slider to change the volume.

Note: Move the slider right or left to increase or decrease the volume, respectively.

10 Tap the Bookmark button to add a bookmark.

■ A small text window appears, enabling you to add a bookmark.

CUSTOMIZE YOUR VIEW

You can choose from four different font sizes for reading your eBooks on your device. Unlike traditional books with an established font size, you can use small or large fonts and change them whenever you want.

You cannot, however, change the font type; the ClearType font is always used in Reader. ClearType uses subpixel font rendering to

create readable fonts that are better than traditional font-smoothing techniques.

You can customize what annotations appear on the display when you are reading eBooks. The Annotations menu enables you to select to view bookmarks, highlights, text notes, or drawings as you read through the book.

Can I change the background color?
✔ No, the background color cannot be changed.

Why does my book now have more pages than before?
✔ The number of pages changes with the size of the font, so it appears that there are more pages with a larger font and fewer pages with a smaller font.

CUSTOMIZE YOUR VIEW

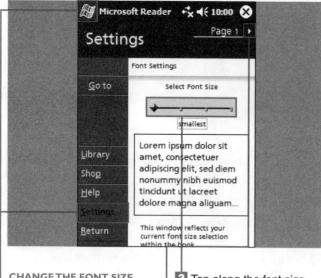

CHANGE THE FONT SIZE

■1 Tap Start ➡ Microsoft Reader.

■2 Tap Settings.

■ The Font Settings display appears.

■3 Tap along the font size bar to choose from one of four sizes.

■ The selected size appears in the preview box.

■4 Tap ▶.

TURN ON ANNOTATIONS

■ The next display in Settings appears.

■5 Tap the annotation choices that you want to appear (☐ changes to ☑).

■ The annotation items that you choose will appear on the display when you view an eBook.

ORGANIZE YOUR BOOKS

I f you have several eBooks loaded on your device, you can use the Sort functionality to organize your books. You can sort books by title, author, the last ones read, book size, and date acquired. Author sorting uses the author's last name.

In most cases, the properties of books are not shown until after the sort method is selected. For example, the book sizes appear under the title when By Book Size is selected as the sort parameter.

Do I have to store my eBooks in the My Documents folder?

✔ No, Windows Mobile 2003 allows eBooks to be placed anywhere in RAM or on your external storage card.

Can I flip the order of the sorting function?

✔ No, the sorting goes from A to Z, most recent to oldest, and smallest to largest. The sorting function cannot be switched from Z to A, and so on.

ORGANIZE YOUR BOOKS

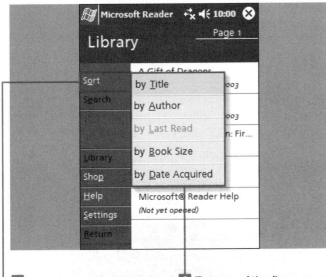

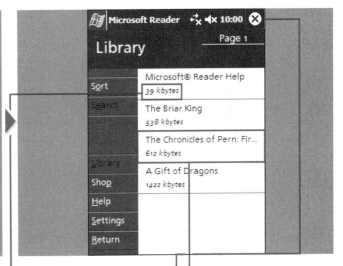

1 In the main Reader Library window, tap Sort.

■ A menu appears.

2 Tap one of the five choices to sort your eBooks.

■ The menu closes, and your eBooks are sorted as selected.

■ The details of the sort parameter appear under the book title.

Note: For example, the size of the book appears if By Book Size is selected.

■ You can tap a book title to open and read the eBook.

3 Tap X.

■ Reader is minimized, and you are taken back to your last active application.

ANNOTATE YOUR BOOKS

You can add highlighting, text notes, and drawings to your eBooks to make reading an interactive experience. These functions are saved as a separate annotation file that is synched on your device. Any annotation made in an eBook can be quickly viewed by using the top drop-down menu and selecting Annotations. An Annotations page appears with

buttons for each type of annotation.

You can highlight words, sentences, or paragraphs in yellow using the Add Highlight functionality.

Text notes that you add to eBooks are clearly noted over in the left margin for later viewing. You can edit, delete, or rename notes after they are created.

The drawing tool enables you to select from 12 colored pens. You then simply draw or write what you want right on the display over the electronic book. The book text is visible underneath the drawing. This tool is helpful for calling out sections of books that you want to review later.

ANNOTATE YOUR BOOKS

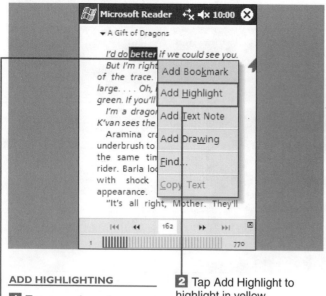

ADD HIGHLIGHTING

1 Tap a word, sentence, or phrase while reading a book.

■ A menu appears with options for annotating the book.

2 Tap Add Highlight to highlight in yellow.

■ The menu disappears, and the selected text is highlighted.

3 Tap more words, sentences, or paragraphs to highlight more of the document.

■ Yellow highlighting appears in the document wherever text is selected.

Can I change the color of the highlighting?
✔ No, yellow is currently the only available color for highlighting.

Can I format the text in the notes?
✔ No, standard text is used in the notes, and no bold, italic, or different-sized fonts are allowed.

Can I change the pen thickness in the drawings?
✔ No, the pen thickness is standard. However, you can select from 12 different pen colors to make your drawing stand out.

Can I name my annotations?
✔ Yes, tapping the top-left title of the book launches a menu from which you can select Annotations. On the Annotations display, you can tap and hold on the annotation titles to delete or rename each one.

Can I filter the annotations that I have?
✔ Yes, on the Annotations display, tap Show from the menu and tap what annotations you want to view.

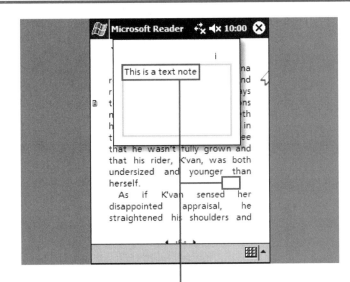

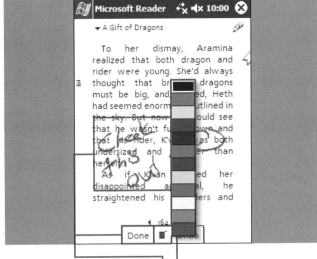

ADD A TEXT NOTE

1 Tap a word, sentence, or phrase.

2 Tap Add Text Note in the menu.

■ A small text window appears over the eBook.

3 Enter text into the text box.

4 Tap anywhere outside the text box when finished.

■ The text box closes, and a small text icon appears in the left margin.

ADD A DRAWING

1 Tap a word, sentence, or phrase.

2 Tap Add Drawing in the menu.

■ A pencil icon appears in the upper-right corner, and a small toolbar appears.

3 Tap the color box and select a pen color.

4 Create your drawing on the eBook.

■ You can tap Undo to erase drawing pieces.

5 Tap Done when finished.

■ The drawing toolbar disappears.

SIGN IN TO AND OUT OF MSN MESSENGER

One of the great features of Windows Mobile 2003 is the capability to stay in touch with your MSN (Microsoft Network) Instant Messenger contacts; the MSN Instant Messenger application is included in Windows Mobile 2003. MSN Messenger requires you to have a Hotmail e-mail account or a .NET Passport account, both of which are free. Hotmail (www.hotmail.com) is an e-mail service provided by Microsoft. The .NET Passport service (www.passport.com) enables you to create one username and password to sign in to all the .NET Passport-participating Web sites and services, including Hotmail.

MSN Messenger connects to the Internet using your default connection that was set up in the Connections Manager. You can learn more about setting up an Internet connection in Chapter 10. Phone Edition devices typically connect via their wireless Internet connection.

After you create your .NET or Hotmail account, you can sign in to and out of MSN Messenger on your device.

SIGN IN TO AND OUT OF MSN MESSENGER

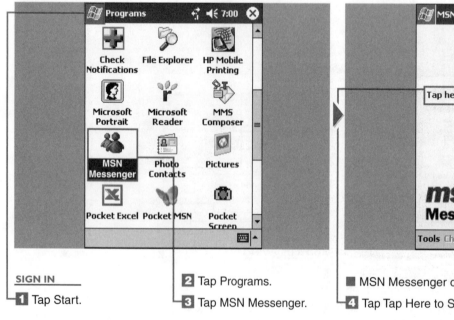

SIGN IN

1 Tap Start.

2 Tap Programs.

3 Tap MSN Messenger.

■ MSN Messenger opens.

4 Tap Tap Here to Sign In.

■ The MSN Messenger sign-in screen appears.

Can I use my own e-mail address to log in to MSN Messenger?

✔ Yes. To do so, create a .NET Passport account and use the e-mail account that you want to use for MSN Messenger during the account-creation process. Using your desktop PC, you can find more information about .NET Passport accounts at www.passport.com.

A friend of mine logged in to MSN Messenger using my device; now my login name no longer appears. What happened?

✔ MSN Messenger remembers the last account used to log in to the MSN Messenger service on your device. You need to reenter your account name and password to log back on.

My company uses Exchange Instant Messaging. Can I log in to that service using MSN Messenger on my device?

✔ Yes. On the Accounts tab of the Messenger options, check the Enable Exchange Instant Messaging check box and then enter your Exchange Instant Messenger account sign-in name and password.

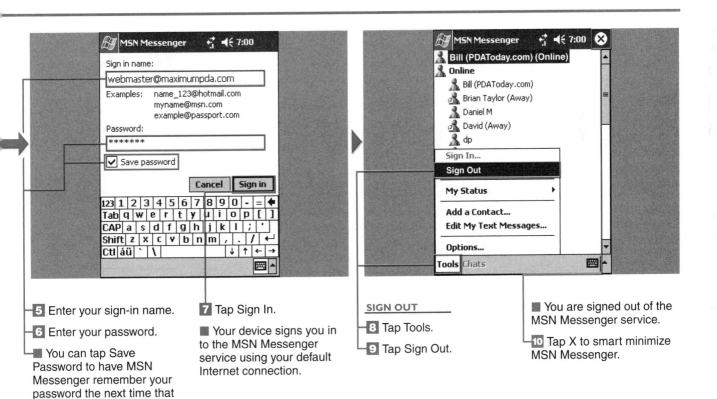

–5 Enter your sign-in name.

–6 Enter your password.

■ You can tap Save Password to have MSN Messenger remember your password the next time that you log in to the service (☐ changes to ☑).

7 Tap Sign In.

■ Your device signs you in to the MSN Messenger service using your default Internet connection.

SIGN OUT

8 Tap Tools.

9 Tap Sign Out.

■ You are signed out of the MSN Messenger service.

10 Tap X to smart minimize MSN Messenger.

CREATE AN MSN MESSENGER CONTACT

After you have an MSN sign-in name and password, you are ready to create MSN Messenger contacts.

You create new contacts by adding them to your MSN Messenger account. Adding MSN Messenger contacts to your account is an easy and effective way to stay in touch

with your family, friends, and colleagues — just about anyone with whom you want to communicate while using your device.

You need to be connected to the Internet in order to add contacts to your MSN Messenger account, and the contacts that you create must

also have an MSN Messenger account and software before you can chat with them.

If you are logging in to an existing MSN Messenger account and already have contacts associated with that account, they will appear in your contact list.

CREATE AN MSN MESSENGER CONTACT

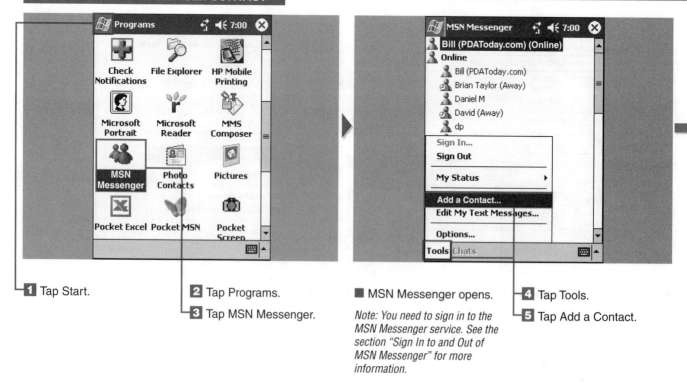

■ 1 Tap Start.

2 Tap Programs.

3 Tap MSN Messenger.

■ MSN Messenger opens.

Note: You need to sign in to the MSN Messenger service. See the section "Sign In to and Out of MSN Messenger" for more information.

4 Tap Tools.

5 Tap Add a Contact.

Why did MSN Messenger say "Failed" when I tried to add a contact?

✔ There can be a couple of reasons for this: You may have mistyped your contact's e-mail address, or your contact may not have an MSN Messenger account. Remember that your contact needs to have a .NET Passport or Hotmail e-mail account to be added to your contact list.

How do I delete a contact that I no longer want on my list?

✔ To delete a contact from your contact list, tap and hold the contact and select Delete. When you are asked if you want to permanently delete your contact, tap Yes. Note that the contact will also be deleted from any other computer on which you use MSN Messenger.

Can I send e-mail to an MSN Messenger contact?

✔ Yes. With your stylus, tap and hold the contact that you want to e-mail and select Send E-mail. Your Inbox is launched, and a new e-mail message is opened with the contact's name already in the To field. For more information on sending e-mail, see Chapter 15.

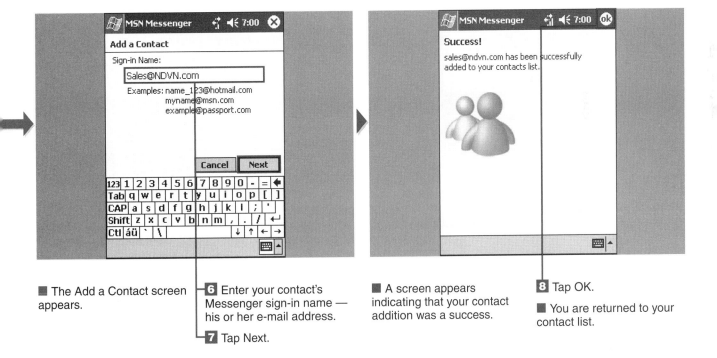

■ The Add a Contact screen appears.

6 Enter your contact's Messenger sign-in name — his or her e-mail address.

7 Tap Next.

■ A screen appears indicating that your contact addition was a success.

8 Tap OK.

■ You are returned to your contact list.

SEND AND RECEIVE INSTANT MESSAGES

After you have entered contacts into your MSN Messenger account, you can select a contact and chat with him or her. Your MSN Messenger contact must be logged in to the MSN Messenger service in order for you to send him an instant message.

Your MSN Messenger contacts that are online and available to chat with appear as green icons in your contact list and are listed under Online. When a contact is offline, she appears as a red icon and is listed under Not Online. You cannot chat with contacts that are not online.

Any of your contacts can send you an instant message if you are listed as one of their contacts, but you must be logged in to the MSN Messenger service to be able to receive the instant message. Your device notifies you when a message is being received.

SEND AND RECEIVE INSTANT MESSAGES

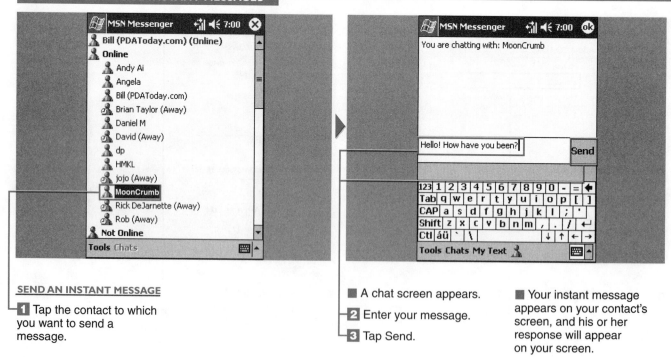

SEND AN INSTANT MESSAGE

1 Tap the contact to which you want to send a message.

■ A chat screen appears.

2 Enter your message.

3 Tap Send.

■ Your instant message appears on your contact's screen, and his or her response will appear on your screen.

What is My Text, and how can I use it?

✔ My Text is a collection of commonly used phrases that you can send to the person you are chatting with. Just tap My Text and select the text that you want use. From Tools, you can tap Edit My Text Messages and add your own phrases or edit the built-in phrases. See the section "Edit My Text Messages" for more information.

How do I add other people to an existing chat?

✔ Tap Tools and select Invite. A list of currently logged on MSN Messenger contacts is displayed. Tap the contact that you want to join your chat, and he or she is added to your current chat.

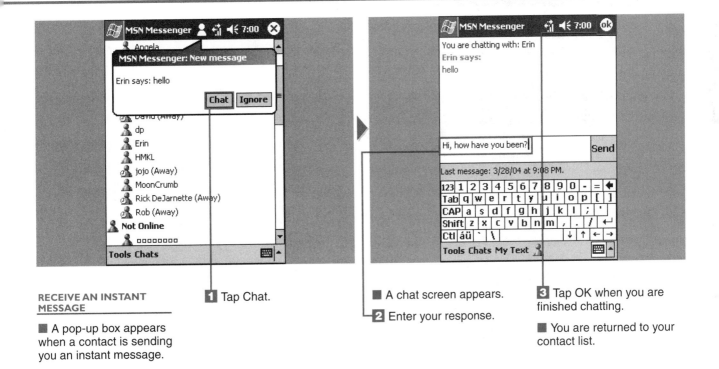

RECEIVE AN INSTANT MESSAGE

■ A pop-up box appears when a contact is sending you an instant message.

1 Tap Chat.

■ A chat screen appears.

2 Enter your response.

3 Tap OK when you are finished chatting.

■ You are returned to your contact list.

MODIFY MSN MESSENGER OPTIONS

MSN Messenger has many options that enable you to optimize your online instant messaging experience. You can modify the name displayed when you are online. Changing your display name can alert your contacts to information about your location, mood, or just about anything you want your contacts to see. A good example of this is changing your display name to

"your name (Pocket PC)" to alert your contacts that you are online with your Windows Mobile device.

You can set MSN Messenger to automatically log on to the MSN Messenger service when you initiate an Internet connection with your device. Note that you should be careful with this if you are using a wireless service that requires you to pay by the amount of data that is

sent or received because automatically logging on must send and receive data to work.

You can set up a block list that shows your status as offline and prevents selected contacts from sending you messages or knowing your online status. This can be useful when you only want to initiate chats with certain contacts and do not want them to initiate a chat with you.

MODIFY MSN MESSENGER OPTIONS

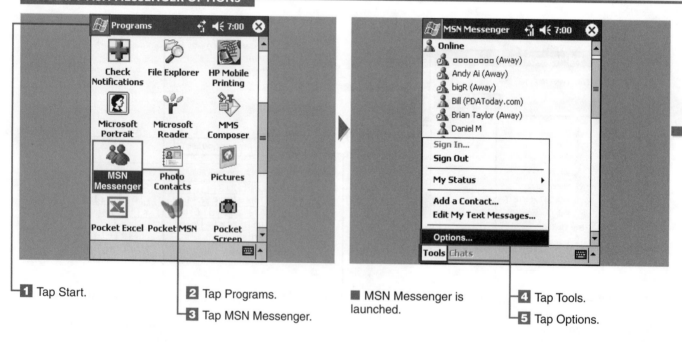

1 Tap Start.

2 Tap Programs.

3 Tap MSN Messenger.

■ MSN Messenger is launched.

4 Tap Tools.

5 Tap Options.

MASTER IT

How do I change my displayed status when I am online?

✔ Tap Tools and select My Status. You can select from seven status options: Online, Busy, Be Right Back, Away, On the Phone, Out to Lunch, and Appear Offline. After you select your new online status, your contacts see the new status in parentheses after your screen name.

Can I tell who has me added to their contact list?

✔ Yes. From the Privacy tab of the options, tap View. This displays a list of people who have added you to their contact list.

Is there an easy way to view a contact's e-mail address?

✔ Yes. Tap and hold the contact that you want to view and select Properties. The e-mail account that the contact used to sign up for his or her MSN Messenger account is displayed.

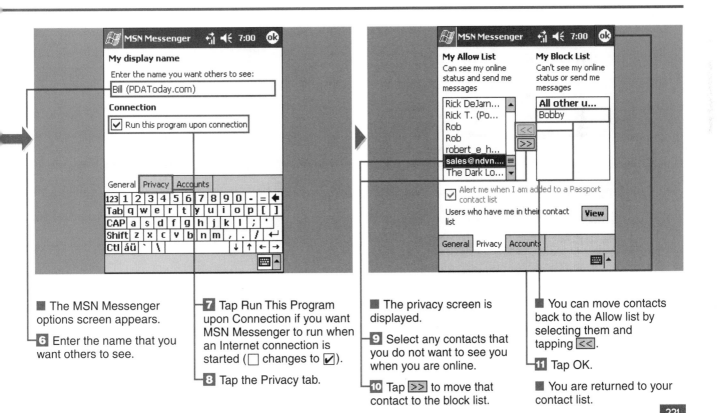

■ The MSN Messenger options screen appears.

6 Enter the name that you want others to see.

7 Tap Run This Program upon Connection if you want MSN Messenger to run when an Internet connection is started (☐ changes to ☑).

8 Tap the Privacy tab.

■ The privacy screen is displayed.

9 Select any contacts that you do not want to see you when you are online.

10 Tap >> to move that contact to the block list.

■ You can move contacts back to the Allow list by selecting them and tapping <<.

11 Tap OK.

■ You are returned to your contact list.

EDIT MY TEXT MESSAGES

You can use the default My Text statements or change them to something else to help speed up chatting with people on your mobile device. My Text statements are designed with the most common phrases or sentences that you would use while chatting to make responses faster and easier than using another input method on your device.

The My Text messages can also be used with the Inbox application, as discussed in Chapter 15, but the databases are different. You can have up to ten My Text messages on your device, and no more can be added through MSN Messenger.

You can enter text or use common emoticon symbols in your My Text messages.

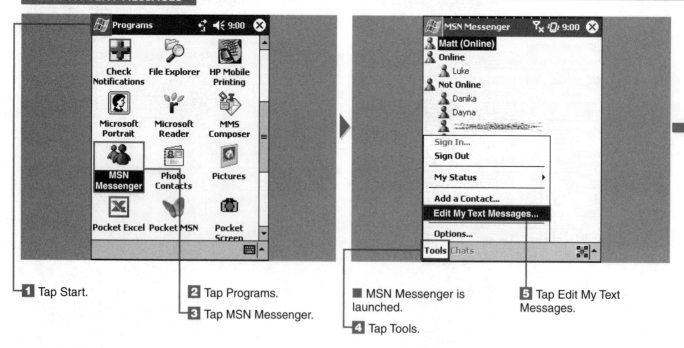

EDIT MY TEXT MESSAGES

1 Tap Start.

2 Tap Programs.

3 Tap MSN Messenger.

■ MSN Messenger is launched.

4 Tap Tools.

5 Tap Edit My Text Messages.

Can I add more than ten My Text messages?

✔ No, there is no ability to add messages. You can only edit existing messages.

Can I change all ten My Text messages to my own messages?

✔ Yes, you do not have to keep any of the default messages in the list.

Can I use any standard editing functions when entering My Text messages?

✔ Yes, you can use use the Cut, Copy, Paste, Clear, Undo, and Select All commands when entering messages. To do so, tap and hold in the text-entry box. The editing menu appears, from which you can tap the function that you want.

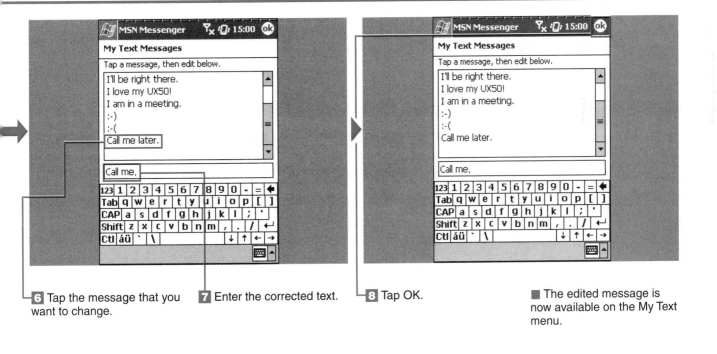

6 Tap the message that you want to change.

7 Enter the corrected text.

8 Tap OK.

■ The edited message is now available on the My Text menu.

USING PICTURES

Your digital camera may have a preview display that is a couple inches wide, and you may want to quickly view photos on a larger display. You may also want to take digital photos with you that are stored on your desktop PC. With the Pictures application, you can transfer images to your device and view them in Thumbnail or Full-Screen view. Pictures also enables you to make minor edits to the images.

Pictures supports viewing images in the .jpg format. It recognizes the DCIM folder created by digital cameras when a compact flash (CF) or secure digital (SD) card is inserted into the external storage slot of your device to allow for quick access to your photos.

You can transfer pictures to your device by placing them in the Windows Mobile 2003 device's My Documents folder on your desktop

and performing a sync operation using ActiveSync. You can also place them on an SD or CF external storage card — from your desktop using a card reader or directly from your camera — and then place the card into your device's external storage slot.

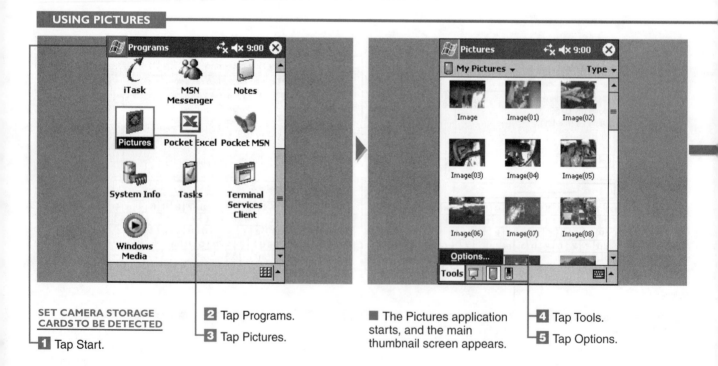

SET CAMERA STORAGE CARDS TO BE DETECTED

1 Tap Start.

2 Tap Programs.

3 Tap Pictures.

■ The Pictures application starts, and the main thumbnail screen appears.

4 Tap Tools.

5 Tap Options.

Do I have to place images in the My Pictures folder inside my mobile device's My Documents folder?

✔ No, Pictures searches for and presents thumbnails of all .jpg formatted images located on your device or external storage cards.

Do I have to enable the digital camera storage card detection option to read photos from my card?

✔ No, Pictures still enables you to view photos from your external storage card. The option just enables the notification message that appears if you insert an external card with images on it to allow for faster launching of Pictures.

Can I transfer images to my device or storage card using the Explore function of ActiveSync?

✔ Yes, you can click the Explore button or File ➪ Explore and transfer images directly to any file you want.

Is there a limit to the number of pictures I can transfer to my device?

✔ If you transfer images to the internal memory of your device, there is a limit to the available storage memory that can be used, which varies by device hardware.

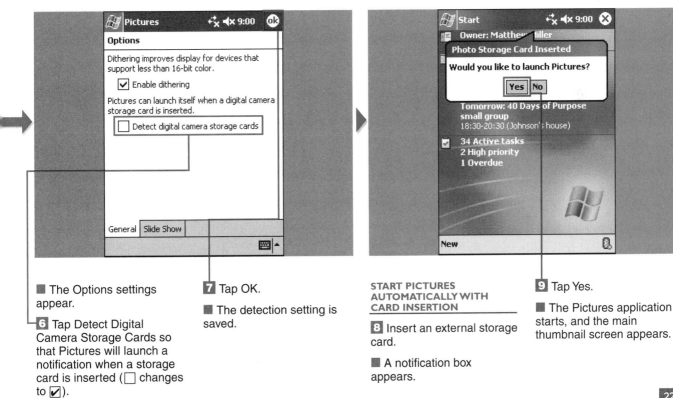

■ The Options settings appear.

■ 6 Tap Detect Digital Camera Storage Cards so that Pictures will launch a notification when a storage card is inserted (☐ changes to ☑).

7 Tap OK.

■ The detection setting is saved.

START PICTURES AUTOMATICALLY WITH CARD INSERTION

8 Insert an external storage card.

■ A notification box appears.

9 Tap Yes.

■ The Pictures application starts, and the main thumbnail screen appears.

225

VIEW IMAGES

After you have images loaded onto your device or external storage card, you can view the images by using the Pictures application. When you first start Pictures, a thumbnail screen appears showing all the images in the selected folder. By default, Pictures starts up with the images loaded in the internal memory of your device located in the My Documents folder. If Pictures is launched using the external storage card notification, the thumbnails for images found anywhere on the storage card appear by default.

You can quickly move between viewing images on your storage card or internal memory by tapping the buttons on the bottom menu bar. You can also filter images by viewing different folder contents on your external storage cards. You can sort the thumbnails by name, date, size, or type.

VIEW IMAGES

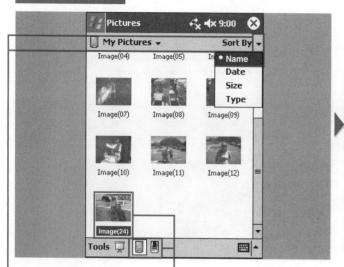

1 Tap ▪.

■ The menu name changes to Sort By.

2 Tap one of the four options to sort the thumbnails.

3 Tap the Pocket PC button or Storage Card button to switch locations.

4 Tap the image that you want to view.

■ Another window appears with the image that you selected.

■ A new bottom menu bar is also visible.

5 Tap OK.

■ The selected image closes, and the thumbnail screen appears.

SEND IMAGES

One of the great things about taking digital photos is the ability to share them with family and friends via e-mail. Using the Pictures application, you can send images via e-mail or infrared to another Pocket PC device.

The Inbox starts automatically when you select the Send via E-mail option, and the picture is attached to an e-mail message. If you choose to beam a picture, the beaming utility launches and instructs you to align ports so that it can find a device and send the photo.

Can I send multiple images via e-mail from within Pictures?

✔ No, you can select multiple images, but when you tap and hold to access the menu, the Send via E-mail function will be grayed out. You can attach multiple images using the Inbox, however, as covered in Chapter 15.

Will Pictures send my images in their original format?

✔ If the image is less than 30KB, it is sent without alteration. If your image is larger than 30KB, Pictures resizes it to 30KB to make it easier to send via wireless connections.

SEND IMAGES

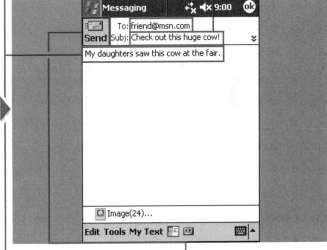

1 After selecting an image, tap Tools.

2 Tap Send via E-mail.

■ The Inbox launches with the selected image as an attachment to an e-mail message.

■ Alternatively, you can tap Beam Picture to send it via infrared.

Note: The beam and e-mail options can also be launched in the Thumbnail view by tapping and holding a thumbnail.

3 Enter a recipient e-mail address.

4 Enter a subject for the e-mail message.

5 Enter the message text.

6 Tap Send.

■ The e-mail is sent, and the main Pictures thumbnail display appears.

VIEW A SLIDESHOW

Your Windows Mobile 2003 device probably has a larger color display than your digital camera; thus viewing photos on your device can be a better experience. You can view the photos in a slideshow that has preset delays between photos. You can also set up a slideshow to play

on your device while it is resting in its cradle.

The slideshow options enable you to set the delay between photos from 1 to 30 seconds. You can also set the screensaver slideshow to start 1 to 30 minutes after your device has been docked in the cradle.

You can also manually advance, pause, or rotate the photos in a slideshow using your stylus. You can use the navigational pad on your device to advance photos and use the Action button to pause and restart the slideshow.

VIEW A SLIDESHOW

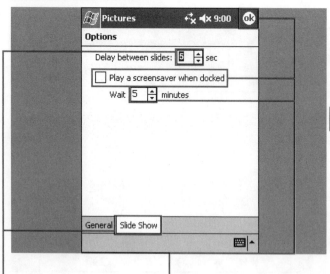

SET SLIDESHOW OPTIONS

1 On the main Pictures thumbnail display, tap Tools.

2 Tap Options.

3 Tap the Slide Show tab.

4 Tap ⏶ or ⏷ to set the delay between photos.

5 Tap Play a Screensaver When Docked (☐ changes to ☑).

6 Tap ⏶ or ⏷ to set the waiting period.

7 Tap OK.

■ The settings are saved, and the main Pictures display appears.

VIEW A SLIDESHOW

8 Tap the location where the photos are stored.

9 Tap ⏷ and select the folder where the photos are located.

10 Tap ⏷ and select a sorting option.

■ The photos appear in the order they are sorted from left to right and down in the Thumbnail view.

11 Tap the Slideshow button to start the show.

■ The slideshow is launched.

Can I specify what photos will be in the slideshow?

✔ No, all photos in the internal memory of your device are shown in a slideshow run from your internal memory. However, if you have photos stored in a specific folder on an external storage card, only the photos in that folder are shown in the slideshow.

Can I save a slideshow and e-mail it to family and friends?

✔ No, slideshows are not files that can be saved, edited, or modified. You can e-mail individual photos as detailed in the section "Send Images."

Can I rotate images through 360 degrees in the Slideshow view?

✔ No, images are displayed in their default view, which is shown in their thumbnail, when a slideshow is started. You can select to rotate the image clockwise 90 degrees. If you select to rotate again, the image returns to its original orientation. All images are rotated in a slideshow if you rotate one image.

■12 Tap anywhere on the display to pause the slideshow.

■ The slideshow control bar appears.

■13 Tap the Play button to restart the show where you left off.

■ The control bar disappears when the show is playing.

■ You can tap the Forward or Back buttons to move through photos manually.

ROTATE A SLIDESHOW

■14 Tap the Rotate button to rotate all images clockwise 90 degrees.

STOP A SLIDESHOW

■15 Tap X to stop the slideshow.

■ The main Pictures display with the Thumbnail view appears.

EDIT IMAGES

You can edit images right on your mobile device. This can be very helpful if you want to take a photo with your digital camera and then make some edits before sending it off to your friends.

You can alter the brightness or contrast using simple button controls. You can rotate your

images counterclockwise through 360 degrees in 90 degree increments. Rotated images are saved in the new orientation.

You can even crop your photos to focus in on particular aspects. You can zoom into photos with different levels that are dependent on the photo resolution and size.

However, you cannot perform color enhancement on your photos, and there is no auto-correct feature for brightness and contrast, but the included features are handy for quick mobile editing.

EDIT IMAGES

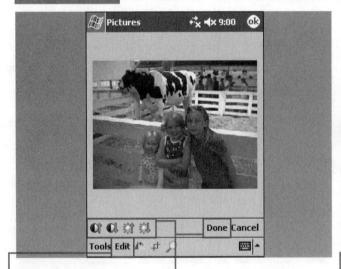

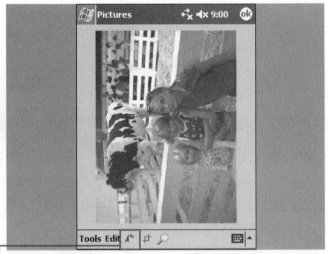

ADJUST BRIGHTNESS AND CONTRAST

1 Tap Edit.

2 Tap Brightness and Contrast.

■ The Brightness and Contrast editing buttons appear on the toolbar.

3 Tap the Brightness and Contrast up and down arrows to adjust the photo.

■ The changes appear automatically.

4 Tap Done to close the toolbar.

ROTATE A PHOTO

1 Tap the Rotate button.

■ The photo rotates 90 degrees counterclockwise with each tap of the button.

After editing a photo, can I save it with a different filename?

✔ Yes. However, you must be careful because if you tap OK after making edits, Pictures asks if you want to save the changes. If you tap Yes, your original photo will be overwritten with the edited photo. If you want to maintain a copy of the original photo, copy the photo by tapping and holding the Thumbnail view in the main Pictures display or by using Save Picture As, as detailed in the next section, "Save an Image."

Can I undo individual levels of brightness and contrast?

✔ No, the Undo and Redo functions do not work with individual levels. You can, however, tap Cancel to undo all the changes that you made to the brightness and contrast.

Are zoom levels saved, or are they just for viewing?

✔ Zooming into a photo is used just for assisting you with editing and is not a photo characteristic that you can save. Cropping a photo has the same effect as zooming into different levels and is saved.

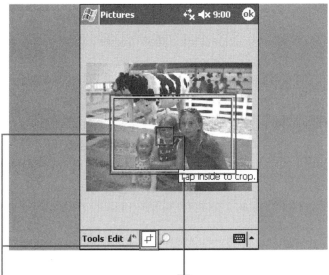

CROP A PHOTO

1 Tap the Crop button.

2 Tap and drag on the area that you want to crop.

3 Tap anywhere inside the cropped guide box.

■ The image is cropped.

ZOOM IN OR OUT

1 Tap the Zoom button.

■ A small zoom control box appears in the lower-right corner.

2 Tap the + or – button to zoom in or out.

3 Tap and drag the red box to center the zoom area.

4 Tap the Best Fit button to return to the full photo view.

■ The image is displayed zoomed out, as it was originally.

SAVE AN IMAGE

I f you are going to make changes to an image and want to keep the original one, it is important that you save the picture with a different filename. You can save your picture using a custom filename on your mobile device.

You can also quickly revert to the saved photo after making further edits if you have not selected to overwrite the photo.

You can select a folder found in your internal memory or select to save the photo onto an external storage card.

Can I save my photo as a different file type?

✔ No, only the `.jpg` image format is supported by Pictures. The file type option is always grayed out and is present just because it is part of the standard Windows Mobile display formatting.

SAVE AN IMAGE

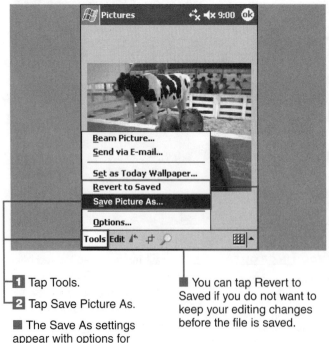

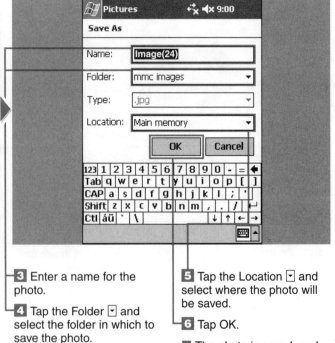

■1 Tap Tools.

■2 Tap Save Picture As.

■ The Save As settings appear with options for saving the photo.

■ You can tap Revert to Saved if you do not want to keep your editing changes before the file is saved.

■3 Enter a name for the photo.

■4 Tap the Folder ⊡ and select the folder in which to save the photo.

■5 Tap the Location ⊡ and select where the photo will be saved.

■6 Tap OK.

■ The photo is saved, and the main Pictures thumbnail display appears.

SET AN IMAGE AS THE TODAY WALLPAPER

As presented in Chapter 2, you can customize your Today screen with different background images or themes. You can use the Today settings option to browse and find a photo to use as the background image. However, that method shows only part of the image if it is larger than the 240 x 320 display.

With the Pictures application, you can select a photo to serve as the Today wallpaper and choose how the photo fits on the Today screen with a transparency level. The transparency level can be set to 0 percent (white screen) or 100 percent (full-color original photo).

How can I change to another Today screen wallpaper?

✔ The selected photo will not appear in the Today settings, and there is no command to undo it. You must select another Today screen background image or theme to remove the Pictures wallpaper.

SET AN IMAGE AS THE TODAY WALLPAPER

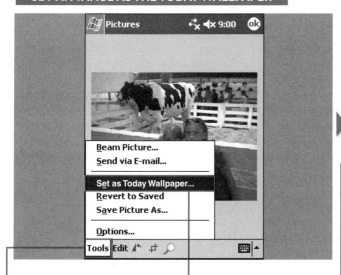

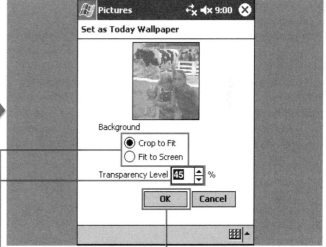

1 After opening the photo that you want to set as the Today wallpaper, tap Tools.

2 Tap Set as Today Wallpaper.

■ The Set as Today Wallpaper settings appear.

3 Tap Crop to Fit or Fit to Screen (○ changes to ◉).

Note: Crop to Fit crops the photo and has it fill the entire Today background. Fit to Screen keeps the entire photo and fits it to the width or height as needed.

4 Tap ⏶ or ⏷ to set the transparency.

■ The preview image shows the transparency level and how it will fit on the display.

5 Tap OK.

■ The Today screen will now have the photo as the wallpaper background image.

CREATE AND SAVE A NEW WORKBOOK

Windows Mobile 2003 includes Pocket Excel in the ROM of every device. You can create new workbooks in Pocket Excel that can be used with your desktop version of Excel. Documents can be saved in the Pocket Excel Workbook (.pxl) or Template (.pxt) formats or in the Excel 97/2000 Workbook (.xls) or Template (.xlt) formats. Pocket

Excel is designed as a mobile version of Excel, but some features have been removed to fit it on the device: There is no support for graphics, the VBA scripting language, pivot tables, embedded objects, embedded passwords, or add-ins.

After you launch Pocket Excel, the Workbook List view appears, which

shows existing workbooks on your device or external storage card that you can open from the My Documents folder. You can save workbooks as templates and use the Tools ⇨ Options menu to open existing templates to speed data entry. There are no templates loaded by default in Pocket Excel as there are in Pocket Word.

CREATE AND SAVE A NEW WORKBOOK

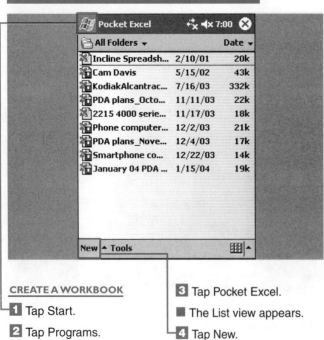

CREATE A WORKBOOK

1 Tap Start.

2 Tap Programs.

3 Tap Pocket Excel.

■ The List view appears.

4 Tap New.

■ A blank workbook or template appears.

5 Tap a cell.

6 Enter data into the cells.

Note: You can use the soft input panel keyboard or an external keyboard to enter data and move around the workbook.

Note: For more information about inputting data in Excel, you can see the section "Enter and Locate Data."

What happens if I tap OK after creating a workbook and do not use the Save As option?

✔ The workbook is automatically saved in the location specified in Options. The workbook is named Book1, Book2, and so on; names already in your workbook list will not be copied.

How do I rename or move a workbook after it is saved?

✔ Tap and hold the workbook in List view and tap Rename/Move.

Can I save workbooks to folders on an external storage card?

✔ No, all workbooks saved to an external card are stored in My Documents.

Can I copy an existing workbook and modify it?

✔ Yes, tap and hold the workbook in List view; you are presented with the options to create a copy or delete a workbook.

Can I password-protect a workbook?

✔ Yes, while you are entering data into the workbook, tap Edit ➪ Password and then enter and verify a password. When you tap to open a password-protected workbook, you will be prompted for the password.

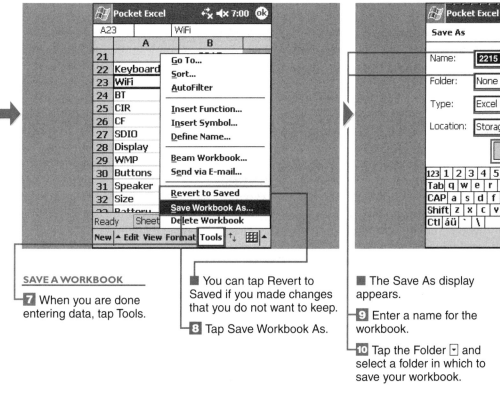

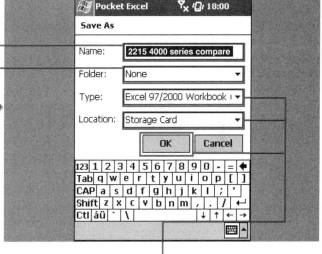

SAVE A WORKBOOK

7 When you are done entering data, tap Tools.

■ You can tap Revert to Saved if you made changes that you do not want to keep.

8 Tap Save Workbook As.

■ The Save As display appears.

9 Enter a name for the workbook.

10 Tap the Folder ⊡ and select a folder in which to save your workbook.

11 Tap the Type ⊡ and select from the list of available types.

12 Tap the Location ⊡ and select where to store the new workbook.

13 Tap OK.

■ The workbook is saved, and the List view appears.

ENTER AND LOCATE DATA

You can enter text, numbers, or formulas into Pocket Excel workbooks using your preferred text-entry method.

Data is entered one cell at a time. After tapping a cell and starting to enter data, you will see the upper data-entry line change to include the cell name, and X, Check Mark, and Fx buttons. Tapping X deletes the contents of the cell, tapping the check mark enters the data into the workbook and checks for valid formula entry, and the Fx button accesses the formula options that are presented in the section "Insert Functions and Symbols."

A powerful feature of Pocket Excel is the capability to quickly locate and replace data. Because the display is limited in size, being able to quickly find information that may be hidden off the viewable screen can be helpful when using your workbooks. You can find items in formulas or in values throughout the workbook.

ENTER AND LOCATE DATA

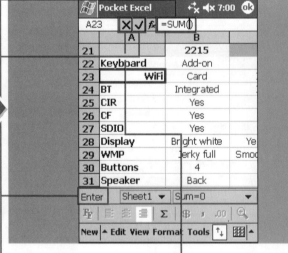

ENTER DATA

1 Tap a cell that you want to work with.

■ The cell is outlined in a bold black line.

2 Enter information into the cell.

■ The status of the sheet changes from Ready to Enter.

3 Tap ☑ to have the data placed into the workbook and check your formulas.

■ You can tap X to clear the cell contents.

Note: For more information about inputting data in Excel, you can see Master Visually Office XP or Teach Yourself Visually Microsoft Excel 2000.

Can I use an external keyboard to enter data?

✔ Yes, you can use any text-entry method supported by Windows Mobile 2003 to enter data in the cells.

Can I move data from the entry line to my workbook without tapping the check mark?

✔ Yes, if you tap or press Enter on a keyboard or if you tab to another cell, the data is entered into the workbook.

When I perform a search, what happens if I keep tapping Next after the term has been found?

✔ The search utility continues to cycle through the found terms until you tap X. If you use the Replace All function, the utility closes automatically after all replacements have been made.

Will Pocket Excel report how many replacements were made?

✔ No, unlike the desktop version of Excel, Pocket Excel does not make a report.

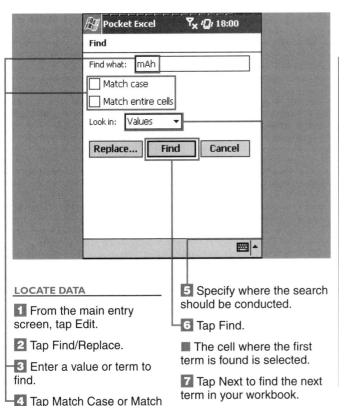

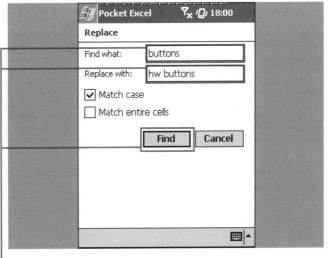

LOCATE DATA

1 From the main entry screen, tap Edit.

2 Tap Find/Replace.

3 Enter a value or term to find.

4 Tap Match Case or Match Entire Cells to limit your search.

5 Specify where the search should be conducted.

6 Tap Find.

■ The cell where the first term is found is selected.

7 Tap Next to find the next term in your workbook.

8 Tap X to close the search utility.

REPLACE DATA

1 Tap Replace.

2 Enter your search term.

3 Enter the replacement term.

4 Tap Find.

■ The cell where the first term is found is selected.

5 Choose to replace the term, replace all matching terms, or just go to the next matching term.

6 Tap Next to find the next term in your workbook.

7 Tap X to close the search utility.

■ The main workbook appears.

EDIT A WORKBOOK

Editing features similar to what you can find in the desktop version of Excel are included in Pocket Excel. You can cut, copy, paste, and paste special between cells and sheets in a workbook. You can clear all characteristics, the formats, or the contents of a cell using the Clear command. The editing options can be accessed through the Edit menu or by tapping and holding a cell.

You can paste all characteristics of a cell or the formulas, values, formats, and everything except the borders by using the Paste Special command. However, you cannot paste links between sheets or between other applications.

You can fill cells horizontally or vertically to quickly copy formulas or data. You can also fill cells in series. You have a choice of

different series formats, including autofill, date, and number. For the date, you can select day, month, or year. The step value for the date and number can also be set when the Fill command is initiated.

EDIT A WORKBOOK

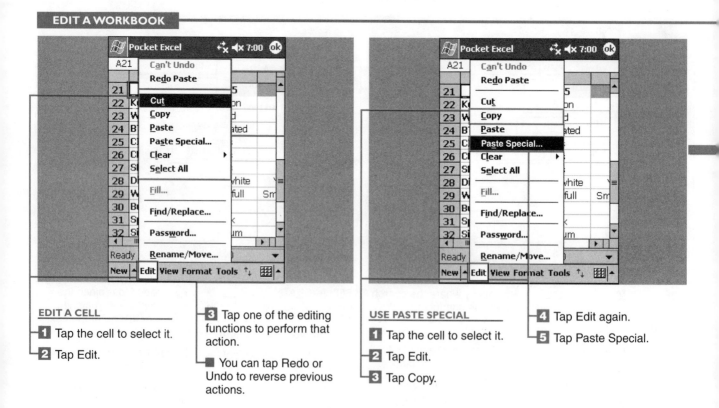

EDIT A CELL

1️⃣ Tap the cell to select it.

2️⃣ Tap Edit.

3️⃣ Tap one of the editing functions to perform that action.

■ You can tap Redo or Undo to reverse previous actions.

USE PASTE SPECIAL

1️⃣ Tap the cell to select it.

2️⃣ Tap Edit.

3️⃣ Tap Copy.

4️⃣ Tap Edit again.

5️⃣ Tap Paste Special.

Why do I not see Paste Special in the menu when I tap and hold a cell?

✔ Paste Special can be accessed only through the Edit menu at the bottom of the display.

If I just tap Paste, what is pasted into the cell?

✔ All the attributes of the copied cell are pasted into the new cell. This also occurs if you select Paste Special and tap All.

In what directions can I fill?

✔ You can fill cells up, down, right, or left of the cell that you selected as the starting point.

Can I use the keyboard Ctrl key to paste into multiple cells that are not adjacent to each other?

✔ No, this desktop function is not available in Pocket Excel.

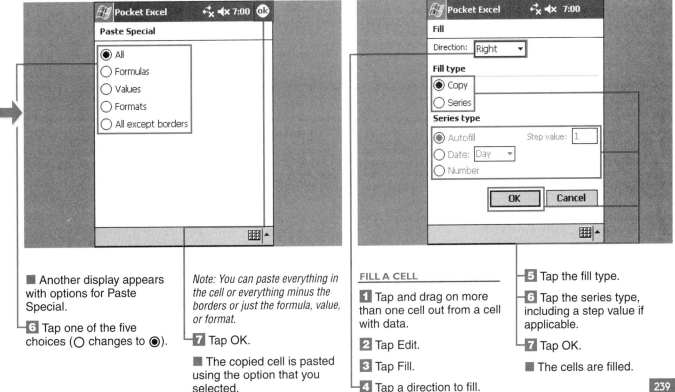

■ Another display appears with options for Paste Special.

6 Tap one of the five choices (○ changes to ◉).

Note: You can paste everything in the cell or everything minus the borders or just the formula, value, or format.

7 Tap OK.

■ The copied cell is pasted using the option that you selected.

FILL A CELL

1 Tap and drag on more than one cell out from a cell with data.

2 Tap Edit.

3 Tap Fill.

4 Tap a direction to fill.

5 Tap the fill type.

6 Tap the series type, including a step value if applicable.

7 Tap OK.

■ The cells are filled.

VIEW A WORKBOOK

You have several options available for viewing Pocket Excel workbooks. You can view the toolbar, the horizontal and vertical scrollbars, the status bar, and row and column headings.

You can access the toolbar using the bottom-right icon in the menu list. The toolbar provides you with

formatting options that are discussed in the section "Format a Workbook."

You can split the workbook display into four quadrants so that you can keep row and column headings visible while you enter data several rows or columns away from the origin.

You can display the workbook in full-screen view, which shows the cell, top cell entry bar, and bottom menu list. You can also zoom the workbook using the five preset levels or specify a custom zoom level from 50 percent to 200 percent.

VIEW A WORKBOOK

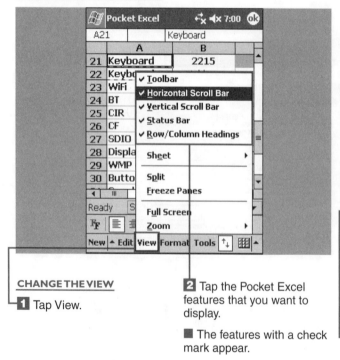

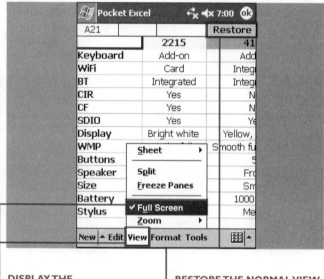

CHANGE THE VIEW

1 Tap View.

2 Tap the Pocket Excel features that you want to display.

■ The features with a check mark appear.

DISPLAY THE FULL-SCREEN VIEW

1 Tap View.

2 Tap Full Screen.

■ The toolbar, scrollbars, status bar, and row and column heads are hidden, giving you a view of data only.

RESTORE THE NORMAL VIEW

3 Tap Restore.

■ The Pocket Excel features that you chose to view appear.

MASTER IT

Can I view workbooks in landscape format?

✔ Not with Windows Mobile 2003, unless you use a third-party application such as Nyditot or JSLandscape. Windows Mobile 2003 Second Edition does provide support for landscape or portrait viewing of Pocket Excel workbooks.

What are the letters to the right of the default zoom levels?

✔ The letters are shortcuts that enable you to quickly change the zoom level of the workbook. Although they are shown as uppercase letters, tapping an upper- or lowercase letter will zoom the workbook to the level that you want.

Why are all the upper View options grayed out and inaccessible?

✔ Check to see if you are working in a cell. If you are entering data into a cell, you can only open the toolbar. If you do open the toolbar, you will notice that only one option is availabe for you to use, the Summation function.

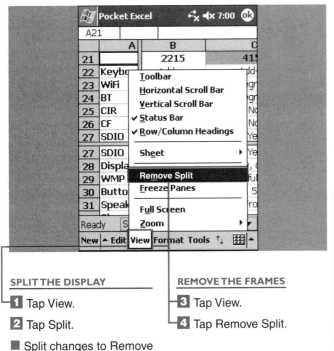

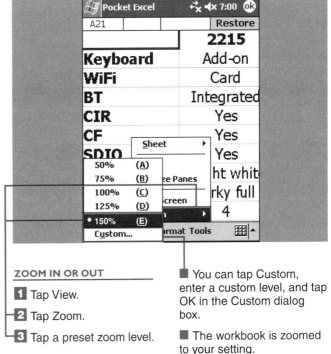

SPLIT THE DISPLAY

1 Tap View.

2 Tap Split.

■ Split changes to Remove Split, and frames appear.

REMOVE THE FRAMES

3 Tap View.

4 Tap Remove Split.

ZOOM IN OR OUT

1 Tap View.

2 Tap Zoom.

3 Tap a preset zoom level.

■ You can tap Custom, enter a custom level, and tap OK in the Custom dialog box.

■ The workbook is zoomed to your setting.

FORMAT A WORKBOOK

Although Pocket Excel is a slimmed-down version of Excel, it has several options for formatting a workbook to make it very usable on a mobile device. You can set the row height and column width; format numbers used in the cells; align the data in the cells; select the font type, color, size, and style; and select the border color and characteristics.

You can also format complete rows or columns using the Format menu.

You can enter a row height from 0 to 409 and a cell width between 0 and 255. You have ten options for formatting numbers in your cells, including a custom formatting category. The categories include Fraction, Scientific, Accounting, Currency, and Date.

You can align cells horizontally or vertically. You can also wrap text within a cell.

You can select 17 different colors for both font and border formats. You can choose from bold, italic, or underline styles of fonts in sizes ranging from 8 to 36. Five border options are available, and you can also select to fill the cell with one of the 17 available colors.

FORMAT A WORKBOOK

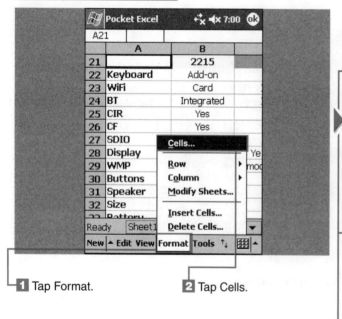

1 Tap Format.

2 Tap Cells.

■ The Format Cells entry screen appears.

3 Tap the Number tab.

4 Tap the number format that you want to use for the cell.

Note: You can use the Size tab to set the size of the row and column, and you can use the Align tab to align the data. The settings are similar to those of Excel on your desktop computer.

How many fonts can I choose from?

✔ Four fonts are preloaded in Pocket Excel — Bookdings, Courier New, Frutiger Linotype, and Tahoma. You can add more fonts, just as you can in Pocket Word. Pocket Excel supports TrueType fonts; you can add `.ttf` font files to the Windows\Fonts directory on your mobile device. If the font is not supported, it defaults to Tahoma.

Can I merge cells as I do in my desktop version of Excel?

✔ No, cells cannot be merged in Pocket Excel.

Can I use the AutoFit command for multiple rows and columns?

✔ Yes, tap and drag in the column or row headings and select those that you want to format. If you tap in the heading of the row or column, the entire row or column is selected. If you tap in the top-left corner of the workbook or tap Edit ➪ Select All, the entire workbook is selected so that you can make changes to the row and column formats. After selecting the row or columns that you want to change, tap Format ➪ Column or Row ➪ AutoFit.

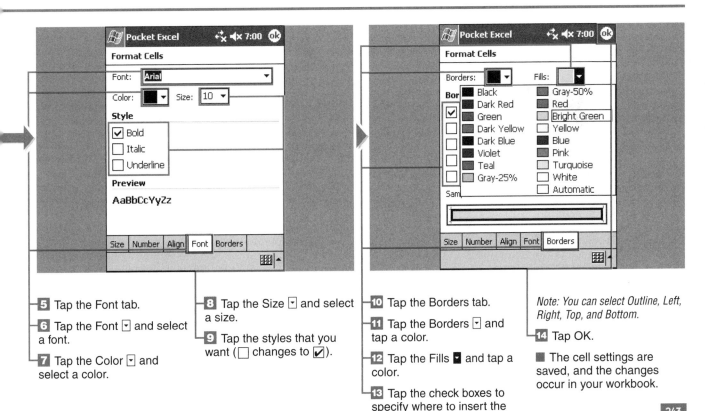

5 Tap the Font tab.

6 Tap the Font ▾ and select a font.

7 Tap the Color ▾ and select a color.

8 Tap the Size ▾ and select a size.

9 Tap the styles that you want (☐ changes to ☑).

10 Tap the Borders tab.

11 Tap the Borders ▾ and tap a color.

12 Tap the Fills ▾ and tap a color.

13 Tap the check boxes to specify where to insert the border.

Note: You can select Outline, Left, Right, Top, and Bottom.

14 Tap OK.

■ The cell settings are saved, and the changes occur in your workbook.

WORK WITH CELLS AND MULTIPLE SHEETS

You may find that you need to insert or delete cells, rows, or columns as you work with and edit your workbooks. Pocket Excel provides the tools to complete these tasks with a couple taps. You may also need to work with multiple sheets in a workbook, so Pocket Excel provides that functionality as well.

When you insert cells, you have the options to shift the cells to the right or down and to insert an entire row or column.

You can rename, insert, delete, or move sheets around in the order that they appear using the Modify Sheets function.

When you are working with multiple sheets, Pocket Excel makes it easy to quickly jump to the various sheets by tapping the sheet name in the status bar or by tapping View ⇨ Sheet.

WORK WITH CELLS AND MULTIPLE SHEETS

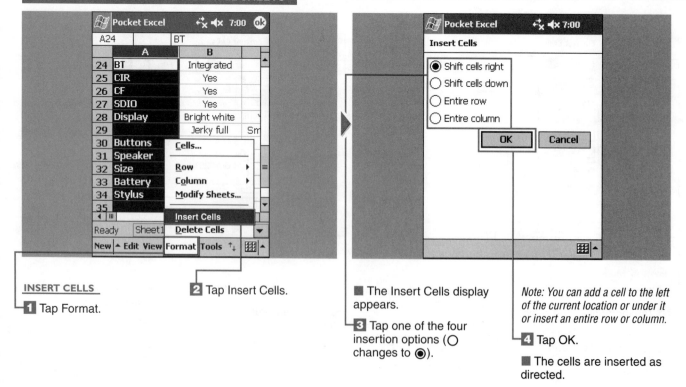

INSERT CELLS

1 Tap Format.

2 Tap Insert Cells.

■ The Insert Cells display appears.

3 Tap one of the four insertion options (○ changes to ⦿).

Note: You can add a cell to the left of the current location or under it or insert an entire row or column.

4 Tap OK.

■ The cells are inserted as directed.

Can I display multiple sheets at one time?

✔ No, only one sheet can be viewed or edited in Pocket Excel.

Where does Pocket Excel place the new sheet when I select to insert one on the Modify Sheets display?

✔ By default, the new sheet is inserted at the top of the list. You can change the order of the sheets by using the Move Up or Move Down buttons on the right of the Modify Sheets display.

What does Pocket Excel name the sheet when I insert one?

✔ Pocket Excel names the sheets Sheet1, Sheet2, and so on by default. You can select a new sheet and rename it in the Modify Sheets display.

If I choose to insert an entire row and column, where is the new row and column placed?

✔ New rows are placed under the cell that you selected when you chose to insert a row. New columns are added to the left of the cell that you selected.

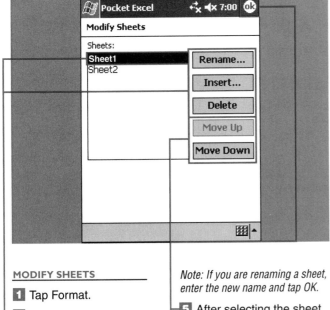

MODIFY SHEETS

1 Tap Format.

2 Tap Modify Sheets.

3 Tap the sheet name.

4 Tap Rename, Insert, or Delete to perform that action.

Note: If you are renaming a sheet, enter the new name and tap OK.

5 After selecting the sheet name, tap Move Up or Move Down to set the order in which the sheet appears.

6 Tap OK.

JUMP TO ANOTHER SHEET

1 Tap the sheet name.

■ A list of all the sheets in the workbook appears.

2 Tap the sheet that you want to jump to.

■ The selected sheet appears.

USE GO TO AND SORT DATA

Because not much data can be shown on the viewable display without zooming, Pocket Excel provides a tool that enables you to quickly go to a specific cell or region — the Go To command. Using Go To, you can go to any cell in the spreadsheet or back to the currently selected region.

Another helpful tool to manage the data in your spreadsheet is the Sort function. Sort enables you to sort your data by designated columns in an ascending or descending manner. You can refine the sort by selecting one to three columns. The second and third column sorts can be thought of as "then by" lists; for example, you can sort by the date of entry and then by the number of items.

USE GO TO AND SORT DATA

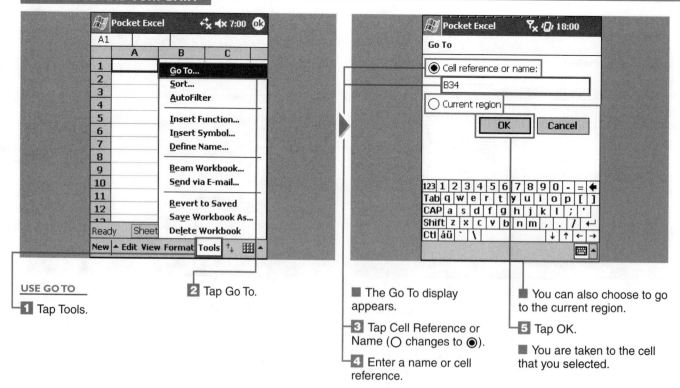

USE GO TO

1 Tap Tools.

2 Tap Go To.

■ The Go To display appears.

3 Tap Cell Reference or Name (○ changes to ⦿).

4 Enter a name or cell reference.

■ You can also choose to go to the current region.

5 Tap OK.

■ You are taken to the cell that you selected.

Can I enter the name of the cell in the Go To settings if I cannot remember the cell reference designation?

✔ If the cell has a designated name, you can go to it. The text in the cell is not considered the cell name.

How do I name a cell?

✔ Select the cell and then tap Tools ➪ Define Name. Enter a name for the cell, and you will see the letter and number cell designation replaced by your custom cell name.

What is the difference between a cell and a region, and where do I go if I select Current Region in the Go To settings?

✔ A *region* is a collection of cells that are immediately adjacent to the active cell and continuous around the active cell until an empty cell, column, or row is found. If you select Current Region, all cells that have values in the area where your active cell is located will be selected.

Can I sort by rows?

✔ No, sorting can be carried out only on columns.

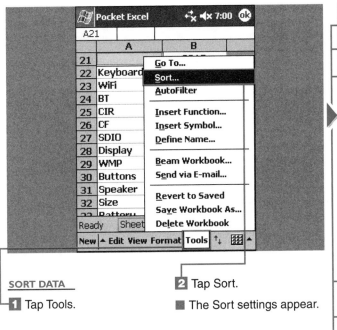

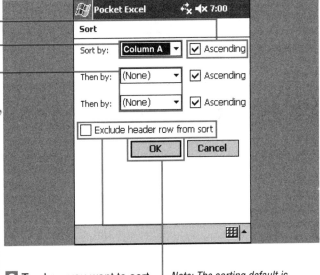

SORT DATA

1 Tap Tools.

2 Tap Sort.

■ The Sort settings appear.

3 Tap how you want to sort the workbook.

■ You can also choose to sort with secondary or tertiary filters.

4 Tap Ascending if you want the values in ascending order (☐ changes to ☑).

Note: The sorting default is descending order.

5 Tap the check box to exclude the header row from the sort (☐ changes to ☑).

6 Tap OK.

■ Your workbook is sorted as specified.

INSERT FUNCTIONS AND SYMBOLS

Y ou can use 109 functions from 9 categories to create your workbook. You can enter a function using text input, or you can use the Insert Function tool to quickly place a function in a cell. After a function is placed in the cell, you must enter the required values for the function to perform its purpose; when you

insert a function, Pocket Excel places the name of the required information between parentheses.

Symbols are often used to designate different variables, so Pocket Excel includes the Insert Symbol tool, which enables you to insert a large number of symbols from 65 subsets. The subsets include Latin,

Greek, and Cyrillic. Not all the subsets that are supported in the full version of Excel are supported in Pocket Excel.

If you add custom fonts to your device, the symbol subsets also present more choices from which to select. You can insert symbols into a cell along with other text.

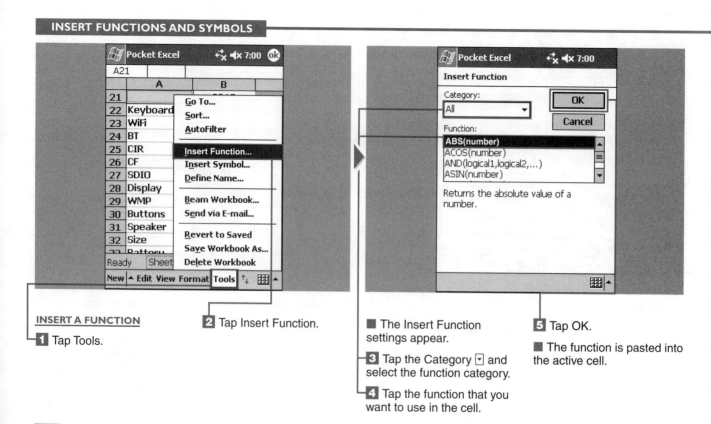

INSERT A FUNCTION

1 Tap Tools.

2 Tap Insert Function.

■ The Insert Function settings appear.

3 Tap the Category ⊡ and select the function category.

4 Tap the function that you want to use in the cell.

5 Tap OK.

■ The function is pasted into the active cell.

What happens if invalid information is placed in a function?

✔ You may receive a #NAME? or #VALUE! error. You may also see a pop-up dialog box appear stating that there is an error in the formula. You must make the corrections or delete the cell to work with another cell.

Is there another way to access the available functions, aside from tapping Tools ⇨ Insert Function?

✔ After you select a cell that you want to work with, the Fx symbol appears in the text-entry line at the top of the page. Tapping Fx brings up the Insert Function display.

What is the Summation button on the toolbar used for?

✔ The Summation button is used for summing numbers, which is a common function in Pocket Excel. This button makes the summation function readily available for easy insertion into your workbook.

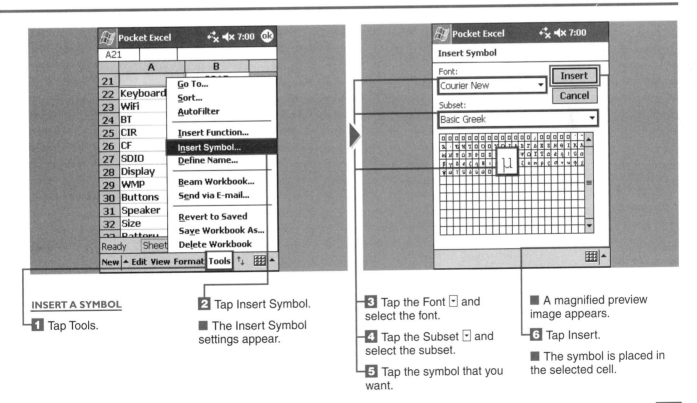

INSERT A SYMBOL

1 Tap Tools.

2 Tap Insert Symbol.

■ The Insert Symbol settings appear.

3 Tap the Font ⊡ and select the font.

4 Tap the Subset ⊡ and select the subset.

5 Tap the symbol that you want.

■ A magnified preview image appears.

6 Tap Insert.

■ The symbol is placed in the selected cell.

SEND A WORKBOOK

You can send your workbook to others using the beam functionality through the infrared port or via e-mail using the Inbox application.

You can e-mail only one workbook at a time using the Pocket Excel Inbox

option. You can send multiple workbooks if you send them as attachments through the Inbox application instead of sending them directly through the Pocket Excel interface. You can also beam only one workbook at a time.

Will recipients without a Pocket PC device be able to read my sent workbooks?

✔ Workbooks are sent in the saved format, so if a workbook is saved as a Pocket Excel (`.pxl`) document, the recipient needs a Pocket PC to read the file. The recipient can also read the file on his desktop if he has ActiveSync installed to perform the conversion. You should save the workbook as an `.xls` file if you are going to send it to others.

SEND A WORKBOOK

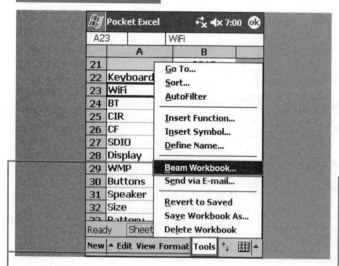

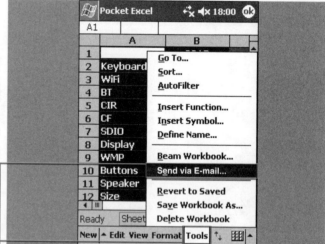

BEAM A WORKBOOK

1 Tap Tools.

2 Tap Beam Workbook.

■ The Beam utility appears and starts searching for devices.

3 Tap the device to which you want to send the workbook.

4 Tap OK.

■ The workbook is sent to the selected device.

E-MAIL A WORKBOOK

1 Tap Tools.

2 Tap Send via E-mail.

■ The Inbox is launched with the workbook as an attachment.

3 Fill in the recipient's e-mail address in the To: line.

4 Tap Send.

■ The workbook is sent if you are connected to the Internet or placed in the Outbox if you are not connected.

SET POCKET EXCEL CONVERSION OPTIONS

Pocket Excel files can be synched to your desktop through ActiveSync and the My Documents folder created when you installed ActiveSync and set up your partnership. You can specify the conversion settings in ActiveSync.

If you receive an Excel e-mail attachment on your

device without its going through ActiveSync, your device will perform a conversion to Pocket Excel format. However, if you view the document without making any changes and then close it, you can still transfer or e-mail it and have it retain the full desktop Excel formatting.

What happens to the attributes of a full Excel spreadsheet when they are run through the ActiveSync conversion?

✔ All attributes not supported by Pocket Excel are deleted from the document. If you are going to make changes to a spreadsheet, save it with a different filename so that the version on the desktop does not lose its formatting when you sync up again.

SET POCKET EXCEL CONVERSION OPTIONS

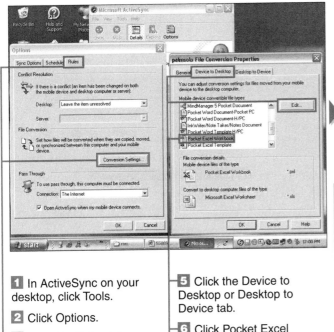

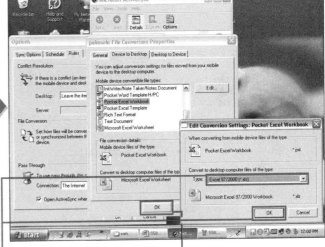

1 In ActiveSync on your desktop, click Tools.

2 Click Options.

3 Click the Rules tab.

4 Click Conversion Settings.

5 Click the Device to Desktop or Desktop to Device tab.

6 Click Pocket Excel Workbook.

7 Click Edit.

■ The Edit Conversion Settings dialog box appears.

8 Click the Type ▼ and select the format that you want to convert to.

9 Click OK.

10 Click OK in the File Conversion Properties dialog box.

11 Click OK in the Options dialog box.

■ The File Conversion properties are saved.

CREATE AND SAVE A NEW DOCUMENT

Windows Mobile 2003 includes Pocket Word in the ROM of every device. You can create new documents in Pocket Word that can be used on your desktop version of Word. Documents can be saved in the following formats: Pocket Word (.psw), rich text format (.rtf), plain text (.txt), Word 97/2000 document (.doc), or Word 97/2000 template (.dot). You may notice

that Pocket Word is a less robust companion to the desktop version of Word and not all features are supported on your mobile device.

After you launch Pocket Word, the last document that you were using or a default document may appear. After closing this document, you see the Document List view, which shows all the documents that can be opened in Pocket Word that are

stored on your device or external storage card. This is the display that you start with to create a new document.

In the List view, you can see documents saved in different formats, which can be identified by their icons. Documents with a small disk icon are stored on an external storage card.

CREATE AND SAVE A NEW DOCUMENT

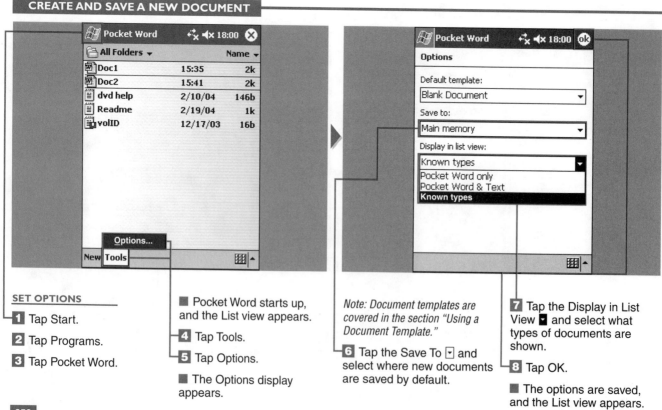

SET OPTIONS

1 Tap Start.

2 Tap Programs.

3 Tap Pocket Word.

■ Pocket Word starts up, and the List view appears.

4 Tap Tools.

5 Tap Options.

■ The Options display appears.

Note: Document templates are covered in the section "Using a Document Template."

6 Tap the Save To ⊡ and select where new documents are saved by default.

7 Tap the Display in List View ⊡ and select what types of documents are shown.

8 Tap OK.

■ The options are saved, and the List view appears.

What happens if I tap OK after creating the document and do not use the Save As option?

✔ The document is automatically saved in the location that you set up in Options in the My Documents folder. The document name will be composed of several characters from your first line of text. If the document is a drawing, a recording, or handwritten, it will be named Doc1, Doc2, and so on.

How do I rename or move a document after it is saved?

✔ Tap and hold the document in the List view and tap Rename/Move to perform the action that you want.

Can I save documents to any folder on an external storage card?

✔ No, all documents saved to an external card are stored in the My Documents folder.

How do I share a new document with others?

✔ Tap and hold the document in the List view to access a menu with options to send the document via e-mail or infrared.

Can I copy an existing document and modify it?

✔ Yes, tap and hold the document in the List view; you are presented with the option to create a copy.

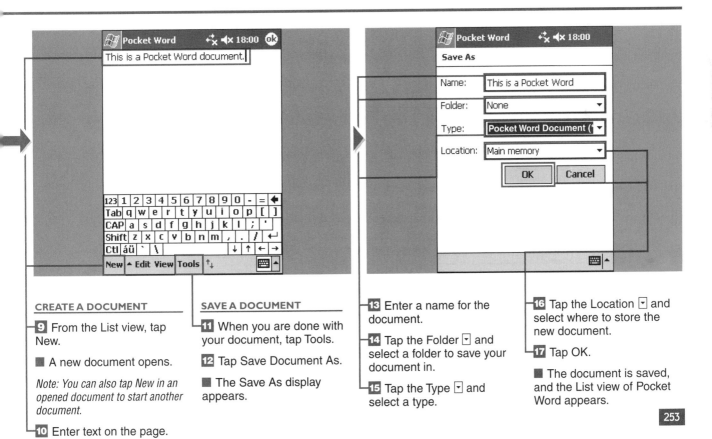

CREATE A DOCUMENT

9 From the List view, tap New.

■ A new document opens.

Note: You can also tap New in an opened document to start another document.

10 Enter text on the page.

SAVE A DOCUMENT

11 When you are done with your document, tap Tools.

12 Tap Save Document As.

■ The Save As display appears.

13 Enter a name for the document.

14 Tap the Folder ⊡ and select a folder to save your document in.

15 Tap the Type ⊡ and select a type.

16 Tap the Location ⊡ and select where to store the new document.

17 Tap OK.

■ The document is saved, and the List view of Pocket Word appears.

USING THE WRITING INPUT METHOD

here are four input methods for creating Pocket Word documents: writing, drawing, typing, and recording. The method that simulates paper the best is the writing input method. In Writing mode, you see lines in the background to help simulate writing on paper. With this method, you use your own handwriting to create documents. A powerful feature of the Windows Mobile 2003 operating system is the capability to later select handwritten text and convert it into typed text via the Recognize function.

You can customize your pen thicknesses and colors to personalize the writing input method. You can undo, clear, copy, and paste what you write. You can highlight, underline, boldface, italicize, or change the color of handwritten text.

All four input methods can also be mixed and matched within a single document, so you can switch to another method after you have started creating a document.

USING THE WRITING INPUT METHOD

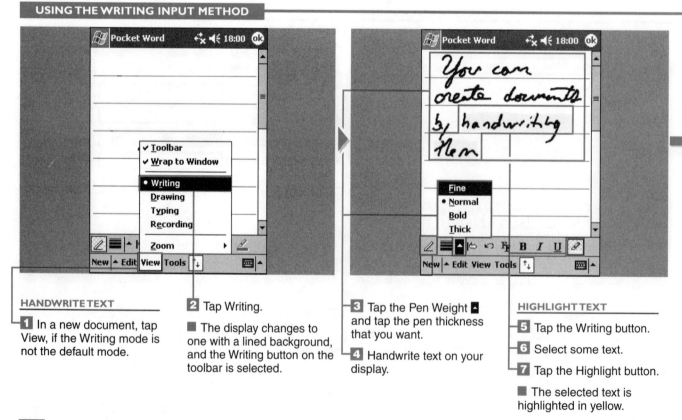

HANDWRITE TEXT

1 In a new document, tap View, if the Writing mode is not the default mode.

2 Tap Writing.

■ The display changes to one with a lined background, and the Writing button on the toolbar is selected.

3 Tap the Pen Weight ■ and tap the pen thickness that you want.

4 Handwrite text on your display.

HIGHLIGHT TEXT

5 Tap the Writing button.

6 Select some text.

7 Tap the Highlight button.

■ The selected text is highlighted in yellow.

MASTER IT

Can I change the color of the pen's ink?

✔ Yes, tap the Format button and select from 16 colors.

Can I change the highlighter color?

✔ No, the highlighter always highlights text in yellow.

How many times can I undo or redo handwriting?

✔ You can use the Undo or Redo function as many times as you want — all the way back to when the document was first created or all the way forward to the last line that you wrote.

What is the Alternates function on the Tools menu used for?

✔ Alternates presents a list of different words that may be the intended words that you handwrote on the display. Tapping a selection changes your handwriting into text as the recognition engine does for the complete selection automatically. Alternates gives you more choices in case your handwriting is difficult for the system to interpret.

What can I do if the Recognize function does not accurately interpret my handwriting?

✔ You can switch to text input and use a keyboard entry system to edit your text, you can try the Alternates function, or you can rewrite the text using better penmanship and try again.

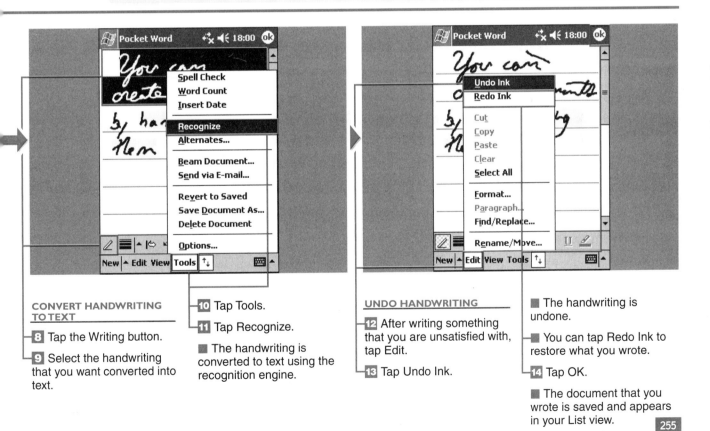

CONVERT HANDWRITING TO TEXT

8 Tap the Writing button.

9 Select the handwriting that you want converted into text.

10 Tap Tools.

11 Tap Recognize.

■ The handwriting is converted to text using the recognition engine.

UNDO HANDWRITING

12 After writing something that you are unsatisfied with, tap Edit.

13 Tap Undo Ink.

■ The handwriting is undone.

■ You can tap Redo Ink to restore what you wrote.

14 Tap OK.

■ The document that you wrote is saved and appears in your List view.

USING THE DRAWING INPUT METHOD

You can create drawings on your device by using your stylus in Pocket Word. Drawings can be helpful when taking down directions, creating room layouts, or trying to present an idea to someone.

Pocket Word includes some shape tools that can convert your hand-drawn shape into a standard rectangle, circle, triangle, or line to help present a clean drawing. These shapes can be resized, filled with color, and moved around the document.

You can add text to the drawing object by tapping the Writing button and using the input panel or a keyboard to type.

You can group or ungroup objects that you draw. Objects can also be aligned to the left, right, top, or bottom of a document, or they can be centered vertically or horizontally.

Sixteen colors are available to set as pen colors or fill colors for items that you draw. Also, you can copy and paste shapes into a document.

USING THE DRAWING INPUT METHOD

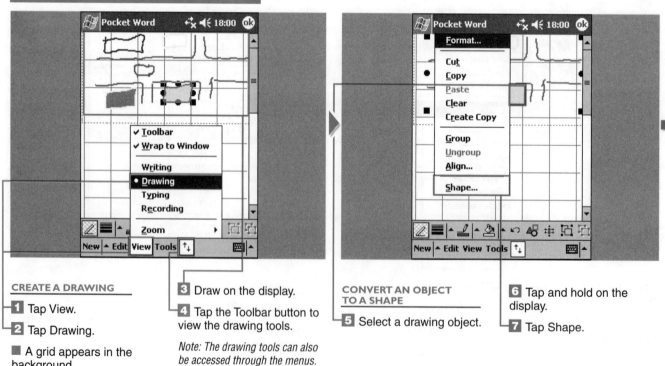

CREATE A DRAWING

1 Tap View.

2 Tap Drawing.

■ A grid appears in the background.

3 Draw on the display.

4 Tap the Toolbar button to view the drawing tools.

Note: The drawing tools can also be accessed through the menus.

CONVERT AN OBJECT TO A SHAPE

5 Select a drawing object.

6 Tap and hold on the display.

7 Tap Shape.

Can I bring an image or photo into Pocket Word to use in my drawing?

✔ No, Pocket Word does not support importing images in documents.

Why would I want to group or ungroup drawing objects?

✔ If you create several smaller objects, it is convenient to group them all together as one drawing so that you can move it around the document or resize it using the buttons that appear when you tap the drawing.

What can I do with the small circles and boxes that appear when I tap on a drawing object?

✔ These drawing tools enable you to resize and reshape the object and rotate the object through 360 degrees.

Can I change the shape of an existing object, such as from a square to a circle?

✔ Yes, if you tap and hold the object and then select Shape from the menu, you can tap one of the four available shapes. The object instantly changes to the new shape.

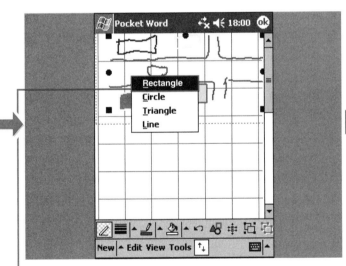

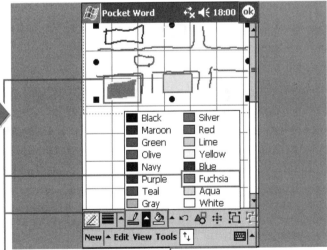

■ A menu appears with four different shape choices.

8 Tap the shape that you want.

■ The object changes to the selected shape.

ADD A COLOR

9 Select a line or shape.

10 Tap the pen button for a line or the fill color palette button for a shape.

■ The color palette appears.

11 Tap a color.

■ Your line color changes, or your shape is filled with the color that you selected.

12 Tap OK.

■ The drawing document closes and is saved, and the Document List view appears.

USING THE TYPING AND RECORDING INPUT METHODS

The most common entry method for Pocket Word is typing. You can enter text by tapping the keyboard keys of the soft input panel or by using an external keyboard designed for your hardware. Typing Pocket Word documents is generally the most accurate method of entry and can be the fastest, depending on the keyboard that you are using.

You can switch between typing and other modes with a couple of taps and include typing in drawing or writing documents. You can perform the standard typing commands such as Cut, Copy, and Paste.

Another useful input method is voice recordings. This method is especially good when you are unable to use your stylus to input data directly on your display. All

Windows Mobile 2003 devices include an integrated microphone for making voice recordings.

Voice recordings can be embedded in documents using other input methods and can be synched or sent to others for listening. You can adjust the recording quality to your preference. Note, however, that the quality impacts the size of the document.

USING THE TYPING AND RECORDING INPUT METHODS

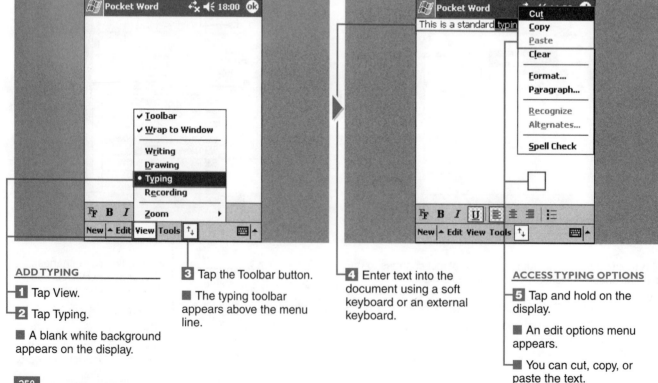

ADD TYPING

1 Tap View.

2 Tap Typing.

■ A blank white background appears on the display.

3 Tap the Toolbar button.

■ The typing toolbar appears above the menu line.

4 Enter text into the document using a soft keyboard or an external keyboard.

ACCESS TYPING OPTIONS

5 Tap and hold on the display.

■ An edit options menu appears.

■ You can cut, copy, or paste the text.

What kinds of keyboards can I use to type in data?

✔ There are full-screen keyboards and keyboards that work with the soft input panel at the bottom right of your display. Fitaly and MessagEase are the two most popular soft input keyboards; they are designed to maximize speed and accuracy with stylus input rather than using the QWERTY keyboard designed for two-handed operation.

Do standard keyboard shortcuts work in typing mode?

✔ Yes, most shortcuts for selecting text and performing editing functions work on the soft input keyboard.

Can I add to an existing voice recording?

✔ No, after a recording has been stopped, a new recording file is created when the Recording function is activated. There is no pause function in Recording mode.

What are the file sizes of recordings?

✔ The lowest quality recording is 8,000Hz mono and records at 2KB per second. The highest quality is 44,100Hz 16-bit stereo and records at 172KB per second; however, you can only listen to stereo recordings through headphones or after transferring the audio file to your desktop. Note: Do not record until your available device memory is full, or you may be unable to use your device.

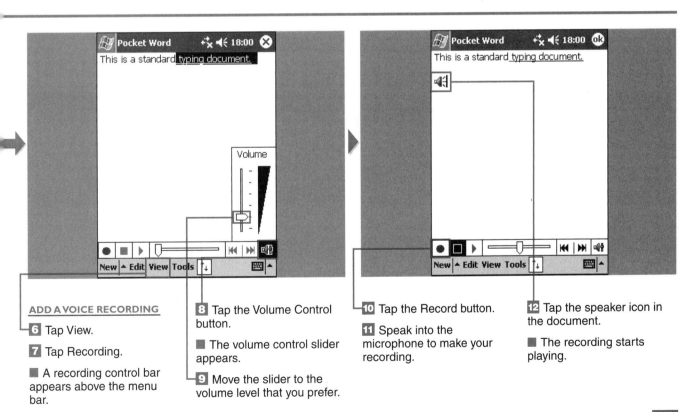

ADD A VOICE RECORDING

6 Tap View.

7 Tap Recording.

■ A recording control bar appears above the menu bar.

8 Tap the Volume Control button.

■ The volume control slider appears.

9 Move the slider to the volume level that you prefer.

10 Tap the Record button.

11 Speak into the microphone to make your recording.

12 Tap the speaker icon in the document.

■ The recording starts playing.

USING A DOCUMENT TEMPLATE

By default, Pocket Word starts a new blank document when you tap New. You can also select from four other templates that help you organize your data and enable the quick input of information — Meeting Notes, Memo, Phone Memo, and To Do. You can also import Microsoft Word templates (.dot) to use in Pocket Word.

The default loaded templates include preformatted text or bullets that you use to fill out with more information. The templates are basic, and generally have about four to five entry fields.

You can combine input methods, such as using the Meeting Notes template in conjunction with voice recordings of the meeting to ensure that nothing was lost in translation.

Templates can only be used by creating a new document; you cannot switch to Template mode while working in a Pocket Word document. Templates are selected in the Options menu, and each subsequent new document will use that template until you change the options.

USING A DOCUMENT TEMPLATE

SET THE DEFAULT TEMPLATE

■1 Tap Tools in the List view.

■2 Tap Options.

■ The Options settings appear.

■3 Tap the Default Template ▼.

■4 Select one of the default templates or one of the templates that you installed.

■5 Tap OK.

■ The template is set as the default.

USING THE MEETING NOTES TEMPLATE

■6 Perform steps 1 to 5, tapping Meeting Notes in step 4.

■7 Tap New.

■ The Meeting Notes template appears.

■8 Enter text into the template.

■9 Tap OK.

■ The document is saved, and the List view appears.

Can I use any desktop Word template on my mobile device?

✔ No, some templates are too complex for Pocket Word. Templates moved from your desktop to Pocket Word go through a conversion process that may strip certain aspects of the template, including macros, headers and footers, and mail-merge features.

Can I change the text in the template within a document?

✔ Yes, the templates primarily provide preformatted text in bold with certain spacing to help format your data. You can edit this text and formatting like any Pocket Word document.

Can I permanently change the template on my device?

✔ No, you cannot change and save the template on your mobile device. However, you can make changes to the template on your desktop and replace the template on your device by editing the template file stored in the Windows directory.

What name is given to my document from a template when I close it without using Save As?

✔ The document is named with the template name — that is, Meeting Notes, Phone Memo, To Do, or Memo. Multiple documents using the same template include parentheses and a number at the end of the filename, such as To Do(4).

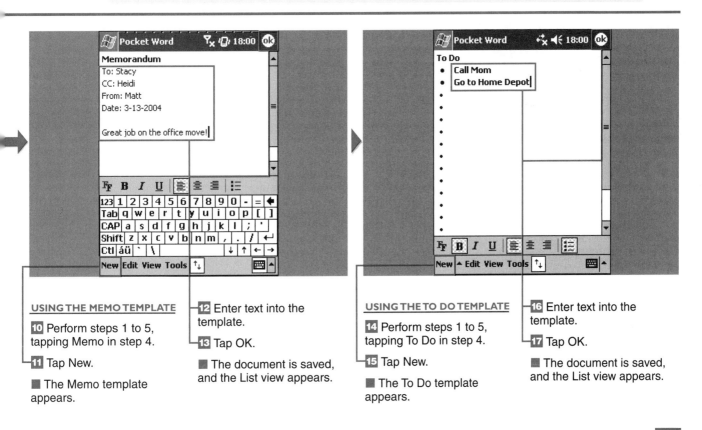

USING THE MEMO TEMPLATE

⑩ Perform steps 1 to 5, tapping Memo in step 4.

⑪ Tap New.

■ The Memo template appears.

⑫ Enter text into the template.

⑬ Tap OK.

■ The document is saved, and the List view appears.

USING THE TO DO TEMPLATE

⑭ Perform steps 1 to 5, tapping To Do in step 4.

⑮ Tap New.

■ The To Do template appears.

⑯ Enter text into the template.

⑰ Tap OK.

■ The document is saved, and the List view appears.

EDIT A DOCUMENT

Basic editing features are included in Pocket Word that should be familiar to desktop Word users. You can change the formatting, change paragraph alignment and indentation, and find and replace words in your document. You can also perform the common text-editing functions mentioned in previous sections, such as Cut, Copy, Paste, and Select All.

The Format options enable you to change the font, font size, pen weight, line and font color, fill color, and attributes of the font such as bold, italic, and underline.

The Paragraph options enable you to change the paragraph alignment to left, right, or center and make the paragraph a bulleted list. You can also set the left and right indentation and set first line or hanging indentations.

The Find/Replace function enables you to search for and replace words and includes the options to match case or match whole words only to help narrow the focus of your search.

You can use the Undo function or Undo button to undo text entry or ink entry or to move back to when the document was first created.

EDIT A DOCUMENT

EDIT TEXT

1 While working in a document, select some text with your stylus.

2 Tap Edit.

3 Tap one of the editing options to perform that action.

Note: You can tap Cut, Copy, Paste, Clear, or Select All.

FORMAT TEXT

4 Tap Edit.

5 Tap Format.

■ The Format settings appear.

6 Tap the Font ▼ and select the font.

7 Tap the Size ▼ and select the font size.

8 Tap the Pen Weight ▼ and select the weight.

9 Tap one or more of the font attributes (☐ changes to ☑).

10 Tap OK.

■ The Format window closes, and the text is formatted according to your selections.

How many fonts and font sizes are included in Pocket Word?

✔ Four fonts are available: Bookdings, Courier New, Frutiger Linotype, and Tahoma. Font sizes can range from 8 to 36 points, and you cannot enter a custom font size.

Can I add more fonts to Pocket Word?

✔ Yes, Pocket Word supports TrueType fonts, so you can add `.ttf` font files to the Windows\Fonts directory on your mobile device. The font should work normally but may default back to Tahoma if it is not compatible.

Can I change line or character spacing?

✔ No, line and character spacing is not an adjustable feature in Pocket Word.

Can I select numbers or letters as my bullet headings?

✔ No, only bullets are included in Pocket Word.

What is the maximum indentation spacing that I can use?

✔ You can set your left or right indentation from 0 to 5.5 inches.

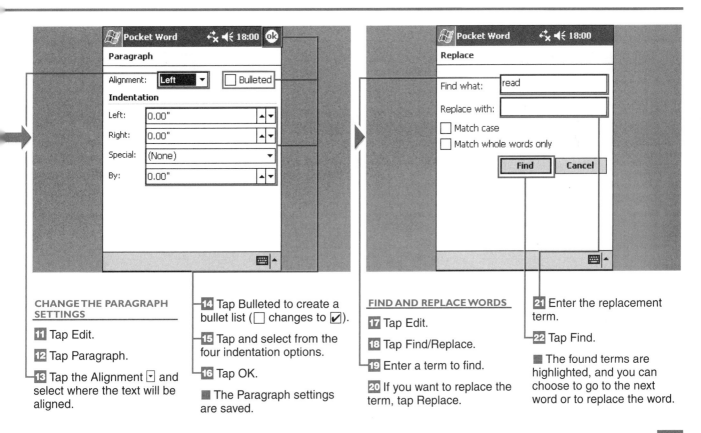

CHANGE THE PARAGRAPH SETTINGS

11 Tap Edit.

12 Tap Paragraph.

13 Tap the Alignment ⯆ and select where the text will be aligned.

14 Tap Bulleted to create a bullet list (☐ changes to ☑).

15 Tap and select from the four indentation options.

16 Tap OK.

■ The Paragraph settings are saved.

FIND AND REPLACE WORDS

17 Tap Edit.

18 Tap Find/Replace.

19 Enter a term to find.

20 If you want to replace the term, tap Replace.

21 Enter the replacement term.

22 Tap Find.

■ The found terms are highlighted, and you can choose to go to the next word or to replace the word.

CHANGE THE VIEW SETTINGS

You can change a few view settings on your device to help you view and work with your documents in the manner that you prefer. You can choose to view the bottom toolbar or close it to view more of the input screen. You can keep the default setting of the document wrapping to fit in the window or have it unwrapped in the full 8.5 x 11–inch paper size.

You can switch between the four input method views of Writing, Drawing, Typing, and Recording. You will notice that text or drawings are grayed out in different views, which means that you must switch back to the view an object or text was created in to edit it. You can also select from five zoom levels ranging from 75 percent to 300 percent.

You can also change the view of a document list by sorting documents according to their name, date, size, or type. You can also select what folder's contents you would like to view.

CHANGE THE VIEW SETTINGS

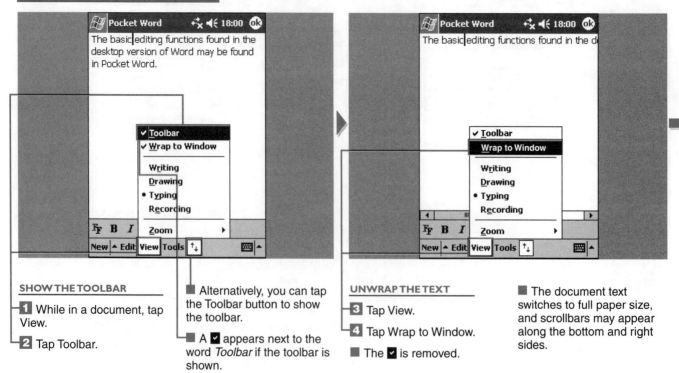

SHOW THE TOOLBAR

1 While in a document, tap View.

2 Tap Toolbar.

■ Alternatively, you can tap the Toolbar button to show the toolbar.

■ A ✔ appears next to the word *Toolbar* if the toolbar is shown.

UNWRAP THE TEXT

3 Tap View.

4 Tap Wrap to Window.

■ The ✔ is removed.

■ The document text switches to full paper size, and scrollbars may appear along the bottom and right sides.

If I uncheck Wrap to Window, how do I navigate in the document?

✔ You can use the scrollbars that appear on the right side and bottom of the display if there is enough text to require them. You can also use your device's direction pad to move through the text, but it will not pan the document as the scrollbars will. The stylus will not pan around the document.

Can I enter a custom zoom level?

✔ No, only the default five zoom levels are supported in Pocket Word.

How can I view documents in Landscape mode?

✔ You cannot view documents in Landscape mode in Windows Mobile 2003. However, support for landscape viewing is included with Windows Mobile 2003 Second Edition or in third-party applications.

How can I view different pages of a multiple-page document?

✔ All documents appear as one long page in Pocket Word; there is no pagination support included. The document will be paginated during the conversion process when synched with your desktop computer.

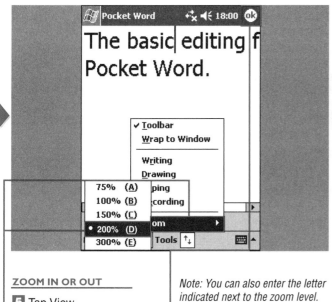

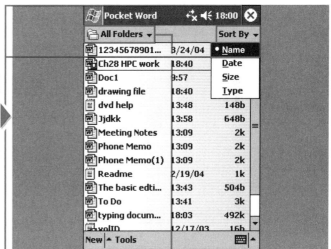

ZOOM IN OR OUT

5 Tap View.

6 Tap Zoom.

7 Tap one of the zoom percentages.

Note: You can also enter the letter indicated next to the zoom level.

■ The text is zoomed to the selected level.

8 Tap OK.

■ The document closes, and the List view appears.

SORT YOUR DOCUMENTS

9 Tap the right ▪.

■ The menu name changes to Sort By, and a menu with four options appears.

10 Tap one of the options to sort the list of documents.

DISPLAY A FOLDER

11 Tap the left ▪ and select a folder to show.

■ Documents within that folder are shown in the list.

SPELL CHECK A DOCUMENT AND COUNT WORDS

There are a couple of additional Pocket Word tools that are helpful for the mobile writer. You can conduct a spell check of your documents and perform a word count. You can even use a custom spell check dictionary on your mobile device.

You can also tap and hold the display in a document and choose to insert the date, or you can choose Tools ⇨ Insert Date. The date will be inserted in short form, such as 08/13/04.

Can I change the format of the insert date function?

✔ Yes, go to Start ⇨ Settings ⇨ System ⇨ Regional Settings and tap the Date tab. Select the Short date block and edit how you want it to appear. This changes the Short date format for all applications, including Pocket Word.

SPELL CHECK A DOCUMENT AND COUNT WORDS

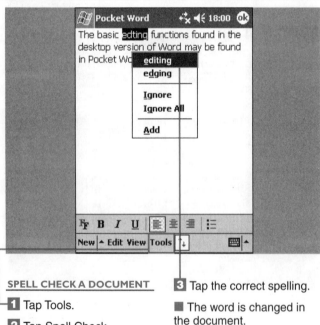

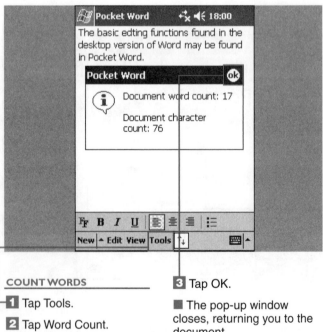

SPELL CHECK A DOCUMENT

1 Tap Tools.

2 Tap Spell Check.

■ Pocket Word finds the first misspelled word after the cursor.

■ A pop-up list appears with alternative spellings.

3 Tap the correct spelling.

■ The word is changed in the document.

Note: You can also choose to ignore the misspelled word or add the word to your device's dictionary for future reference.

COUNT WORDS

1 Tap Tools.

2 Tap Word Count.

■ A window appears showing the document word count and character count.

3 Tap OK.

■ The pop-up window closes, returning you to the document.

SET POCKET WORD SYNCHRONIZATION OPTIONS

You can sync documents back and forth between your desktop and mobile device. However, not all formatting and features of Microsoft Word are supported in Pocket Word, so some things will be removed in the syncing process. Pocket Word does not support passwords, headers and footers, tables,

and other advanced features. Image support is provided but is limited.

When you move or copy documents from your desktop to the My Documents folder of your Pocket PC, a conversion through ActiveSync takes place. You have the option of choosing the conversion settings on your desktop.

I opened a document on my mobile device that had an image on my desktop, but the image has disappeared; what happened?

✔ If you open a Word document in Pocket Word that has not gone through ActiveSync — that is, was stored directly on a storage card — then images are removed during device conversion.

SET POCKET WORD SYNCHRONIZATION OPTIONS

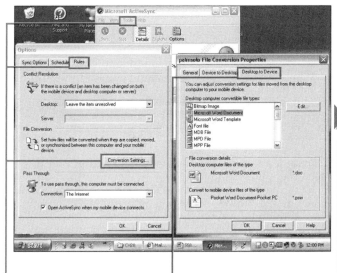

1 On your desktop computer, open ActiveSync.

2 Click Tools.

3 Click Options.

4 Click the Rules tab.

5 Click Conversion Settings.

■ The File Conversion Properties dialog box appears.

6 Click the Desktop to Device tab.

Note: The settings for the Device to Desktop tab are very similar.

7 Click Microsoft Word Document.

8 Click Edit.

■ The Edit Conversion Settings dialog box appears.

9 Click the Type ▼ and select the format that you want to convert into.

10 Click OK.

11 Click OK in the Properties dialog box.

12 Click OK in the Options dialog box.

■ The conversion settings are saved and used during the next ActiveSync.

CREATE A NEW TASK

With the Tasks program, you can create a task list or to-do list of things that you need to accomplish or track. You can then update and track your tasks while on the go.

When creating a new task for your task list, select a descriptive subject that you will understand later, such as "clean the garage" or "purchase

concert tickets." The subject title appears in your task list.

You can specify what date the task is to start and whether it is to be completed by a specific date. The start and end date can appear on your task list to remind you of upcoming deadlines. You can also set a reminder alarm to alert you to an upcoming deadline.

Tasks enables you to specify the priority of a task. Assigning a priority to your task can help you organize your task list.

You can also add text notes to a task to provide you with additional task details as well as voice notes.

CREATE A NEW TASK

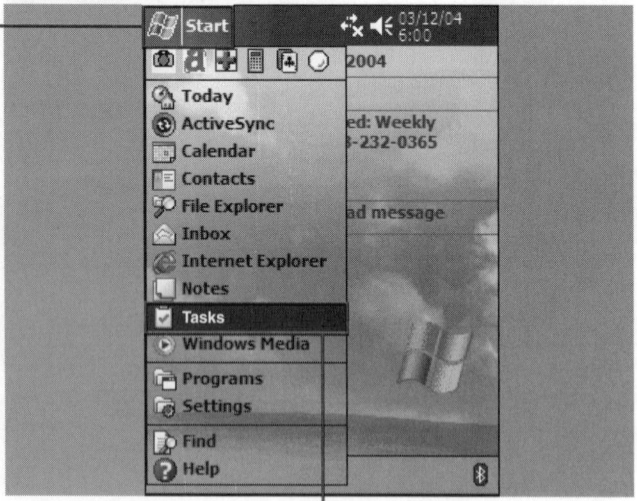

1 Tap Start.

2 Tap Tasks.

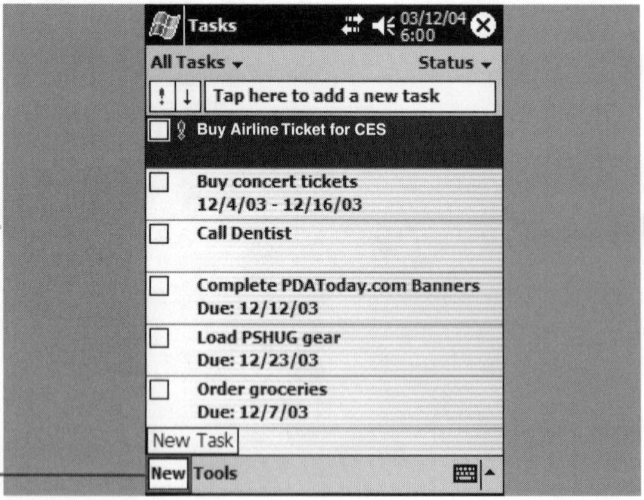

■ The Tasks list appears.

3 Tap New.

■ The new task window appears.

How do I edit a task?

✔ Tap the task that you want to edit and then tap Edit to display the task's properties. Modify the task's properties as needed and tap OK.

Is there a way to display the start and due dates on the task list?

✔ Yes. From the task list, tap Tools and then tap Options. You can select to show the start and due dates for your task list.

Why is the Reminder option gray in my task, and I am unable to set it?

✔ The reminder is disabled and therefore gray because the reminder has not been set. To set a reminder, you need to first assign a start date, and then you can tap Reminder to set a reminder alarm.

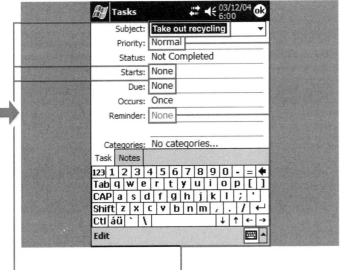

4 Enter a subject for the new task.

5 Tap Starts to set a starting date of your task.

6 Tap Due to set a due date for your task.

Note: If you place no start or due date, these are set to None.

7 Tap Priority to change your task's priority.

Note: Your choices are High, Normal, and Low.

8 Tap Reminder to turn on the reminder alarm.

■ After you turn on the reminder, you can set a reminder date.

9 Tap the Notes tab.

10 Enter any notes for your task.

11 Tap OK to save the new task.

■ The task appears in the task list.

Note: You can find more information on adding text and voice notes in Chapter 17.

SET A TASK TO REOCCUR

With the Tasks program, you can define whether a task occurs only once or on a regular schedule. This can be helpful if you want a task to reoccur on a regular pattern such as every Thursday.

You can also specify a recurrence pattern. A recurrence pattern

enables you to automate when a task that does not follow one of the preset patterns appears on your list.

The Occurs Pattern Wizard is available to help you create your own custom occurrence patterns. You can specify when the pattern is to start and end and the duration of

the pattern. You can set whether the pattern is daily, weekly, monthly, or yearly and what day of the week the pattern occurs.

You can also set a specific time for the pattern to end after a set number of occurrences. This can be useful for a task that you need to complete only a set number of times.

SET A TASK TO REOCCUR

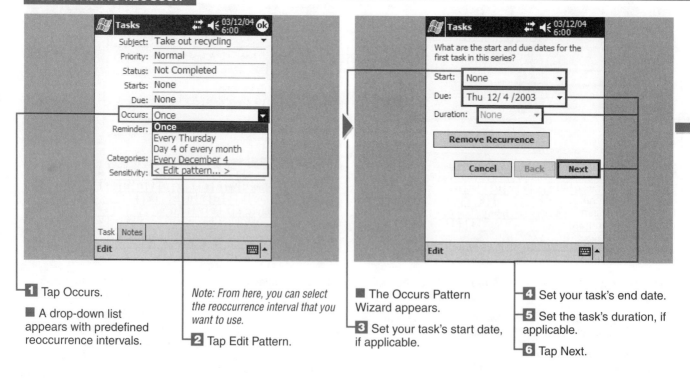

1 Tap Occurs.

■ A drop-down list appears with predefined reoccurrence intervals.

Note: From here, you can select the reoccurrence interval that you want to use.

2 Tap Edit Pattern.

■ The Occurs Pattern Wizard appears.

3 Set your task's start date, if applicable.

4 Set your task's end date.

5 Set the task's duration, if applicable.

6 Tap Next.

MASTER IT

How do I remove a custom occurrence from a task?

✔ Start the Occurs Pattern Wizard for the task from which you want to remove the custom pattern. Tap Remove Recurrence when the wizard starts.

Can I set a reminder for a reoccurring task?

✔ Yes, you can set a reminder just as you would for a one-time task. To do so, set the reminder for the first date of the task when you want it. Then the reminder will reset itself for subsequent occurrences. See the section "Create a New Task" for more information.

How do I add a note to a reoccurring task?

✔ You add a note to a reoccurring task the same way that you would for a one-time task; see the section "Create a New Task."

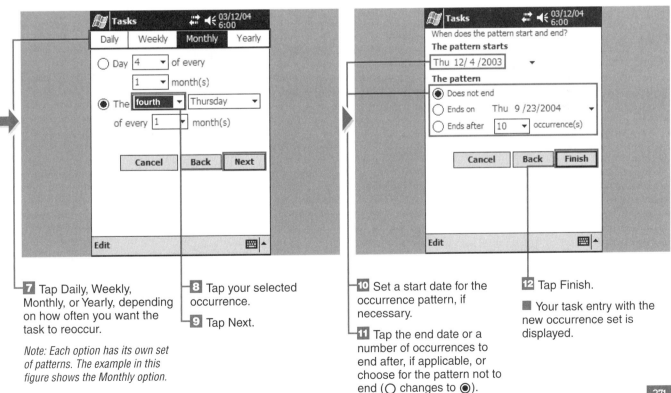

7 Tap Daily, Weekly, Monthly, or Yearly, depending on how often you want the task to reoccur.

Note: Each option has its own set of patterns. The example in this figure shows the Monthly option.

8 Tap your selected occurrence.

9 Tap Next.

10 Set a start date for the occurrence pattern, if necessary.

11 Tap the end date or a number of occurrences to end after, if applicable, or choose for the pattern not to end (○ changes to ⊙).

12 Tap Finish.

■ Your task entry with the new occurrence set is displayed.

MANAGE A TASK LIST

You can manage a task list by sorting the list a number of different ways. You can show your tasks defined by category, active tasks, all tasks, and completed tasks. You can further sort your task list by priority, subject, start date, or due date.

When you complete a task, you can place a check in the check box next to the task to mark it as complete. You can also delete a task when you no longer need it on your list. Remember, however, that there is no way to recover a deleted task. Make sure that you do not delete a

task if you think that you may need information from it later. On the other hand, you also do not want to keep too many tasks in your task list that you have already completed, giving you too much to scroll through.

MANAGE A TASK LIST

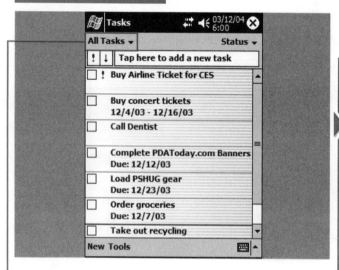

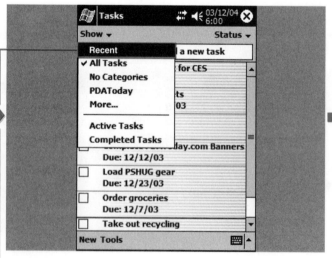

SHOW TASKS

1 Tap All Tasks.

■ A drop-down menu labeled Show appears.

2 Tap the option for how you want your tasks to be displayed.

■ Your task list is shown according to your selection.

Is there a quick way to tell if a task is past due?

✔ Yes, your task appears red in the task list when it becomes past due.

I use Tasks in Outlook on my PC; can I synchronize that list with my mobile device and vice versa?

✔ Yes. Tasks entered in Outlook on your PC or on your device get copied to one another during synchronization with ActiveSync. You can find more information on ActiveSync and synchronization in Chapter 12.

Can I make the task list text appear larger?

✔ Yes. You can do so by selecting Use Large Font on the Options screen. This option is covered later in this chapter in the section "Set Task Options."

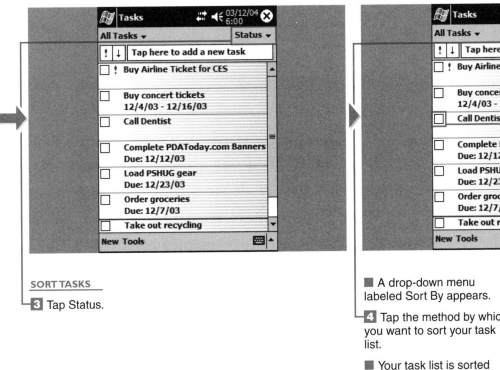

SORT TASKS

3 Tap Status.

■ A drop-down menu labeled Sort By appears.

4 Tap the method by which you want to sort your task list.

■ Your task list is sorted according to your selection.

MARK A TASK AS COMPLETED

5 Tap the box next to a task that you have completed.

■ A check appears in the box to indicate that the task is completed (☐ changes to ☑).

273

CREATE A CUSTOM CATEGORY

You can organize your tasks by assigning them to any of the existing categories. The built-in categories are Business, Holiday, and Personal. Additionally, you can create custom categories. Creating custom categories can help you keep your tasks organized in far greater detail.

After you create a custom category in Tasks, you will be able to use this category in Calendar and Contacts, and vice versa. The categories are also synchronized to the desktop.

Can I delete custom or existing categories?

✔ Yes. You can delete any category listed. Tap the category that you want to delete and then tap Delete. This can be useful for removing unused categories.

CREATE A CUSTOM CATEGORY

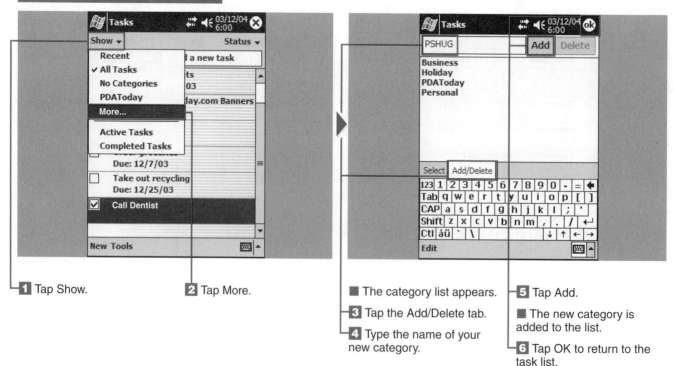

1 Tap Show.

2 Tap More.

■ The category list appears.

3 Tap the Add/Delete tab.

4 Type the name of your new category.

5 Tap Add.

■ The new category is added to the list.

6 Tap OK to return to the task list.

SET TASK OPTIONS

You can turn on or off several options in the task list.

You can set Tasks to always use reminders for new items. When this option is turned off, you will not be able to add a reminder to your tasks.

You can set Tasks to show a start and due date for tasks on your task list. Setting this option to off helps to display more of your list on the screen at one time.

You can set Tasks to display the task list using large fonts. This can be helpful if you are having trouble reading the list.

Is there a way to change the font colors for my task list?

✔ Your task list fonts are controlled by the Windows Mobile system and cannot be changed here. There are third-party tools that can alter system font colors.

SET TASK OPTIONS

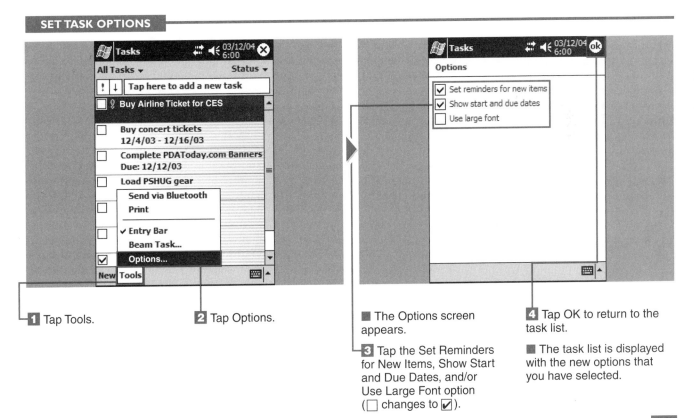

1 Tap Tools.

2 Tap Options.

■ The Options screen appears.

3 Tap the Set Reminders for New Items, Show Start and Due Dates, and/or Use Large Font option (□ changes to ✓).

4 Tap OK to return to the task list.

■ The task list is displayed with the new options that you have selected.

SEND A TASK

I n Tasks, you can send a task to another Windows Mobile device via the built-in infrared port or, if your device is equipped with Bluetooth, via the Bluetooth radio. Sharing tasks with another Windows Mobile device is a quick and easy way to send a task to a colleague.

When sending a task to another device via Bluetooth, you need to

make sure that the other device is able to receive a Bluetooth signal. Sometimes this setting is called *Discoverable mode.* Additionally, you should ensure that your Bluetooth radio is turned on. You can find more information about the Bluetooth radio and Bluetooth Manager in Chapter 8.

When sending a task to another device via infrared, you need to

ensure that the device to which you are sending the appointment has the Beam utility set to receive all incoming beams. You can find more information about receiving infrared beams in Chapter 9.

SEND A TASK

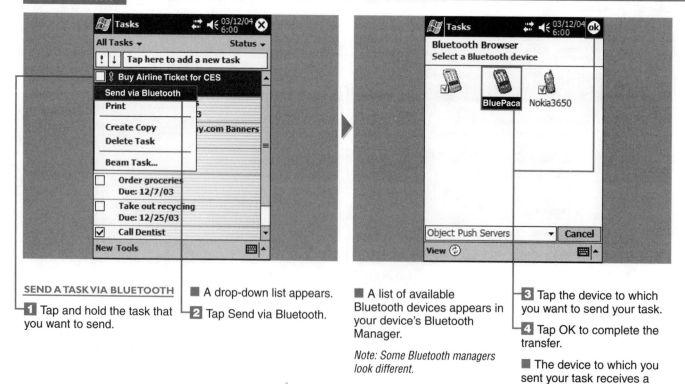

SEND A TASK VIA BLUETOOTH

1 Tap and hold the task that you want to send.

■ A drop-down list appears.

2 Tap Send via Bluetooth.

■ A list of available Bluetooth devices appears in your device's Bluetooth Manager.

Note: Some Bluetooth managers look different.

3 Tap the device to which you want to send your task.

4 Tap OK to complete the transfer.

■ The device to which you sent your task receives a notification dialog box asking if it wants to save your task to its task list.

Can I send a task via Bluetooth when the task is open?

✔ No, the Send via Bluetooth option appears only when the task list is open.

Can I send more than one task at a time?

✔ Yes. You can select as many tasks from your task list as you want to send to the other device before tapping Send via Bluetooth.

Can I send a task using just the stylus?

✔ Yes. Find the task that you want to send on your task list and then tap and hold the item with your stylus. Select the method with which you want to send your task.

How come when I try to send a task to the office next to me via Bluetooth, it only connects intermittently?

✔ Most Bluetooth radio-enabled devices beam information only about 10 meters (about 30 feet).

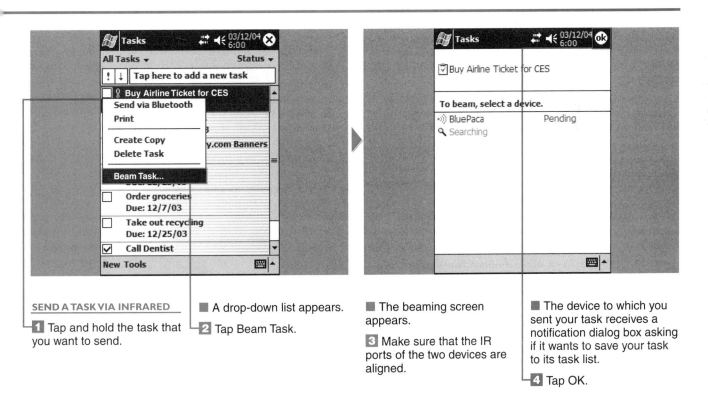

SEND A TASK VIA INFRARED

1 Tap and hold the task that you want to send.

■ A drop-down list appears.

2 Tap Beam Task.

■ The beaming screen appears.

3 Make sure that the IR ports of the two devices are aligned.

■ The device to which you sent your task receives a notification dialog box asking if it wants to save your task to its task list.

4 Tap OK.

CONNECT TO TERMINAL SERVICES

Using the Terminal Services Client on your Windows Mobile 2003 device, you can log on to a desktop computer and use all the applications, files, and such on that computer. The desktop computer needs to run Terminal Services or Remote Desktop to allow a connection.

Terminal Services enables you to run applications that cannot be used on your mobile device. It is also helpful when you are traveling because you can gain access to all the files on your work computer.

You can also use the Terminal Services client to access Terminal servers as clients and administer Windows 2000 or 2003 Exchange servers.

When would I want to limit the size of the desktop to fit the mobile device?

✔ When you run applications on your remote desktop that have been sized for Windows Mobile devices. If you run an application that is not formatted for the display, you will not be able to navigate and may become frustrated with the results.

CONNECT TO TERMINAL SERVICES

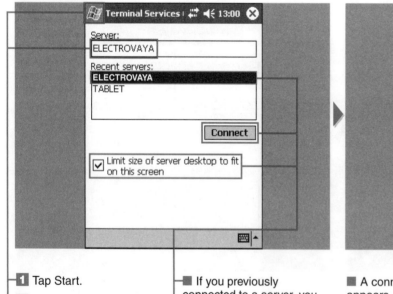

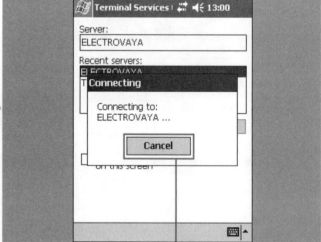

1 Tap Start.

2 Tap Programs.

3 Tap Terminal Services Client.

4 Enter the name or IP address of the remote server or computer to which you will be connecting.

■ If you previously connected to a server, you can tap the name from the Recent Servers list.

5 Tap the check box to fit the desktop to your device (☐ changes to ☑).

6 Tap Connect.

■ A connection status box appears.

■ The status box disappears when the connection is established.

■ You can tap Cancel to stop the connection.

DISCONNECT A SESSION

After connecting with Terminal Services, you will find that there are no menus on your device. You can end a session only by performing a couple of actions on your remote desktop via the Terminal Services client on your device.

You can disconnect from your desktop without ending a session, or you can disconnect and end a session. Both options are accessed via your remote desktop's Start menu. There is no option on the mobile device's Start menu to disconnect a session.

I disconnected from a session, but the next time I logged in, the session was reconnected. What happened?

✔ Check with your network administrator to see if he or she has configured Terminal Services to reconnect to disconnected sessions. If so, you will always be reconnected to them the next time that you log in.

DISCONNECT A SESSION

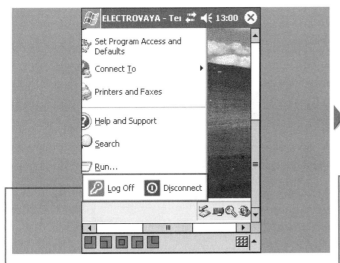

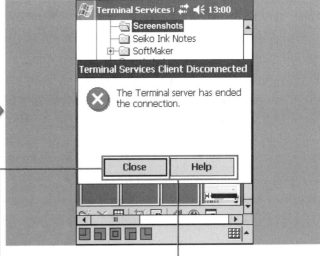

1 Tap Start on your remote desktop via the Terminal Services Client window.

2 Tap Log Off or Disconnect.

Note: Log Off disconnects and ends your session. Disconnect disconnects without ending the session.

Note: You may have to tap Shutdown and then Disconnect or Log Off, depending on your desktop operating system.

■ A dialog box appears, informing you that the Terminal Services Client has disconnected.

3 Tap Close to close the dialog box and go back to using your mobile device.

■ You can tap Help to access the Help file.

Note: You can find more information about Help files in Chapter 3.

NAVIGATE WITHIN THE TERMINAL SERVICES CLIENT

Viewing a large desktop display on a 320 x 240 mobile device display can be challenging. You can use a couple of navigational tools to move around the larger remote display.

The Terminal Services Client has five navigational buttons along the bottom of the display that enable you to quickly jump to parts of the remote display. These buttons are

the fastest way to move around the display, but are not present if you selected to fit the remote desktop into the mobile device's display size.

There are scrollbars along the right side and bottom of the Terminal Services window. You can also find scrollbars on the desktop in many applications and must be careful to move along the scrollbar that you intended to if you use this navigation technique.

If you selected to have the remote desktop fit to the mobile device screen, there will be no means of navigating around the display. To undo this selection, uncheck Limit Size of Server Desktop to Fit on This Screen when you first connect to Terminal Services. See "Connect to Terminal Services" for more information.

NAVIGATE WITHIN THE TERMINAL SERVICES CLIENT

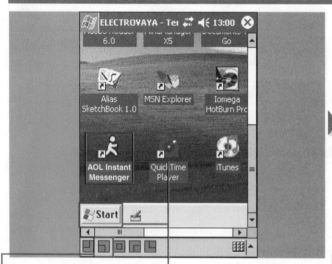

WITH THE NAVIGATIONAL BUTTONS

1 Tap any of the five navigational buttons to quickly jump to that sector of the remote display.

■ The window on your mobile device changes to the location indicated by the button.

■ You can double-tap an application or tap the Start menu to operate the remote desktop.

2 Tap more navigational buttons to move around the display.

■ Different sectors of the desktop display appear on your mobile device.

MASTER IT

Can I add more navigational sectors to the five current buttons?

✔ No, the five buttons cover the display, and you cannot create more buttons for more specific locations.

Is there anything that I can do to make the appearance better and navigation easier on my mobile device?

✔ Yes, you can maximize programs on the desktop computer to get the best view on your mobile device.

Can I use my stylus or mobile device hardware navigational pad to navigate around the remote desktop?

✔ Yes and no. You can control your desktop using double-taps on your display that simulate double-clicks of your mouse with your desktop. However, the hardware navigational pad does not function in Terminal Services.

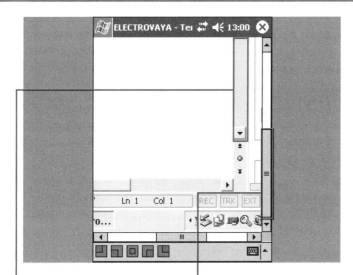

WITHIN AN APPLICATION

■1 Use your stylus to move the scrollbar.

Note: Notice the separate scrollbars in the application and in the mobile device's Terminal Services Client window.

■2 Use your stylus to move the scrollbar in the Terminal Services Client window.

■ The display moves according to the amount of scrolling that you perform.

WITHOUT THE NAVIGATIONAL BUTTONS

Note: When you have the check box for fitting to your mobile device selected, notice that there are no navigational buttons.

■1 Double-tap an application to launch it on your remote desktop.

■ You can tap Start to access programs not shown on the fitted display.

IMPROVE TERMINAL SERVICES CLIENT PERFORMANCE

Operating a remote desktop from a much smaller window presents some readability and usability challenges, even with a high-speed data connection. You can perform a couple of steps to improve the performance of the Terminal Services Client. These steps are all performed on the desktop that you will be connecting with from your mobile device.

In order to improve the display performance, you can go into your Display settings via the Control Panel and clear the transition effects for menus and ToolTips. This decreases the time that it takes for the screen to be refreshed.

If you plan to use the Terminal Services Client to browse via your desktop's more powerful version of Internet Explorer, you can make a change to the Advanced options that also decreases the time that it takes for Web pages to be refreshed on your desktop computer.

IMPROVE TERMINAL SERVICES CLIENT PERFORMANCE

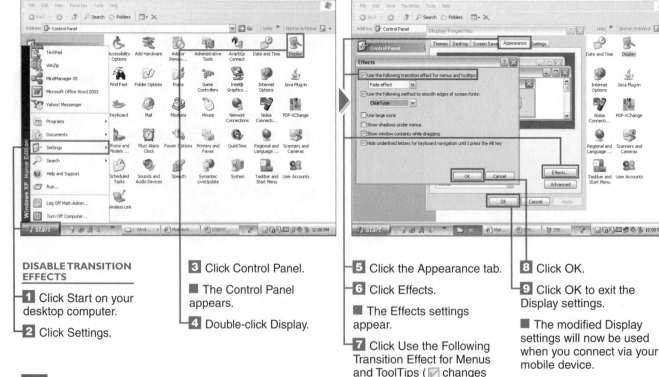

DISABLE TRANSITION EFFECTS

1 Click Start on your desktop computer.

2 Click Settings.

3 Click Control Panel.

■ The Control Panel appears.

4 Double-click Display.

5 Click the Appearance tab.

6 Click Effects.

■ The Effects settings appear.

7 Click Use the Following Transition Effect for Menus and ToolTips (☑ changes to ☐).

8 Click OK.

9 Click OK to exit the Display settings.

■ The modified Display settings will now be used when you connect via your mobile device.

Are there other steps that I can take to improve the performance of the Terminal Services Client?

✔ Yes. You can exit applications on your device that you are no longer actively using to ensure that adequate memory is available. Also, you can change the settings for the display to be smaller on your desktop, such as 640 x 480, so that you can more easily view the applications (because they would be larger). Another method is to reduce the number of colors on your screen to 256 so that it takes less time to update. You can also set up your system to allow single clicks in Windows XP to make navigation easier; to do so, open My Computer and click Tools ➪ Folder Options and then change Click Items as Follows to Single Click. Finally, you can perform all of these enhancements as a new user so that they do not affect your everyday user account. The downside is that you need to navigate to your My Documents folder for your everyday account.

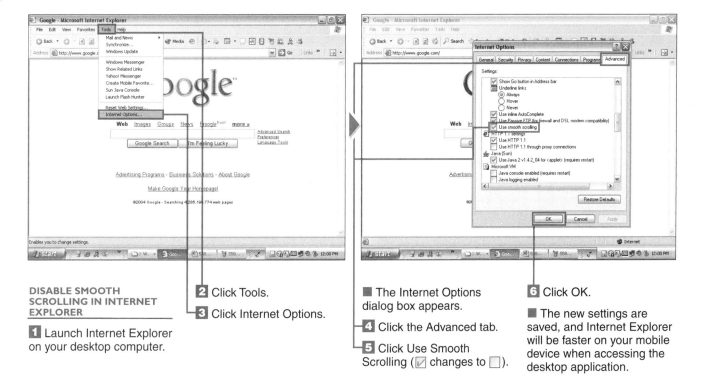

DISABLE SMOOTH SCROLLING IN INTERNET EXPLORER

1 Launch Internet Explorer on your desktop computer.

2 Click Tools.

3 Click Internet Options.

■ The Internet Options dialog box appears.

4 Click the Advanced tab.

5 Click Use Smooth Scrolling (☑ changes to ☐).

6 Click OK.

■ The new settings are saved, and Internet Explorer will be faster on your mobile device when accessing the desktop application.

TURN PHONE FUNCTIONALITY ON AND OFF

You can turn phone functionality on and off and still use the Pocket PC features of your device. Also, you can leave the phone on when you turn off the Pocket PC device and still receive calls. You have to turn the phone off to stop receiving calls.

When the phone is on, you can quickly switch back to the phone features from any Pocket PC application by pressing the Talk hardware button on your device.

Is there any other way to turn on my phone, instead of tapping the signal strength indicator?

✔ Yes, if you tap Start ⇨ Settings and then the Personal tab, you will see a Phone icon. Tapping this icon launches a notification asking if you want to turn wireless on.

TURN PHONE FUNCTIONALITY ON AND OFF

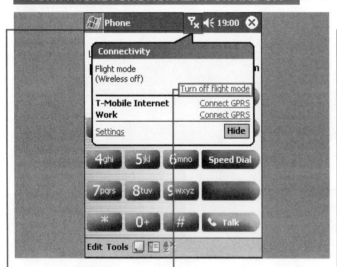

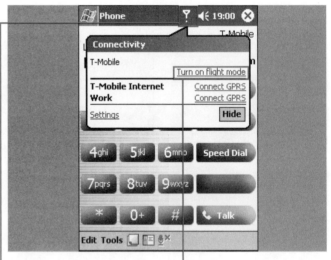

TURN YOUR PHONE ON

1 Press the Talk hardware button to start the Phone application.

Note: The Talk button is usually the green-colored button on the device.

2 Tap the signal strength indicator.

Note: If the phone is off, the indicator shows an antenna with an X to the right of it.

3 Tap Turn Off Flight Mode.

■ The X in the indicator changes to bars numbering from 1 to 4 for the signal strength.

TURN YOUR PHONE OFF

1 Tap the signal strength indicator.

■ The Connectivity notification pops up with the name of your service provider on the left.

2 Tap Turn On Flight Mode.

■ The bars indicating the signal strength change to an X in the indicator, and the Connectivity notification shows that wireless is off.

SET UP YOUR SPEED DIAL LIST

You can set up a list of frequently called numbers on your device for speed dial. Each contact must be in your Contacts database.

You can edit the name that appears in your speed dial list, and it will still be associated with the contact that you initially set it up with. You can also specify what speed dial location the contact is assigned to, and the list does not have to be in sequential order.

Is there a limit to the number of speed dial numbers that I can set up?

✔ Yes, you can set up a maximum of 99 speed dial numbers going from 1 to 99.

Can I move an entry up or down my speed dial list?

✔ Yes, but if the spot that you move the contact to is taken, you will be prompted to overwrite the existing contact.

SET UP YOUR SPEED DIAL LIST

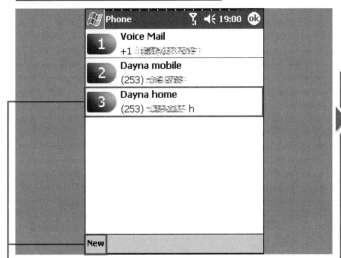

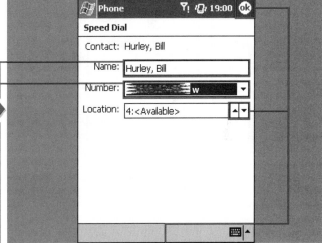

1 Press the Talk hardware button to start the Phone application.

2 Tap Speed Dial.

3 Tap New to create a new entry.

■ You can tap and hold an existing speed dial entry to edit or delete the contact.

■ Your Contacts list appears.

4 Select a contact from the list.

Note: You can also tap and hold a contact name in Contacts and select Add to Speed Dial.

5 Enter a display name for your speed dial list.

6 If there is more than one number associated with the contact, tap ▾ to select the number that you want to use.

7 Tap ▴ or ▾ to select a location to assign to your contact.

8 Tap OK.

■ The contact appears in your speed dial list.

ANSWER OR IGNORE A CALL

I f the wireless functionality is turned on, you can receive phone calls directly to your mobile device. If the device is turned off but the radio is on, you can still receive phone calls.

When you receive a call, the signal indicator icon changes to a right-leaning phone, and a notification

appears with the caller ID information (if you set this up with your provider) and two actions that you can take — Answer or Ignore.

If you answer the call, simply use your headset or device directly to talk with the caller. If you choose to ignore the call, the ringing or vibrating stops, and the call is

forwarded to your voice mail, if that is available from your provider. You will also receive a notification that a call was missed.

You can also set up to have your calls answered automatically, which is discussed in the section "Change Your Phone Settings."

ANSWER OR IGNORE A CALL

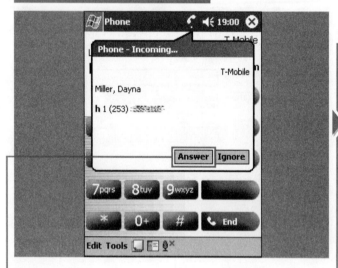

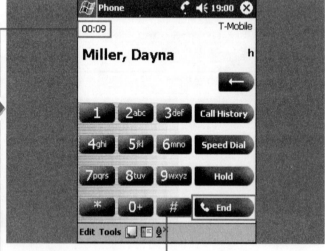

ANSWER A CALL

Note: When someone calls your device, the signal indicator changes to a phone, and a notification appears.

1 Tap Answer.

Note: You can also press the Talk hardware button to answer the phone or have your device answer automatically after a set number of rings. This option is discussed in the section "Change Your Phone Settings."

■ The notification disappears.

■ The green Talk button changes to a red End button, and the signal indicator switches from a phone icon to a radio signal icon.

■ A call timer also appears.

2 Use your headset or device to talk.

3 Tap End to end the call.

■ The red End button changes back to a green Talk button.

Can I answer or ignore a second call that may come in?

✔ Yes, the notification box appears, and you can place your first call on hold while you answer the new call. Details on call management are covered in the section "Manage a Call in Progress."

What is the difference between just ignoring a call and tapping the Ignore button?

✔ If you tap Ignore, the ringing or vibrating stops. If you just physically ignore the call, the ringing or vibrating continues for a few rings.

Will my caller know that I tapped the Ignore button?

✔ No, the caller will eventually receive your voice mail message and probably assume that your phone was off or you were on another call.

Can I clear my missed calls list?

✔ Yes, you can tap and hold the Tools menu and then select Delete All Calls.

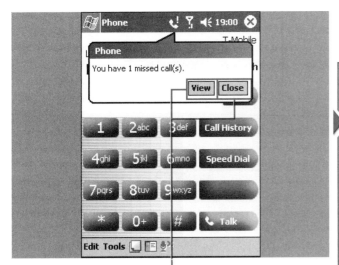

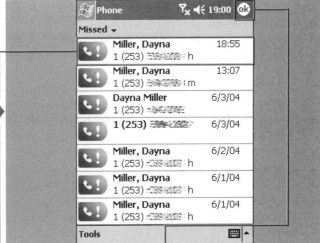

IGNORE A CALL

■1 When the incoming call notification appears, tap Ignore.

■ The signal indicator changes to a phone with an exclamation point, and a missed call notification appears.

■2 Tap View if you want to see the missed call details.

■ You can tap Close to close the notification.

■ A list of the recently missed calls appears.

■3 Tap a contact name.

■ The time, date, and duration of the call is shown in a pop-up window.

Note: The duration for missed calls is shown as 00:00.

Note: You can tap and hold a name to delete the missed call information, call the contact back, or send him or her an SMS message.

■4 Tap OK.

■ The missed Call History window closes, and the main phone entry display appears.

PLACE A CALL

In addition to receiving calls, you can place an outgoing call several different ways. You can call using the keypad, using speed dial, from Call History, and from your Contacts list.

Microsoft has designed the buttons on the Phone Edition devices to be large enough so that you can comfortably tap on a phone number with your finger. You can also use your stylus on the buttons to dial.

With Windows Mobile 2003 Second Edition, you can dial phone numbers from the Today screen using Transcriber or an external keyboard.

If you miss a call, a notification bubble appears, and you can place a call by tapping Call in the notification.

PLACE A CALL

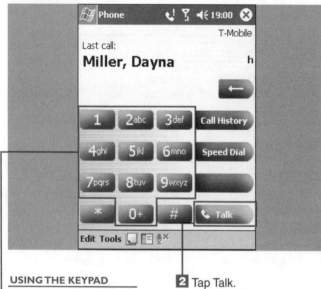

USING THE KEYPAD

1 Tap the number to be dialed.

■ The phone number appears on the entry line as you tap numbers.

2 Tap Talk.

Note: Alternatively, you can press the Talk hardware button.

■ The call is initiated.

USING SPEED DIAL

1 Tap and hold the number corresponding to the contact that you want to call in your Speed Dial list.

Note: See the section "Set Up Your Speed Dial List" for more information.

■ The keypad color scheme may change as the number is dialed.

What can I do if I enter an incorrect digit?

✔ You can tap the Backspace button, and after each tap the right-most digit will disappear. You can then enter the correct digit on the number entry line. You can also tap and hold the Backspace button to clear the entire entry line.

Can the Edit menu assist me when I am placing a call?

✔ Yes, if you copy a phone number from another application and place it into the Clipboard, you can paste the number into the entry line. You can also tap Edit ⇨ Clear to clear the entire number entry line with one command.

Can I make a call using voice recognition?

✔ There is no voice calling functionality included in the operating system. However, Microsoft developed and sells Voice Command software that enables you to call contacts and dial numbers using voice recognition. There are other third-party solutions for voice dialing as well, such as the Fonix products.

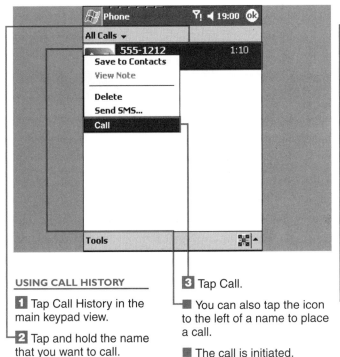

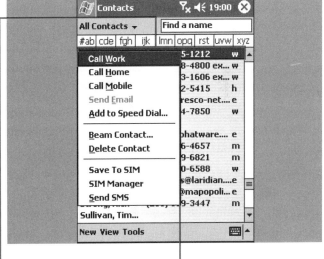

USING CALL HISTORY

1 Tap Call History in the main keypad view.

2 Tap and hold the name that you want to call.

3 Tap Call.

■ You can also tap the icon to the left of a name to place a call.

■ The call is initiated.

USING YOUR CONTACT LIST

1 While in the Contacts application, tap and hold a name.

Note: See Chapter 14 for more information about using Contacts.

2 Tap the number that you want to dial.

■ The call dialog box opens, and your call is placed if a cellular signal can be achieved.

MANAGE A CALL IN PROGRESS

A dvanced call-management features are included in the Windows Mobile operating system for the Pocket PC Phone Edition. You can mute a caller, place a call on hold, quickly switch between callers, and manage a conference call with a few quick taps on your display.

The Mute button is available only when a call is in progress. When you mute a call, a notification will appear in the top-right corner to let you know the mute status. When you can place a call on hold, the status will again appear at the top of the window.

Another powerful feature is the ability to quickly set up a three-way conference call. When you are

placing a conference call, the Conference and Swap buttons become available. You can use these to have all three callers talk, or you can choose to swap the two callers and speak to each individually. However, you will be billed for the minutes used for each caller on a three-way call.

MANAGE A CALL IN PROGRESS

MUTE A CALL

1 While you are on a call, tap the Mute button.

■ A small mute symbol appears here.

PLACE A CALL ON HOLD

1 While you are on a call, tap Hold.

■ Hold changes to Resume, and (On Hold) appears in the status window.

2 Tap Resume to continue the call.

■ Resume changes back to Hold.

Can I put a conference call or other call on speaker phone?

✔ Yes, simply press and hold the Talk hardware button, and a speaker phone notification will pop up stating that the speaker phone is on.

Can I have more than two other people on the line at the same time?

✔ No, the operating system supports only three-way conferencing calling and does not support adding more calls.

When I am in a conference call, can I put both of the callers on hold?

✔ Yes, to place both of the callers on hold, simply tap the Hold button. You can tap the Resume button to continue the call with all three participants.

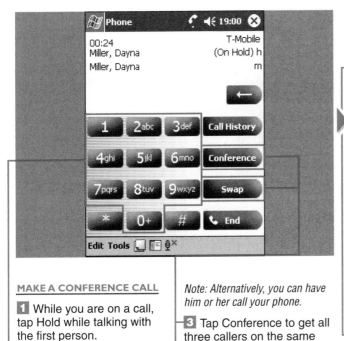

MAKE A CONFERENCE CALL

1 While you are on a call, tap Hold while talking with the first person.

2 Dial the second person.

Note: Alternatively, you can have him or her call your phone.

3 Tap Conference to get all three callers on the same line.

■ You can tap Swap to switch the hold from one person to the other.

■ The Conference button changes back into Speed Dial.

■ The names and numbers of the other two people are replaced by the word Conference.

4 Tap End to end the conference call.

■ The call ends, and the keypad view appears.

MANAGE YOUR CALL HISTORY

Y ou can view the time and duration of missed, outgoing, and incoming calls using your Call History. You can view all the calls in your history or filter the list by missed, outgoing, or incoming calls or by caller.

Any notes that you have attached to a call show up as a pencil and paper icon in the Call History list. You can tap and hold a call to access the menu to view the note.

You can individually delete a call, or you can delete all the calls in the list in the view that you have filtered on your device. If you want

to hold on to some calls but do not want to keep every call, you can use the Call Timers display to set how far back calls will be deleted to.

The Call Timers display shows the duration and number of calls that have been made on your device. You can reset the Recent Calls numbers and track just a set period of time.

MANAGE YOUR CALL HISTORY

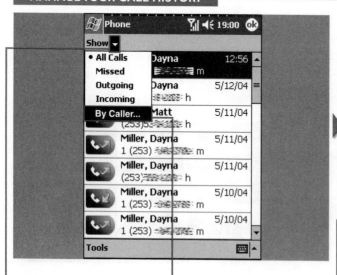

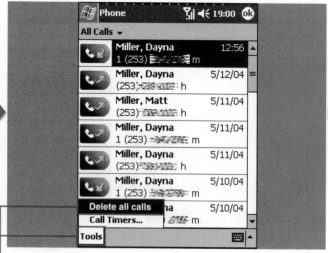

FILTER CALL HISTORY

1 From the main keypad display, tap Call History.

■ Your Call History, showing all calls, appears.

2 Tap ▾.

■ The category name changes to Show.

3 Tap how you want the calls filtered.

■ Just the calls in the category that you selected appear in the list.

DELETE ALL CALLS

4 Tap Tools.

5 Tap Delete All Calls.

■ A confirmation dialog box appears, asking if you want to delete all the calls permanently.

6 Tap Yes.

■ All the calls are deleted, and a blank Call History page appears.

If I filter my Call History by contact name, how will I know what type of calls the history contains?

✔ The icons on the left side of the display indicate if the call was missed, outgoing, or incoming.

Can I export my call history for future reference?

✔ No, however, you can take screen shots, with IA Screenshot or Developer One Screensnap, for example, of the Call History pages and save those for later viewing.

What order are calls listed in Call History, and can I reverse the order?

✔ The Call History shows the newest calls at the top, down to the oldest calls at the bottom. You cannot reverse the order of the calls in the history.

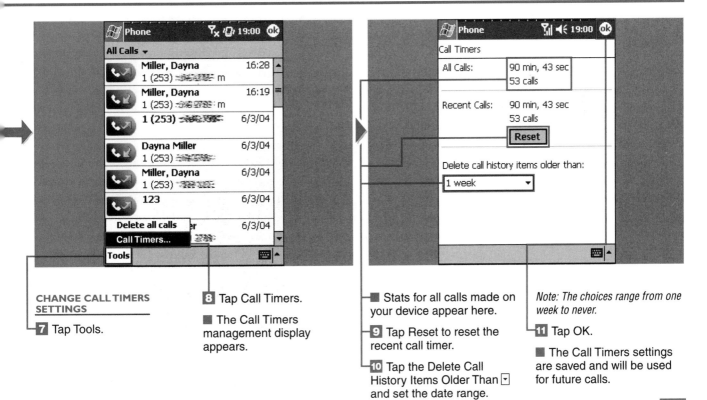

CHANGE CALL TIMERS SETTINGS

7 Tap Tools.

8 Tap Call Timers.

■ The Call Timers management display appears.

■ Stats for all calls made on your device appear here.

9 Tap Reset to reset the recent call timer.

10 Tap the Delete Call History Items Older Than ▾ and set the date range.

Note: The choices range from one week to never.

11 Tap OK.

■ The Call Timers settings are saved and will be used for future calls.

SEND AN SMS MESSAGE

Y ou can send SMS (Short Message Service) messages from your GSM/GPRS-enabled Phone Edition device to others with the ability to receive SMS messages. SMS messages are short text messages with a 160-character limit. SMS is similar to paging a person but is more interactive and can be used for instant messaging.

SMS messages are sent to a cell phone number and not an e-mail address, so they do not go through the Internet but through the wireless provider's network.

What happens when I receive SMS messages on my device?

✔ When an SMS message is delivered to your device, a notification appears with the options of replying to the message, calling the person who sent the message, deleting the message, or closing the message. The body of the message appears in the notification as well.

Can I send an SMS message to multiple recipients at one time?

✔ Yes, just separate the addresses with a semicolon.

SEND AN SMS MESSAGE

1 Tap Tools.

2 Tap Send SMS.

■ The Inbox is launched, and a new message appears.

Note: You can also send SMS messages by starting from the Inbox application.

3 Enter an SMS address.

4 Enter a subject.

5 Enter the message body.

■ A running character count appears to ensure that you do not exceed the 160-character limit.

6 Tap Send.

■ The message is sent, if you are connected, or placed in the Outbox, to be sent when you reconnect.

TAKE NOTES DURING A CALL

You can take handwritten or text notes on your device while talking with someone on the phone. The notes that you take during the call are attached to that call. When you view the call in your Call History, you can also view the attached note. Notes are also saved in the Notes application, filed under the Calls folder.

If I delete all the calls in my Call History, will my notes be deleted too?

✔ No, your notes can still be found in the Calls folder of the Notes application. However, they will no longer be attached to a specific call. The note automatically includes the caller, phone number, and date and time of the call.

Can I make multiple note files in one call?

✔ Yes, you just need to tap New from the Notes page.

TAKE NOTES DURING A CALL

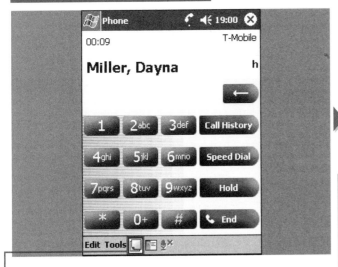

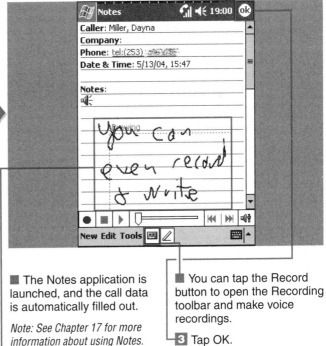

1 Tap the Create New Note button while on a call.

■ The Notes application is launched, and the call data is automatically filled out.

Note: See Chapter 17 for more information about using Notes.

2 Enter your note using your preferred text-entry method.

■ You can tap the Record button to open the Recording toolbar and make voice recordings.

3 Tap OK.

■ The note is saved and associated with the call in Call History.

CHANGE YOUR PHONE SETTINGS

Y ou can select from several settings for your Phone Edition device to customize the phone features according to your preferences.

You can select the ringer type and tone, how the keypad taps sound, security features, various phone services, network settings, broadcast channels, and automatic pickup.

You can use custom ring tones to truly make your device unique. You can assign a PIN number to your phone to add additional security and prevent unauthorized use. You can also view available networks in case your network is unavailable or you travel and need access to multiple networks.

The automatic pickup feature tells your phone to pick up after a set amount of rings, from 1 to 10. You

may also see the option to turn off all buttons except for the On/Off button; if you bump your Phone Edition device and initiate calls by accident, you may want to enable this feature.

The phone service settings are specific to your wireless provider, and the subscription services that you pay for will vary from other users.

CHANGE YOUR PHONE SETTINGS

PHONE SETTINGS

1 From the main keypad view, tap Tools.

2 Tap Options.

■ The Phone settings appear.

3 Tap the Ring Type ⊡ and select a type.

4 Tap the Ring Tone ⊡ and select a tone.

■ You can tap Play and Stop to test the ring tone.

5 Tap the Keypad ⊡ and select how the keypad will sound.

6 Tap the check box to enable security.

SERVICES SETTINGS

7 Tap the Services tab.

8 Tap the service that you want to set up.

9 Tap Get Settings.

■ Your device connects to your wireless provider and automatically configures your settings.

What is my original PIN?

✔ This varies depending on your wireless provider. Contact your provider to find out what PIN was assigned to your device.

Is there another method to manage ring tones, outside of the Phone settings?

✔ Yes, tap Start ➪ Settings and choose the System tab; then tap on Add Ring Tone. Windows Mobile 2003 searches for and returns a list of all acceptable audio types. Then you can test the types and select the ones that you want to be included in your Phone Settings Ring Tone drop-down list.

What type of sound files can I use for ring tones?

✔ You can use .wav, .mid, or .wma files as ring tones. You may want to manage the size of the audio file because the ring tones need to be stored in the RAM of your device.

What are the different ring types?

✔ The ring types are Ring, Increasing Ring, Ring Once, Vibrate, Vibrate and Ring, Vibrate Then Ring, and None.

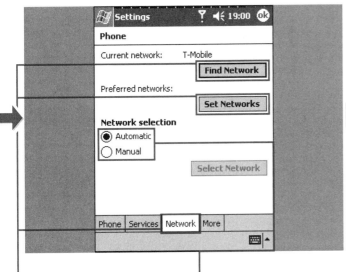

NETWORK SETTINGS

⓾ Tap the Network tab.

⓫ Tap Find Network.

■ Your device connects and verifies your current network.

■ You can tap Set Networks to set up how a secondary network can be accessed.

⓬ Tap how you want your network to be selected — either automatically or manually.

Note: If you choose Manual, you have to tap Select Network and then tap the network name to connect with.

MORE SETTINGS

⓭ Tap the More tab.

⓮ Tap the first check box to set automatic pickup and tap ▾ to select how many rings will occur before pickup.

⓯ Tap Enable to enable broadcast channels.

⓰ Tap Settings to specify what type of channels you will receive.

⓱ Tap OK.

■ Your Phone settings are saved.

Note: Your device may also have the option to lock the hardware buttons.

INDEX

continued

INDEX

INDEX

Read Less – Learn More®

Visual

Visual Blueprint™

For experienced computer users, developers, and network professionals who learn best visually.

Extra

Apply It "Apply It" and "Extra" provide ready-to-run code and useful tips.

Title	ISBN	Price
Access 2003: Your visual blueprint for creating and maintaining real-world databases	0-7645-4081-5	$26.99
Active Server Pages 3.0: Your visual blueprint for developing interactive Web sites	0-7645-3472-6	$26.99
Adobe Scripting: Your visual blueprint for scripting Photoshop and Illustrator	0-7645-2455-0	$29.99
ASP.NET: Your visual blueprint for creating Web applications on the .NET Framework	0-7645-3617-6	$26.99
C#: Your visual blueprint for building .NET applications	0-7645-3601-X	$26.99
Excel Data Analysis: Your visual blueprint for analyzing data, charts, and PivotTables	0-7645-3754-7	$26.99
Excel Programming: Your visual blueprint for building interactive spreadsheets	0-7645-3646-X	$26.99
Flash ActionScript: Your visual blueprint for creating Flash-enhanced Web sites	0-7645-3657-5	$26.99
HTML: Your visual blueprint for designing effective Web pages	0-7645-3471-8	$26.99
Java: Your visual blueprint for building portable Java programs	0-7645-3543-9	$26.99
Java and XML: Your visual blueprint for creating Java-enhanced Web programs	0-7645-3683-4	$26.99
JavaScript: Your visual blueprint for building dynamic Web pages	0-7645-4730-5	$26.99
JavaServer Pages: Your visual blueprint for designing dynamic content with JSP	0-7645-3542-0	$26.99
Linux: Your visual blueprint to the Linux platform	0-7645-3481-5	$26.99
MySQL: Your visual blueprint to open source database management	0-7645-1692-2	$29.99
Perl: Your visual blueprint for building Perl scripts	0-7645-3478-5	$26.99
PHP: Your visual blueprint for creating open source, server-side content	0-7645-3561-7	$26.99
Red Hat Linux 8: Your visual blueprint to an open source operating system	0-7645-1793-7	$29.99
Unix: Your visual blueprint to the universe of Unix	0-7645-3480-7	$26.99
Unix for Mac: Your visual blueprint to maximizing the foundation of Mac OS X	0-7645-3730-X	$26.99
Visual Basic .NET: Your visual blueprint for building versatile programs on the .NET Framework	0-7645-3649-4	$26.99
Visual C++ .NET: Your visual blueprint for programming on the .NET platform	0-7645-3644-3	$26.99
XML: Your visual blueprint for building expert Web pages	0-7645-3477-7	$26.99

with these two-color Visual™ guides

 "Master It" tips provide additional topic coverage.

Title	ISBN	Price
Master Microsoft Access 2000 VISUALLY	0-7645-6048-4	$39.99
Master Microsoft Office 2000 VISUALLY	0-7645-6050-6	$39.99
Master Microsoft Word 2000 VISUALLY	0-7645-6046-8	$39.99
Master VISUALLY Adobe Photoshop, Illustrator, Premiere, and After Effects	0-7645-3668-0	$39.99
Master VISUALLY Dreamweaver 4 and Flash 5	0-7645-0855-5	$39.99
Master VISUALLY Dreamweaver MX and Flash MX	0-7645-3696-6	$39.99
Master VISUALLY FrontPage 2002	0-7645-3580-3	$39.99
Master VISUALLY HTML 4 and XHTML 1	0-7645-3454-8	$39.99
Master VISUALLY Office 2003	0-7645-3994-9	$34.99
Master VISUALLY Office XP	0-7645-3599-4	$39.99
Master VISUALLY Photoshop 6	0-7645-3541-2	$39.99
Master VISUALLY Web Design	0-7645-3610-9	$39.99
Master VISUALLY Windows 2000 Server	0-7645-3426-2	$39.99
Master VISUALLY Windows Me Millennium Edition	0-7645-3496-3	$39.99
Master VISUALLY Windows XP	0-7645-3621-4	$39.99
Master Windows 98 VISUALLY	0-7645-6034-4	$39.99
Master Windows 2000 Professional VISUALLY	0-7645-3421-1	$39.99

For visual learners who want an all-in-one reference/tutorial that delivers more in-depth information about a technology topic.

The Visual™ series is available wherever books are sold, or call 1-800-762-2974.

Outside the US, call **317-572-3993**